CONSTELLATING HOME

INTERSECTIONAL RHETORICS
Karma R. Chávez, Series Editor

Constellating Home

Trans and Queer
Asian American Rhetorics

V. Jo Hsu

THE OHIO STATE UNIVERSITY PRESS
COLUMBUS

Library of Congress Cataloging-in-Publication Data
Names: Hsu, V. Jo, author.
Title: Constellating home : trans and queer Asian American rhetorics / V. Jo Hsu.
Other titles: Intersectional rhetorics.
Description: Columbus : The Ohio State University Press, [2022] | Series: Intersectional
    rhetorics | Includes bibliographical references and index. | Summary: "Examines
    counterstories where queer, trans, and disabled Asian Americans recover and reimagine
    shared histories, connecting individual experiences into grounds for solidarity and
    disruptions of dominant narratives. Focuses on three archives of trans and queer Asian
    American storytelling, including oral histories, photography, performances, personal
    essays, and poems"—Provided by publisher.
Identifiers: LCCN 2022018846 | ISBN 9780814214886 (cloth) | ISBN 0814214886 (cloth) |
    ISBN 9780814282359 (ebook) | ISBN 0814282350 (ebook)
Subjects: LCSH: Asian American sexual minorities—Social conditions. | Pacific Islander
    American sexual minorities—Social conditions.
Classification: LCC HQ73.3.U6 H78 2022 | DDC 306.76089/95073—dc23/eng/20220611
LC record available at https://lccn.loc.gov/2022018846
Other identifiers: ISBN 9780814258453 (paper) | ISBN 081425845X (paper)

Cover design by Nathan Putens
Text design by Juliet Williams
Type set in Adobe Minion Pro

CONTENTS

ACKNOWLEDGMENTS

This book would not exist without the organizers, artists-activists, teachers, and visionaries who trusted me and allowed me into their spaces. Thank you to Celeste Chan, Mia Nakano, Un Jung Lim, MLin, and Jasmin Hoo for creating sites where wayward queers like me could find a bit of home. Thank you for your imagination, for your leadership, and for the worlds you are building.

Ever since The Ohio State University Press announced its Intersectional Rhetorics series, I knew there was no editor I would trust with this book more than Karma Chávez. I did not know all the other things I would learn from Karma along the way—about scholarship, about inhabiting this profession with conviction and compassion, and about keeping my humor and humanity throughout the journey. The final iteration of this book also owes a tremendous debt to Adela Licona, whose insightful and encouraging feedback helped clarify and strengthen my ideas. I hope our paths continue to cross and that we have future opportunities to create together. Thank you, too, to Amy Sueyoshi and Jian Neo Chen, who not only provided invaluable counsel but whose writings were my doorways into trans and queer Asian American studies. Other individuals and organizations who have been instrumental to this book are Yi-Ting Chang, who remains a cherished interlocutor, Fereshteh Abbasi, for her expertise in Persian, and *Color Bloq,* who were the first to publish my thoughts on homing and who provide a brilliant example of QTPOC worldmaking. These pages also would not be in your hands without the thoughtful guidance of Taralee Cyphers and those at OSU Press. I hope that one day I get to meet my readers: whoever you are, I am grateful for your time and feedback. Finally, thanks to the units that have provided the time, community, and resources necessary to complete a book: the Department of English and the Gender Studies Program at the University of Arkansas and the Department of Rhetoric and Writing, the Center for Asian American Studies, the Center for Women and Gender Studies, and the Office of the Vice President for Research at the University of Texas at Austin.

I am fortunate to benefit and learn from a generous, deeply caring intellectual community. All my love to Toni Jensen, from whom I have learned more about rhetoric, writing, and surviving the university than would fit into a book, let alone this meager section. GPat Patterson and Christina Cedillo taught me to forge kinship in defiance of settings that actively discourage such intimacy. Anjali Vats, Vani Kannan, Ersula Ore, Sharon Yam, Andrea Riley-Mukavetz, Lisa King, and Niq Johnson—your care has carried me through the hardest parts of this journey. The list of relations who continue to encourage, uplift, and inspire me is too long to provide in its entirety, but I must also acknowledge Lore LeMaster, E Cram, Remi Yergeau, Elaine Richardson, Aja Martinez, Morris Young, Al Harahap, Stephanie Kerschbaum, and Jay Dolmage for all the ways you have supported me personally and professionally. You make this work possible and meaningful. To Alex Hidalgo, Kim Wieser, LuMing Mao, Ada Hubrig, Hil Malatino, Terese Monberg, Jen Wingard, Jennifer Nish, Isaac West, Jeff Bennett, Bryan McCann, Ashley Mack, Jonathan Alexander, Carmen Kynard, John Lynch, Ashley Hall, David F. Green, Seth Kahn, and Shinsuke Eguchi: thank you for your openness to connection and for your commitment to building spaces better than the ones we were given.

My venture into rhetoric began at Penn State, due in large part to Debbie Hawhee, whose generous mentorship provides a model to which I can only aspire. To Ebony Coletu: I am forever grateful for the ways you challenged me to become more than I was willing to settle for. Your lessons continue to shape who I am as a scholar. Other teachers and guides from PSU include Suresh Canagarajah, Rosemary Jolly, Tina Chen, Keith Gilyard, Kit Hume, and Elizabeth Kadetsky, each of whom have significantly impacted my thinking over the years. To Laura Brown and Sarah Adams: your friendship is one of the best things I got to take away from State College. I love that we have remained in each other's lives. Thanks also to Jenny Padilla for the workouts, the writing dates, and the tattoo adventures, and thank you to Laura Vrana, Michelle Huang, and Jayme Peacock for your lasting camaraderie.

I am fortunate to have been surrounded by brilliant and thoughtful colleagues at the University of Arkansas and the University of Texas at Austin. Lisa Corrigan was a singular force in my first years as an assistant professor and the reason I finally found harbor in gender studies. Thanks, too, to Constance Bailey, Niketa Reed, Injeong Yoon, Yajaira Padilla, Lissette Szwydky-Davis, Geffrey Davis, Mohja Kahf, Brody Parrish Craig, and K. C. Cross for the spaces of belonging you carved out in that corner of Arkansas. Annie Hill, Alison Kafer, and Ana Schwartz: thank you for going far out of your way to help me find my place in Austin. Likewise, Donnie Sackey, Casey Boyle, Rasha Diab, Jackie Rhodes, Diane Davis, Scott Graham, Holly Schwadron, Sara Casselberry, Stacey Sowards, Josh Gunn, Lisa Moore, Grayson Hunt, Lina Chhun, Pavithra Vasudevan, Hiʻilei Hobart, Chelsi West Ohueri, Ashanté Reese, Bedour Alagraa, Ashley Farmer, Roger Reeves, Mónica Jiménez, Eric Tang, Tony Vo, and all my colleagues in the DRW and CAAS: I am so grateful for the welcome, and I hope for many more opportunities to work with and learn from you. One of the great wonders of this profession is that I spend my days with brilliant, intellectually courageous colleagues and students. I am certain I will have forgotten someone. If you aren't here by name, please know that I value the gift of your time and attention, and I know I am better for it.

Finally, but not at all least, thank you to the ones I call home. Michelle Howe and Laura Starkston were the first people with whom I asked hard questions. David Stoll and Mayra Martinez were grounding forces amid my queer meanderings. Gloria Chang gave me the comfort and confidence that comes with belonging. Lin Shu and Yung Hsu, my parents, taught me to carry home across borders; I thought of you with every one of these pages, and I hope you can see yourselves in them. To Susan Scott and David Eggers, thank you for inviting me into your beautiful, vibrant family spaces. Talidog and Nomi can't read but need to be thanked anyway for taking me on daily walks, (re)teaching me how to play, and reminding me to never take myself too seriously. I end with Mck, who always gets the last word: you are my how and my why. I came to you with all the armor of resilience, and you taught me about love.

Constellating Home

Storytelling, Diasporic Listening, and (Re)Defining Commonplaces

Ghost Passages: A Prologue

The journey from Arkansas to California crosses two time zones. In Fayette-ville I wake at 4:30 a.m. to catch the earliest flight, which reclaims two extra hours in midair so that I land in San Francisco at 9:30 a.m. My body, however, knows that it is 11:30 a.m. in Arkansas. It knows that we got up seven hours ago—that we haven't been sleeping well all week. It remembers waking to the smell of smoke one week ago. It remembers evacuating our house on the one snowy morning of the year. It remembers inhaling soot and ash when I step past our door, and the scream of sirens—the first time I hear that sound as a sign that help is coming.

"Trauma time is cyclical," a friend cautions on the day of the fire, while my dog and I are recovering on someone else's living room floor. We spend a week on air mattresses, coffee shop porches, and other borrowed spaces as I try to clear the smoke from the house and our lives. Time doesn't slow for unanticipated misfortune, though, and I have a trip scheduled—five days of interviews, gallery visits, and writing workshops. It is my first year in a new faculty position, and I have invested nearly all my research funds in this book. So even though everything I own still smells like smoke, even though I cannot stop looking for the exit of every room that I am in, even though the sound of sirens sends my body into a panic, I pack my most professional-looking clothes, drop off the dog at the sitter's, and prepare to leave for San Francisco.

My first evening in the Bay Area, I attend Writing Rainbow, a "free school" for queer and trans people of color (QTPOC). It meets at The Flight Deck, a theater space dedicated to "radical acts of imagination."[1] I arrive in Oakland a little before class begins, just in time to meet Celeste Chan outside the main entrance. We had been corresponding for a while over email and telephone, but this is our first time meeting in person. In Chan's own words, she is "a queer artist, writer, and organizer, schooled by DIY and immigrant parents from Malaysia and the Bronx."[2] She carries that DIY ethos into her many projects, which provide artistic and educational platforms for QTPOC. Without the infrastructure of traditional schools, she has produced entire educational programs from scratch by designing curricula, recruiting students, arranging for classroom spaces, applying for grants, and actually teaching the classes. Tonight, though, she gets a brief respite from one of those roles.

Tonight's workshop is run by guest-facilitator Nancy Au, "a queer, bisexual writer, artist, and teacher" based in Oakland.[3] Both Chan and Au live and work at the intersections of writer, teacher, artist, and community-builder. In addition to Writing Rainbow, Chan helms the writing segment of the Queer Ancestors Project, an annual (also free and grant-funded) workshop for trans and queer youth ages eighteen to twenty-six. Au co-founded The Escapery, a "writing and other arts unschool," whose playful and experimental curriculum "re-center[s] women/NB, queer/trans artists, and artists of color."[4] The Escapery's website adds: "No famous white men, no tear-down workshops, zero-tolerance for micro or macro aggressions."[5]

When a member of The Flight Deck lets us inside, Au leads us up a narrow stairway and to an attic space lined with posters from old shows. We push the tables together into a large, shared writing surface. Chan lays out trail mix and Trader Joe's cookies. Au begins by invoking the ghosts of our pasts, inviting us to think about the ways we encounter them. Some ghosts, she says, we cannot see or hear, and their presence is only faintly sensed. Some are more identifiable and speak to us. Other ghosts haunt. For the next three hours, my ghosts rise in droves. In a series of "writing experiments," we amass a chorus of reverberant memories—of forced migration, estrangement, longing, love, and *be*longing. We read excerpts from queer and POC writers, and we answer

---

1. "The Flight Deck."
2. Chan, "Bio."
3. Au, "About."
4. Beker, Au, and King, "The Escapery."
5. Beker, Au, and King.

their calls. Ocean Vuong's *Night Sky with Exit Wounds* tears open a lifetime of calloused flesh. The stanza breaks and I, too, am a queer kid on the cusp of adolescence, discovering "the cost / of entering a song—was to lose / your way back."

I come to this space as an academic. I am funded by a university grant and compelled by a tenure clock that began ticking when I started a job eight months ago. The title *assistant professor* feels too new to be real and too authoritative to be mine. In almost all academic settings, I am presumed a student. Here, though, the academic job feels like a millstone. Here, *assistant professor* stands for starkly different forms of learning and for the inaccessible spaces that have necessitated DIY curricula in borrowed rooms. I wish the title was something I could have left at the door, but that would be an indefensible exercise of privilege—to shed my identities at will.

I have no single line of argument to convey the value of this rainy evening. I could quantify the number of queer spaces I had been in before where the majority were POC (zero); or I could count for you the number of Asian American spaces I had visited where the majority were queer (zero); I could number the trans Asian Americans featured in Hollywood blockbusters (zero) or who've made a run for US president (Ha! Please.). None of those statistics, though, could place you, reader, here with us, in a room that feels like a homecoming, the first time in twenty-nine years I ever felt "Asian American."

There are reasons for that—why race is most apparent beyond the bounds of acceptable gender and other corporealities. The following chapters explore and expose some of the discursive and structural forces that occlude racial logics and their imbrications with other vectors of identity. This prologue, however, and other // *ghost passages* // that visit upon subsequent chapters, invoke the power of these spaces. That is, the gift of not having to explain, or to constrict experience and relationships to point and counterpoint. These ghost passages story experiential knowledge alongside the rhythms of more conventional theory and analysis to explore insights made possible by more inclusive intellectual genealogies and by understanding that knowledge is not the sole province of universities but something we borrow from and give back to the communities that support us.

Spending time in rooms filled with trans and queer family, exchanging stories rather than arguments, and pursuing communion rather than cure— these are everyday acts of defiance.[6] The archives explored in this book honor such moments as substantive and political acts. *Constellating Home* is named for the term I give to this deliberate storytelling: homing. As writing practice,

---

6. Though of course there are times and places for both arguments and action.

homing animates personal experience into social analysis, collective politics, and mobile sites of belonging. Through narrative, homing asks readers to sit with moments of incongruity and discomfort and to allow those feelings to open up new possibilities—that seemingly distant histories and experiences might relate to our own; that we do not and cannot know everything; but also that we can move closer to and make time for one another's truths.

In the attic of The Flight Deck, I am invited into learning that is not shaped by market pressures and meritocratic benchmarks for productivity. We dwell for however long we need on each reading and exercise. The conversation moves with an ebb and flow that is equally comfortable in silence and spirited debate. I think about how academic fields now disciplined and canonized in textbooks on intersectional feminism, ethnic studies, and disability studies began in such spaces. The knowledge codified by our disciplines was first written in zines and manifestos and on cardboard signs. In Writing Rainbow the histories, social phenomena, and cultural tensions examined in academic monographs and journal articles are experienced in their vernacular names and affective journeys. Here is the truth that feminists of color, queer of color critics, crip poets, artists, and other activists from the margins have insisted in languages endemic to *and* external to the academy: that theory takes many forms, and that knowledge is made in languages fractured and fluent, jargonistic and poetic, textual and embodied.

Inspired by these wide-ranging traditions, this book speaks in a mongrel tongue—what Jack Halberstam has termed a *scavenger methodology*— a queer way-of-knowing that fuses methods often assumed incompatible or antithetical.[7] In doing this work, I am indebted to the deep wells of knowledge built by DIY radicals, feminist organizers, and trans, queer, and disabled visionaries and worldmakers. This book owes just as much to the communities outside of universities with even longer legacies, who have trusted me with their stories and their ways of teaching and learning through story. I am, of course, not the first to blend narrative, analysis, and criticism. Many of the scholars who established gender and sexuality studies, ethnic studies, and disability studies did so by drawing from their experiences within communities historically excluded from formal academic institutions. Despite the stories these scholars established as intellectual knowledge, many academic fields remain suspicious of narrative, experience-based, and affective methodologies. Meanwhile, many community organizers, artists, and other creators— including some whose labor and generosity made this book possible—have been alienated by academic language and its sterile treatment of histories both

7. Halberstam, *Female Masculinity*, 12.

traumatic and tender. I hope this book pulls together these discursive communities—not seamlessly, but in a manner that maps those seams, conscious of and attending to legacies of harm. Let this be a stitch toward the closing of a wound.

Asian Americans and Rhetorics of Home

David Eng and Shinhee Han describe Asian Americans like me—migrant children "displaced in a global system"—as particularly vulnerable to the condition of being "psychically nowhere."[8] In a groundbreaking study, Eng, a professor of English, and Han, a psychotherapist, define psychic nowhere as "the absence of a clear geographic belonging or destination."[9] I prefer the words of writer-activist Celeste Chan, though: "How do you make a home when no one wants you there? In some ways that's the story of Asians and people of color in America. How do you make a home when no one wants you there, or when you're constantly told to get out?"[10] Eng and Han examine diaspora as a possible answer to such questions. In their study displacement opens the psychic space for "creative play," where Asian Americans approach identity as a relational process. Asian Americans can then place their individual experiences in dialogue with communal histories, politics, and courses of action, repurposing diaspora as a transitional space where social identities and conditions of belonging can be continually revised.[11]

When I interviewed Celeste Chan after Writing Rainbow, she described building communal writing spaces as "a form of activism. It's about knowing what's possible—knowing our lineages, knowing that people like us always existed, knowing what past generations did or how they organized, how they networked."[12] Writing Rainbow and the three archives of trans and queer Asian American and Pacific Islander (QTAPI)[13] rhetorics I examine in this book dwell within this unsettling space of diaspora. These storytelling projects reach into "psychic nowhere" to take hold of communal wisdoms long withheld by normative racial frames. With home as relational and reflexive

---

8. Eng and Han, *Racial Melancholia, Racial Dissociation*, chap. 3.
9. Eng and Han, chap. 3.
10. Chan, personal interview.
11. Eng and Han, *Racial Melancholia, Racial Dissociation*, chap. 3.
12. Chan, personal interview.
13. QTAPI is the commonly accepted acronym for Queer and Trans Asian Americans and Pacific Islanders. I at times use the phrase *trans and queer Asian Americans* to foreground the inclusion of trans folks, who have often been neglected within mainstream "LGBTQ+" politics.

making, these stories network personal experiences with those of others and broader histories, establishing communities that extend across and trouble presumed boundaries. Tracing the insights of these stories, I demonstrate how QTAPI storytelling intervenes in normative understandings of US citizenship, enables interpersonal connections that drive community organizing, and communicates the needs, desires, and interlocking vulnerabilities that shape the places where we belong.

Taken together, QTAPI rhetorics offer crucial disruptions of Asian American racialization in the US. These histories are deeply implicated in the evolution of settler colonial capitalism and its seepage into racial, sexual, and gender politics. Rhetoricians Kent Ono and Vincent Pham discuss *yellow peril* and *model minority* as mutually imbricated discourses that entwine to construct Asian Americans as threats to the nation. For my purposes, these discourses can be seen as interwoven storylines that form the normalizing narrative of Asian Americans in the US—a narrative about unfeeling automatons as efficient workers and unruly subjects as foreign menaces. Like Ono and Pham, I emphasize that the storylines that circulate about Asian American identity and belonging are rhetorical in that they shape public perception and thus the ways people and governing bodies "make sense of immigration, international relations, economic downturns" and other social and political phenomena.[14] That is, while these stories are fabricated by cultural exigencies, they have material impact on public policy, interpersonal engagement, and the psychology and experiences of Asian Americans.

My approach to rhetoric derives from Jay Dolmage's memorable definition, which considers rhetoric "as the strategic study of the circulation of power through communication."[15] Stories, in this view, are conduits of power. The model minority is a plot that leverages select instances of Asian American "success" to delegitimize antiracist movements, whereas yellow peril situates the minority exemplar as perpetually external to the nation. White heteropatriarchal dominance of media outlets—from news media to Hollywood films to major literary platforms—further enables the circulation of hegemonic worldviews through major cultural institutions. For example, during the 2020 COVID-19 outbreak, the president, Republican leaders, and conservative media insisted on phrases such as *Chinese virus* and *kung flu*, inciting an upsurge of anti-Asian hate crimes. These monikers deflected blame for the US government's egregious mishandling of a public health crisis, playing on extant fears of Asian bodies as foreign contagion. Throughout his re-election

---

14. Ono and Pham, *Asian Americans and the Media*, 43.
15. Agnew et al., "Octalog III," 113.

campaign, Donald Trump blamed the "Chinese Plague" for the devastating loss of human lives and livelihoods experienced under his administration.[16] This racist and xenophobic storyline enabled Trump to avert responsibility for the ravages of the pandemic, despite how it traveled through and exploited inequalities in US health care, housing, and employment—inequalities actively exacerbated throughout his presidency.

Amid the intensifying political tensions of 2020 and 2021, Asian Americans, many of whom were not Chinese, were verbally and physically assaulted. A Hmong family was stabbed at a Sam's Club in Texas—including a toddler and a six-year-old—because the assailant "thought the family was Chinese, and infecting people with Coronavirus."[17] Meanwhile, presidential hopeful Andrew Yang penned an opinion piece for the *Washington Post* enjoining Asian Americans to lean harder into model behaviors and respectability politics. Yang reminded readers that interned Japanese Americans volunteered for military service during World War II, and that Asian Americans compose "some 17 percent" of doctors in the US. Following these examples, Yang argues, Asian Americans "need to step up, help our neighbors, donate gear, vote, wear red white and blue."[18] Yang's argument misses the mutuality of yellow peril and model minority, and the ways both are embedded in and required of US racial injustices. As opposed to replacing the explicitly xenophobic narratives of yellow peril, model minority contains difference by providing a narrow tract for US assimilation and rendering any deviants as threats to the nation—a narrative continually weaponized against nonconforming Asian Americans and other POC. What Yang should have noticed about the sharp pivot against Asian Americans was how even high-profile personalities such as himself stand on the cusp of ostracization, conveniently ejected as external threats to (implicitly white) US Americans when it is politically expedient.

Despite all that scholars and activists have done to debunk the Janus-faced stereotype of yellow peril / model minority, it remains, in the words of historian Ellen Wu, the "Energizer Bunny."[19] It keeps going. Its perdurance exemplifies the power of *stock stories*—a term coined by critical race theorist Richard Delgado to describe accounts that "justif[y] the world as it is."[20] Stock stories select from available facts to support extant conditions of inequality and are

16. Walsh, "Trump Is Demanding China Pay 'Big Price' for Covid-19."
17. Johnson, "FBI May Charge Man Who Attacked Asian Americans over Coronavirus with Hate Crime."
18. Yang, "We Asian Americans Are Not the Virus, but We Can Be Part of the Cure."
19. Wu quoted in Chow, "Racial Wedge."
20. Delgado, "Storytelling for Oppositionists"; see also Martinez, *Counterstory,* 33–38.

often taken for granted as the natural order. (*Of course* Asians are more likely to be doctors—that's just in their nature.) The suasive force of hegemonic stories means that both speakers and audiences are likely to align events with these stock explanations. In both real-world and fictional contexts, stories of or by Asian Americans are continually routed through yellow peril or model minority frames—both of which are premised on a distant, monolithic culture of self-discipline.

For example, figure skater Michelle Kwan was frequently adored as a "role model" who exemplified Asian culture's emphasis on hard work, despite her being born in California. When the 1998 Olympics pitted Kwan against fellow US skater Tara Lipinski, MSNBC reported the results as "American beats Kwan."[21] The headline captured the contingency of Asian American belonging, and the reality that it is secondary to and in service of whiteness. Over time, such stories adhere together, rendering the Asian American body what Sara Ahmed calls a *sticky sign*—a sign *stuck* in a particular narrative of foreignness, trapped between disciplined complacency and devious threat.[22] The accumulation of these stories—the repetition-with-difference of yellow peril / model minority exemplars—builds a gravitational pull so that new information is drawn into its orbit. This way, single stories do not need to directly endorse any element of dominant stereotypes. Rather, readers are simply more likely to channel new data through normalizing frames.

Like gravity, the narrative pull of stock stories is an ambient force. We obey it without conscious effort. For this reason, all stories contain—and to a degree, *need*—certain normalizing elements. As anthropologist Dorinne Kondo explains, "intelligibility means that it's legible [. . . and] to the extent that anything is legible, it's reinscribing convention."[23] Stories build on established reference points, and it is not possible, or perhaps even desirable, to abandon all points of familiarity. In Kondo's words, "stereotypes are always haunting"[24] the ways we speak and listen; there is no ideologically pure representation. The goal of this book, then, is not to tell a single story of resistance but to listen for, connect, and amplify a range of diverse counternarratives[25] and to build a critical mass of (gender)queer possibilities that can resist the gravitational pull of the model minority and its social forms.

---

21. Kawai, "Stereotyping Asian Americans," 117.

22. Ahmed, *The Cultural Politics of Emotion*, 89–92.

23. Thobani, "Dorinne Kondo."

24. Thobani.

25. Delgado, "Storytelling for Oppositionists"; Solórzano and Yosso, "Critical Race Methodology." In rhetorical studies, the power of counterstories has been notably demonstrated through the work of Aja Martinez (*Counterstory*). See Jian Neo Chen for more on trans of color critique through autobiographical writing.

This chorus of narratives invites readers to understand home as more than location. With the wisdom of diaspora, homing emphasizes that belonging is not stable, guaranteed, or predictable. Instead, it approaches home as a constellation of stories that determine with whom, where, and how we belong. Diaspora also brings to homing an imagination that expands the bounds of one's possible communities, and an ethics that prioritizes sheltering and caring for those made most vulnerable by narratives of displacement. Homing then regards home as the difficult, collaborative, at times contradictory practice of re-placement, reimagining, and relating across distance and difference.

Homing Practices

In Mandarin, my first language, the word for *family* and for *home* is the same: 家. To go home, 回家, is to return to your family. For all my life, this has been true for my parents. Though they moved to the US shortly before my birth, nearly everyone they considered family/home remained in Taiwan. My mother is the middle child of six, and my dad the youngest of four brothers. Blood ties have been the strongest tethers in their lives. For as long as I can remember, they have looked forward to a homecoming that restores a bit of their past. I have envied that certainty—anchored in a land, a history, and a people they know as theirs. What, though, is the meaning of home for an only child born on stolen land, half a world from their parents' place of birth? What is family when blood ties strain across geographical and cultural distance? What family/home will stand on decades of silence and centuries of erasure?

Aptly, the term for *writer* in Mandarin is 作家. Split into its constituent parts, 作 means *to make* and 家 means *home*. Translated literally, 作家 means *to make a home*.[26] Throughout this book, I articulate *homing* as a critical approach to storytelling that (re)makes family/home as ongoing practice. Homing stories situate individual experiences in relation to relevant histories and events, (re)composing 家 with the mutability of our growth and movements. This storytelling deliberately confronts systems of power and representation, paying particular attention to the author's relations and responsibilities.[27] Homing enables diasporic subjects to deconstruct, co-construct, and maneuver among sites of (un)belonging. It exposes the nar-

---

26. I first wrote on this concept in *Color Bloq* (Hsu, "Chinese Roots, Queer Kinships").
27. Riley-Mukavetz, "Developing a Relational Scholarly Practice."

rative and structural forces that constrain and expand the possibilities for intimacy, security, and kinship.

In migratory animals, homing is the ability to navigate toward an originary location through unfamiliar territory. For diasporic subjects without a physical place of return, homing can be both movement toward and creation of such shelter—a narrative mapping that establishes the grounds for communities to come together. Through homing, QTAPI locate and create alternative intimacies and belongings in defiance of our structured isolation, composing foundations for ground-up, relationship-driven collaboration. As homes transform with each departure and arrival, homing enables storytellers to trace and affect the evolution of the spaces and relations that constitute family/home. Refusing any static homeland, homing instead explores locations, communities, and nations as combinatory formations (re)made through the narratives we tell.

Sociologists Avtar Brah and Anne-Marie Fortier have explored "homing desires" in queer diaspora, wherein "the desire to *feel at home* [is] achieved by physically or symbolically (re)constituting spaces which provide some kind of ontological security in the context of migration."[28] Rhetorical studies can build from this foundation a more nuanced vocabulary for how narratives respond to and intervene in discourses of identity and belonging. As a rhetorical technology, story can slow down, hold still, redefine, and/or reimagine our physical movements to renegotiate their shared meanings. The QTAPI narratives throughout this book, and my own self-storying, provide different accounts of homing that I constellate into a wide array of stories and perspectives. What results are dynamic, contingent configurations of LGBTQ+ Asian American experience—an always-incomplete map of LGBTQ+ Asian American belonging that invites new arrivals, challenges, and expansions. While this book necessarily focuses on one particular set of texts and interpretations, homing as concept offers an understanding and method of storytelling that can examine and remake communal identities and the values and aspirations that hold people together.

I owe the term *constellation* to Leanne Betasamosake Simpson, Malea Powell, and the Cultural Rhetorics Theory Lab. In Nishnaabeg thought, constellation names a knowledge system based in relationality.[29] When applied to rhetoric, constellations permit "multiply-situated subjects to connect multiple discourses at the same time, as well as for those relationships (among

---

28. Fortier, "'Coming Home,'" 409–10; emphasis original; Brah, *Cartographies of Diaspora*. See also Sandibel Borges's exploration of homing as resistance against patriarchal, capitalist, and ableist systems by LGBTQ+ Latinx migrants. Borges, "Home and Homing as Resistance."

29. Simpson, *As We Have Always Done*.

subjects, among discourses, among kinds of connections) to shift and change without holding a subject captive."[30] Throughout this book, I map constellations of life stories, assembling individual narratives into broader networks of shared meaning. Like the connections we plot in the night sky, rhetorical constellations can act as homing guides for those forging life trajectories without charters.[31] Each constellation is only one possible configuration among infinite permutations, but it draws meaning from the connections we agree upon.[32] Rhetorical constellations are not about declaring a singular truth but about listening for and accommodating a multiplicity of relationships and responsibilities.

Central to homing and constellating—to storying life's meanderings and to mapping broader assemblages from such trajectories—is *diasporic listening*. Like Romeo García's "community listening," diasporic listening is "a reaffirmation of a debt, and imagining the possibilities of new stories in and with others."[33] For me, this communal imagination is guided by queer diaspora's attention to "promiscuous intimacies."[34] Inspired by the work of M. Jacqui Alexander, David Eng, Eithne Luibhéid and Lionel Cantú, Gayatri Gopinath, José Esteban Muñoz, and Chandan Reddy, I listen for the submerged and forgotten elements of shared pasts and for resonances among seemingly distinct histories.[35] Put more simply, diasporic listening is a critical orientation attuned to reciprocities ignored or obscured by normative frames. In search of these promiscuous relations, I connect QTAPI stories to relevant historical moments and cultural touchstones, drawing from my own background in Asian American, queer, and disabled rhetorics; my experience as a trans, queer, and disabled Taiwanese American; and my encounters with these archives and storytellers. While diasporic listening is more deliberate about seeking and foregrounding possible connections, it is also a reminder that reading and listening are always rhetorical. Audiences bring embodied knowledges, beliefs, and values to their interpretations of new information—and thus have an ethical imperative to understand the cultural and histori-

---

30. Powell et al., "Our Story Begins Here."

31. "Only within the interdependency of different strengths, acknowledged and equal, can the power to seek new ways to actively 'be' in the world generate, as well as the courage and sustenance to act where there are no charters." Lorde, "The Master's Tools Will Never Dismantle the Master's House," 95.

32. Powell et al., "Our Story Begins Here"; Bratta and Powell, "Entering the Cultural Rhetorics Conversations"; Del Hierro, Levy, and Price, "We Are Here."

33. García, "Creating Presence from Absence," 13.

34. Gopinath, *Unruly Visions*, introduction.

35. Alexander, *Pedagogies of Crossing*; Eng, *Racial Castration* and *The Feeling of Kinship*; Luibhéid and Cantú, *Queer Migrations*; Gopinath, *Impossible Desires* and *Unruly Visions*; Muñoz, *Disidentifications* and *Cruising Utopia*; Reddy, *Freedom with Violence*.

cal contexts of the stories they receive. Diasporic listening attempts to "hold ourselves, the people that we work in close community with, and our broader community, accountable"[36] to the many ways our lives come into contact and tension with others.

Intentionally linking gender, race, and disability, my listening practice responds to the conspicuous absence of disability in Asian American studies[37] as well as the corresponding whiteness of disability studies.[38] In fact, given how notions of contagion have been attached to Asians, and how physical and cognitive difference have been used to control migration, Asian American history is inevitably bound up with disability.[39] I build from Robert McRuer's crip theory to argue that "compulsory ableism"[40] is integral to the normative family forms embedded in model minority life trajectories. The gender norms scripted onto "model" Asian bodies demand a superhuman capacity for labor, exposing ableism as an always-deferred ideal alongside paradigmatic hetero-sexism. Model immigrants are expected to thrive in work and educational environments that presume always-well, neurotypical bodyminds. The narratives and valuations that shape race, heteronormativity, and the bodies that make up the US body politic are inevitably entwined.

Queerness, too, is interpolated in this history. On the flip side of the model minority myth, opponents of Asian immigration often decried the "moral and racial pollution" of (presumed) women prostitutes and the perceived deviance of Chinatown bachelor societies.[41] Medical inspections at Ellis Island included questions about sexual preferences and histories, and "abnormal sex instincts" were categorized as "constitutional psychopathic inferiority."[42] On the West Coast, Chinese migrant men were viewed as "slave dealers" and women as "degraded sex slaves."[43] Sexual and gender nonconformity enmeshed with mental and physical illness to cast Asian bodies as a danger to the health of the nation. Both model minority and yellow peril tropes were and remain integral to managing national borders, marking particular bodies and intimacies as desirable and others as fundamentally opposed to the nation-state. Diasporic listening searches for the collisions and collusions among these scripts,

---

36. Nakano, personal interview.
37. Ho and Lee, "The State of Illness and Disability in Asian America."
38. Bell, "Introducing White Disability Studies"; Schalk, "Coming to Claim Crip."
39. Shah, *Contagious Divides*; Dolmage, *Disabled upon Arrival.*
40. McRuer, *Crip Theory.*
41. Lee, *America for Americans*, 82.
42. Dolmage, *Disabled upon Arrival*, 11.
43. Lee, *The Making of Asian America*, 70.

recognizing that they are not altogether silent but resonate at lower frequencies than we are accustomed to hearing.[44]

While focusing on the relational and systemic, my approach does not dismiss the significance of the personal. I am guided by the founding principles of Black feminism, which has been integral to the evolution of queer studies, trans studies, and crip theory and politics. Even while I understand terms like *queer* and *disabled* as "fluid and ever-changing,"[45] I find it important to ground my analysis in the needs and lived experiences of those deeply affected by the consequences of racism, compulsory heterosexuality, and ableism. My discussions of how bodily and behavioral norms entwine in conceptions of "deserving" citizens attempt to center the voices of trans and nonbinary folks, South Asians and Pacific Islanders, disabled folks, and others often overlooked in conceptions of US citizenry. Their stories demonstrate the inextricability of Asian American activism from queer politics, disability activism, and racial justice.

The importance of this principle—drawn from Black feminism's lessons on centering those most impacted—continues to be overlooked throughout mainstream pushes for social change, including those for and by Asian Americans. In 2020–21 Asian American politicians and celebrities helped expedite the passage of the COVID-19 Hate Crimes Act, despite the protestations of more than one hundred Asian American and LGBTQ+ groups. A joint letter signed by organizations including GAPIMNY—Empowering Queer & Trans Asian Pacific Islanders, the National Queer Asian Pacific Islander Alliance (NQAPIA), and the Blasian March emphatically "reject[s] hate crime legislation that relies on anti-Black, law enforcement responses to the recent rise in anti-Asian bias incidents across the US."[46] As the signatories point out, the Hate Crimes Act provides no resources for actual communities targeted by anti-Asian violence, instead facilitating hate crime reviews and hate crime reporting. Solutions that centered LGBTQ+ and disabled Asian Americans, sex workers and low-wage workers, and undocumented Asian Americans would have channeled resources toward better health care, community-based trauma centers, and housing and food security. To the exclusion of these voices, prominent Asian Americans have backed a measure that further endangers those most vulnerable and that impedes solidarity with other and overlapping structurally marginalized communities.

---

44. The metaphor of *frequencies* comes from Tina Campt's *Listening to Images,* which attends to the "lower frequencies" of vernacular photographs of Black diaspora.

45. Sandahl, "Queering the Crip or Cripping the Queer?," 27.

46. 100+ Asian American and LGBTQ Organizations, "Statement in Opposition."

While I work to center the narratives of historically underrepresented Asian Americans, I am also mindful that bringing their stories into academic conversations is not a neutral or straightforward task. I am wary of how readers and I may replicate the historic violences of academic researchers who have extracted from communities without reciprocity or accountability. I am wary of the gravity of stock stories—how even writers and readers with the best intentions will carry with them the weight of normative plots. In an attempt to deflect such possibilities, I incorporate practices of "refusal" modeled by scholars in Indigenous and decolonial studies.[47] Refusal is a generative stance against colonialism's "regimes of representation,"[48] which reiterate damaging myths about the Majority World. Eurocentric researchers have often subjected the stories entrusted to them to distortive frames that presume "the disappearance of Indigenous people, the enslavability and murderability of Black people, [and] the right to make interdictions on Othered lives."[49] These representations not only define marginalized communities by their wounds but also suggest that the mere witnessing of this harm by majoritarian audiences is progress. At best, such representational practices expect dominant cultures to confer the changes required to repair that damage. More often, these representations are consumed in ways that support sentiments of white generosity without creating any substantive change at all.

More than just a flat *no,* refusal is "a type of investigation into 'what you need to know and what I refuse to write in.'"[50] Refusal "turns the gaze back on power,"[51] exposing colonial appetites for spectacles of trauma while denying the audience just that. There are moments throughout this book when I pivot the gaze away from my community partners, or from passages of my own experience, knowing that true events still get folded into appropriative falsehoods. As the practice of writing toward alternative sites of belonging, homing is more than just shelter *for*; it is also shelter *from*. The goal of my narration is not to convey some "authentic" story of QTAPI experience to detached audiences but to demonstrate how QTAPI rhetors and rhetorics (1) provide incisive critiques of US mythologies regarding formations of self, family, and nation; and (2) provide visionary vocabularies for other forms of being and of togetherness. Toward this end, refusal shifts the spotlight away from pain and toward the privilege that feels entitled to consume that pain. It is a method

47. Simpson, "On Ethnographic Refusal."
48. Tuck and Yang, "R-Words," 244.
49. Tuck and Yang, 244.
50. Simpson quoted in Tuck and Yang, 223.
51. Tuck and Yang, "Unbecoming Claims," 817.

based not in the display of knowledge but in interrogating what you do not, should not, or cannot know.

Listening for (Counter)Hegemonic Histories

As normalizing rhetorics, model minority and yellow peril tropes conspire to enable the success of *particular* Asian Americans whose stories support the myth of meritocracy. Meanwhile, those outside the protections of middle-class heteronuclear families face social and systemic discrimination narrativized as personal failure. This braided thread of Asian American stereotyping reveals how racism enlists hetero/cissexism and ableism in its construction of deserving US citizens. The foundation and legacies of Asian American gendered racialization can be traced to Euroamerican expansion in the 1800s—to the British conscription of Chinese and Indian indentured laborers in the West Indies and the exploitation of Chinese migrants for the US transcontinental railroad. Both historical developments positioned Asians as instruments in colonial conquest and as a labor force to supplant or suppress insurrectionary Africans, establishing rhetorics that have scaffolded North American racial politics well into the present.[52] While I cannot do justice to the deep history of Asian Americans in the US in this section, I offer a brief gloss of that trajectory. Through diasporic listening, I search for and emphasize the intimacies among Asian American racialization and other marginalizing scripts in US history. These stories establish a narrative constellation on which subsequent chapters expand.

Impelled by colonialism's need for disposable labor, Asians in the West were complicit in Indigenous dispossession. As historian Patrick Wolfe explains, settler colonialism is "first and foremost a project of replacement. Settlers come to stay."[53] Staying on stolen land requires the removal or assimilation of Indigenous peoples. Early colonial occupations then sought to eliminate Native Americans while simultaneously filling their land with alien labor. As defined by Iyko Day, "alien" status (as opposed to Native or settler) positioned enslaved Africans and Asian migrants as a fungible labor force, establishing race as an organizing principle that distinguished settlers from the excludable and deportable alien.[54] The alienness of differently racialized peoples—documented relentlessly through artistic and journalistic media as well as governmental correspondence—enabled settler states to profit from their

52. Shah, *Contagious Divides*; Lowe, *Intimacies*; Day, *Alien Capital*; Chen, *Trans Exploits*.
53. Wolfe, *Traces of History*, chap. 1.
54. Day, *Alien Capital*, 24.

labor while enfiguring Black and Asian Americans as fundamentally distinct from white settlers. Those distinctions were then formalized through legal and social forms of segregation, disenfranchisement, exploitation, imprisonment, exclusion, and expulsion.

This is not to say that African and Asian Americans had equivalent experiences in settler regimes. While Day demonstrates how heterogeneously racialized "aliens" are distinguished among "settler" and "Native" positions, Claire Jean Kim's "racial triangulation" illustrates how Asian identity maps onto the "Black and White" racial field that predominates contemporary US politics—an imagined binary that enforces the ongoing erasure of Native presence. Departing from the linear "racial hierarchy" approach that places "white" on top and "Black" on the bottom, Kim argues that US racialization operates on at least two axes: superior/inferior and insider/foreigner. As Asian Americans are valorized in relation to Black Americans, they are also ostracized as "immutably foreign and unassimilable,"[55] and thus exogenous to the body politic. While the "alienness" of Black Americans has been narrativized as constitutional and/or cultural inferiority, Asian Americans have been scripted as "other" through a "venerable (if now decrepit) culture."[56] Put more simply, colonialism concentrates power among white settlers by replacing Indigenous peoples on their own land with alien labor, and framing those laborers as either unhuman chattel or so indelibly foreign that they must be "aliens ineligible to citizenship."[57]

Though Kim's analysis begins in the mid-1800s, with the conscription of Chinese workers for US railroad companies, Chinese (and soon Indian) "coolies" arrived as early as 1807 to help transition British colonies from slavery to ostensibly "free" labor. The "Trinidad experiment" of the early 1800s brought Chinese workers to Trinidad to suppress rebellions by enslaved peoples while expanding sugar production. The new class of Asian laborers were described as "free" despite being coerced onto ships akin to those that once carried enslaved Africans, and despite the exploitative working conditions to which they arrived. Correspondence from this period reveals an explicit plot to position the Chinese as a "racial barrier between [the British] and the Negroes."[58] That barrier—that is, the rhetorical boundary that marked Asians as distinct from and superior to enslaved or newly emancipated Africans—was their ability to approximate (but never fully inhabit) white, heteronormative family formations.

---

55. Kim, "Racial Triangulation," 107.

56. Kim, 110.

57. Phrasing from the California Alien Land Law of 1913.

58. Lowe, *Intimacies*, 23.

Reading administrative documents on the design of this new labor structure, Lisa Lowe observes repeated use of Chinese women to symbolize "the capacity of the colonized to develop into a reproductive, family community."[59] Throughout administrative correspondence, Chinese women's sexuality was instrumentalized to resemble the "civility" of European marriage and family, creating an implicit contrast to sexualized representations of African and African-descended women.[60] When Attorney General Archibald Gloster plotted the introduction of Chinese laborers to the West Indies, he imagined that the presence of Chinese women would help establish Chinese families and therefore "secure the 'racial barrier.'"[61] In other words, the formation of Chinese families would prevent racial intermixing and the potential coalitions and resistance that could arise from those relationships. For Gloster, the promise of Chinese migrants was not only their perceived "industrious habits" and "constitutional strength"[62] but also their ability to reproduce the nation through racially segregated nuclear families. Reflecting on his own design, Gloster wrote, "I think it one of the best schemes possible."[63]

The Trinidad experiment presaged racial scripts that would shape Asian American labor and social formations in the US throughout the following centuries. Decades later, the Central Pacific Railroad Company employed Chinese laborers as an "expendable, interchangeable, replaceable" resource, imported from overseas to control the price of labor.[64] Viewed as "animated tools," these "alien" workers laid tracks through Miwok, Ohlone, and Paiute lands, complicit in the project of Indigenous dispossession.[65] Across the country, white Americans began employing Asian laborers to, in the words of one woman, "teach the negro his proper place."[66] Asian workers were used to prevent newly emancipated Africans and African-descended people from asking for or receiving reasonable wages.

When the railroads were complete, Californian administrators scrambled to control the demographics of their burgeoning state. Asian Americans' assumed productivity, which precedented later model minority tropes,[67] became "yellow peril." Responding to anxieties about Chinese labor impact-

---

59. Lowe, 30.
60. Lowe, 33.
61. Lowe, 31.
62. Gloster quoted in Lowe, 30.
63. Gloster quoted in Lowe, 30.
64. Karuka, *Empire's Tracks*, chap. 2.
65. Karuka, chap. 5.
66. Kim, "Racial Triangulation," 112.
67. Though the actual phrase *model minority* did not appear until much later, I use it to emphasize how early framings of Asian immigrants set precedents for later stereotypes.

ing white earning potential, governing officials found it easier to associate Chinese bodies with disease than to contrive an argument for why the once "industrious" workers should be expelled from the dwindling job market.[68] Chinese people were regarded as "a social, moral, and political curse to the community."[69] Chinese women, whose sexuality continued to figure heavily in mainstream discourse, were framed as vectors of disease threatening to contaminate white families.[70] Men and women were viewed as practicing "deviant heterosexuality" in violation of white middle-class family norms.[71] These attitudes fueled the Chinese Exclusion Act of 1882, established to stem the "Asian invasion."[72] This landmark legislation then formalized the operations of continental imperialism: first, the claiming of Indigenous lands and waters; next, the civic exclusion of the aliens who performed this labor.

Asians and Asian Americans are hardly innocent in this history of colonial race-making. Many Asian American attempts at self-advocacy have relied on dominant narratives of US belonging. In their petition against Chinese exclusion, the Chinese Six Companies emphasized that the "greatness" of China and the US were similarly rooted in imperial expansion. A few decades later, advocates for Chinese American assimilation cultivated "conventional gender roles and heterosexual behaviors" in San Francisco's Chinatowns, seeking to reform Chinatown's reputation as a (morally suspect) bachelor society.[73] Contemporary forms of the "model minority" can trace their roots to these values—to the figuration of Asian Americans as compliant workers with "the social potential [. . .] to form 'middle class' families through Christian marriage and reproduction."[74]

The actual phrase *model minority* is attributed to a 1966 essay in *New York Times Magazine* titled "Success Story, Japanese-American Style."[75] Written by sociologist William Petersen, "Success Story" spins a tale of spectacular ascension against all odds, often drawing direct comparisons between Japanese Americans and other racial minorities. The article sets the stage with a long

68. Craddock, "Embodying Place," 355.

69. San Francisco Board of Supervisors quoted in Trauner, "The Chinese as Medical Scapegoats," 70–73.

70. Shah, *Contagious Divides*, 78; Sueyoshi, *Discriminating Sex*, 74.

71. Ting, "Bachelor Society."

72. Karuka, *Empire's Tracks*, chap. 5.

73. Wu, *The Color of Success*, 188. Amy Sueyoshi also offers an in-depth study of how Chinese and Japanese immigrants, previously seen as distinct peoples, were reimagined as one pan-Asian stereotype for the entrenchment of US racial hegemony. Sueyoshi, *Discriminating Sex*.

74. Lowe, *Intimacies*, 33.

75. Petersen, "Success Story, Japanese-American Style."

history of anti-immigrant policies, xenophobia, and the violence of Japanese internment. In Petersen's words, Japanese Americans have been subjected to extreme prejudice "like negroes" and hated as hyperefficient competitors "like Jews."[76] Unlike any of these other groups, however, Japanese Americans have achieved "any criterion of good citizenship [. . .] by almost totally unaided effort."[77] Characterizing Japanese Americans as "the outstanding exception"[78] to the limited socioeconomic mobility of racial minorities, Petersen's article establishes the thematic components of the model minority myth: support of the heteronuclear family, quiet complaisance, and individual uplift through education and hard work.

Petersen extracts from this history a willingness to assimilate that, in his eyes, makes Japanese Americans suitable American citizens. Despite their exclusion from formal citizenship, Petersen notes that Japanese Americans are "exceptionally law-abiding citizens."[79] When denied formal marriage, they developed strong (heteronuclear) families. When Japanese Americans were interned as traitors, the Japanese American Citizens League fought for the right to volunteer for the US military—eventually resulting in the highly decorated, all-Japanese American 442nd Infantry Combat Team. In Petersen's telling, the soldiers of the 442nd were so successful that they inspired an outright draft of Japanese Americans. While Petersen acknowledges the twisted logics behind this decision by government officials, he focuses primarily on Japanese American fortitude: "most accepted as their lot the overwhelming odds against them and bet their lives, determined to win even in a crooked game."[80] Rather than exposing and examining the conditions for Japanese American oppression, Petersen's account provides a roadmap for how particular minorities survive and succeed within the unequal conditions they are given.

As players in the "crooked game," the Japanese Americans of Petersen's article hit all the benchmarks of the model minority myth. They are avid students who conduct their education "like a military campaign."[81] They are more likely to pursue careers in business, optometry, or engineering than in the liberal arts. Among the "nonwhites" Petersen discusses in his brief overview of racial history, Japanese Americans are the only ones to "[climb] out of the slums and [acquire] social respect and dignity."[82] Petersen attributes this

---

76. Petersen, 20.
77. Petersen, 21.
78. Petersen, 41.
79. Petersen, 40.
80. Petersen, 36.
81. Petersen, 40.
82. Petersen, 40.

ascension to what he terms an "achievement orientation" transmitted through the family and religion. Among Japanese American values he says, "none [are] more important than 'Honor your obligations to parents and avoid bringing them shame.'"[83] In connecting achievement and other "model" behaviors to filial piety, Petersen reinforces the family as the space where national values are cultivated through a language of intimacy.

Though Petersen praises Japanese Americans' willingness to "[adapt] to American institutional forms,"[84] he still attributes this assimilability to *shushin* (Japanese moral education) and Buddhist values rather than to the possible *Americanness* of Japanese Americans. As Claire Jean Kim points out, Japanese immigration had been barred between 1924 and 1965, meaning that "the Japanese American population in 1966 consisted almost entirely of native-born U.S. citizens."[85] This is another cornerstone of the model minority myth— that Asians are somehow wired to be more compliant workers than other racial minorities, and that the genetic and/or cultural origins of such wirings are rooted in their perennial foreignness. No matter how assimilable model minorities become, they will never fully homologize with whiteness.[86]

Months after Petersen's publication, *U.S. News World and Report* celebrated another "U.S. success story" in San Francisco's Chinatown, where Chinese Americans were "moving ahead by applying the traditional virtues of hard work, thrift, and morality."[87] As in Petersen's article, that morality was attributed to "a tradition of respect for parents" and distant "Oriental" conventions rather than to survival strategies developed under US working conditions.[88] In 1971 *Newsweek* wrote in similar terms about Japanese Americans "Outwhiting the Whites," and the *Los Angeles Times* revisited Petersen's language in its 1977 "Japanese in U.S. Outdo Horatio Alger."[89] This flurry of Asian American representation came on the heels of the US civil rights movement. In fact, Petersen's article was published the same year Stokely Carmichael coined the term *Black Power*.[90] Racial unrest in the US also spurred the 1965 Immigration

---

83. Petersen, 41.

84. Petersen, 41.

85. Kim, "Racial Triangulation," 119.

86. In the introductory chapter of *Trans Exploits*, Jian Neo Chen offers a detailed account of how model minority mythology entwines with controlling images of the Black matriarch (Moynihan) and Oscar Lewis's notion of a Latinx "culture of poverty" to "activate the neoliberal restructuring of the settler U.S. state and civil society to minimally incorporate previously externalized communities within the national imaginary" (16).

87. "Success Story of One Minority in the U.S.," 7.

88. "Success Story of One Minority in the U.S.," 8.

89. "Success Story: Outwhiting the Whites"; Toth, "Peril to Identity."

90. Blackpast, "(1966) Stokely Carmichael, 'Black Power.'"

and Nationality Act, which not only concluded over eighty years of legislated Chinese exclusion but created preferential categories for those with professional skills or family ties. This particular portrait, then, not only adheres to patterns of Asian and Asian American racialization throughout Euroamerican history but was also explicitly engineered by legislation that favored white-collar workers with strong nuclear families. The influx of Asian migrants after 1965 contributed to homogenizing narratives of Asian America that continue to obscure the diversity of Asian Americans and Pacific Islanders and the needs that attend their particular experiences of colonization, imperialism, and racial discrimination.

The model minority myth, however, is also adept at erasing its own tracks. The hallmarks of "model" behavior—heteronormative "family values"; quiet, abled industriousness; and cultural essentialism—all naturalize racial and gender inequities as matters of individual achievement and cultural difference. In addition to ongoing coverage of Asian American "achievement" (more recently exemplified by the Pew Research Center's 2012 report on "the Rise of Asian America"[91]), the limited visibility of Asian American diversity in popular media has overwhelmingly focused on Asian Americans as racial exception—a success story told with alternating admiration and fear.[92] Asian Americans' achievements are praiseworthy so long as they do not subsume the primacy of white Americans, which is a culturalist compliment wrapped around distrust and derogation. The model minority myth is thus a distinctly (North) *American* success story; this is the narrative through which the US positions itself as a postracial democracy while simultaneously holding all designated "aliens" at bay.[93]

Listening diasporically to this history exposes the entanglements of yellow peril / model minority with other controlling narratives of US history. This storyline used to contain Asian Americans was necessitated both by Indigenous dispossession and by fear of African American freedom. It is inextricable from the ableist, heteropatriarchal, and meritocratic standards contrived to justify subjugating peoples of color. Even as LGBTQ+ Asian Americans inherit racial scripts that erase or punish their genders and sexualities, they—rather, we—step into these historical currents. We inhabit them unequally—with differential affordances, barriers, and vulnerabilities—but we are still too

91. Pew Research Center, *The Rise of Asian Americans*.
92. Ono and Pham, *Asian Americans and the Media*, 81.
93. For much more detailed explorations of how the US refashioned itself as a land of equal opportunity by offering narrow trajectories for racial assimilation, see Lee, *The Making of Asian America*; Wu, *The Color of Success*; Melamed, *Represent and Destroy*; Ferguson, *The Reorder of Things*.

often referenced as a monolith that deflects accountability. What rhetorical strategies, then, are available to us as people whose embodiments, desires, and lives subvert the narratives used to shield white supremacy? How do we negotiate from our varied positionalities a sense of collective power and political purpose? And how do we practice a politics of refusal that prevents our stories from being weaponized against our own or other minoritized communities?

Chapter Contents and Methodology

As described by LuMing Mao and Morris Young, Asian American rhetoric is a "rhetoric of becoming"[94] that examines, critiques, and at times even transforms transnational configurations of power. Most often, these texts come from rhetors exercising the "identity politics" theorized by the Combahee River Collective. Identity politics, as rhetorical practice, builds knowledge from one's own experiences of oppression when dominant vernaculars refuse that reality, and it situates those experiences within networks of "racial, sexual, heterosexual, and class oppression."[95] In this particular understanding, theorizing *from* experience of systemic oppression can expose the discriminatory mechanisms that are unnoticeable to those who benefit from that system. Whereas Mao and Young define Asian American rhetoric as the "use and development *by* Asian Americans of symbolic resources"[96] and Monberg and Young examine "rhetorical activity *by* Asian Americans,"[97] I emphasize that transformative critique is not an inherent trait of stories from the margins. Especially given the ways that colonialism strategically limits and surveils the knowledges available to colonized peoples, critical consciousness requires historically situated, socially engaged analyses of power. The multimodal archives featured in the following chapters offer inventive permutations of such analyses—acting on and at times transforming the experiences of trans and queer folks, disabled folks, Asian Americans, and those who live at the intersections of all those identities.

As a rhetorical critic, I am concerned with how communicative strategies (re)shape the boundaries of political and social belonging. Challenging the ways Asian Americans are disciplined as the well-behaved minority of neoliberal multiculturalism, I trace the compositional strategies through which rhetors invent, construct, and circulate counternarratives of trans and queer

---

94. Mao and Young, *Representations*, 5.
95. Combahee River Collective, *The Combahee River Collective Statement*.
96. Mao and Young, *Representations*, 3; emphasis added.
97. Monberg and Young, "Beyond Representation"; emphasis added.

Asian American experience. My approach is informed by intersectional and transnational feminist theory, finding "connection among meanings"[98] while situating individual stories within "wider systems of historical, cultural, and material local- and geo-politics."[99] Here, stories are the means through which individual experiences accrue social significance.

In fact, story is a methodological tether that brings together the interrelated disciplines of feminist theory, queer of color critique, critical race theory, trans theory, and disability studies. To connect these knowledges as well as the intersectional experiences of those who are marginalized by bodily and behavioral norms, my primary method is story. Using narrative as queer curation, *Constellating Home* documents and *values* the transitory, hushed moments in which queer intimacies thrive. It takes up conversations, performances, memories, and speculations composed of trans and queer Asian American experience, emplacing them together within counternarratives of communal and national (un)belongings. Inquiring into the rhetoricity of archives, this book seeks to confound the chronologies, cartographies, and categorizations that have rendered QTAPI "impossible subjects"[100] in dominant histories. In doing so, *Constellating Home* builds on the narrative traditions through which marginal subjects have revolutionized their experiences into collective knowledge, reparative critique,[101] and coalitional action.

Like many undertakings of queer archival work,[102] story is less invested in singular truth claims than in multiplicities, in imaginative affinities, and in discovering what has been occluded by our discursive boundaries. This ability to balance and make sense of contradiction, as others have argued, makes story an adaptive and sophisticated method. In the words of Terese Monberg, story is "pedagogical and methodological, and therefore deeply theoretical."[103] The narrative archives I explore expose the hidden logics[104] that figure trans and queer Asian Americans as threats to family and nation—thereby providing a *theory* of the world and its machinations. By giving name to those otherwise unspeakable, resonant experiences, these narratives triangulate a set of values through which to channel Asian American politics—providing a *method* of communal organizing. Finally, by making available and continuing

98. Lugones, *Pilgrimages/Peregrinajes*, 29.
99. Dingo, "Networking the Macro and Micro," 532.
100. Ngai, *Impossible Subjects*.
101. Kondo, *Worldmaking*, 50.
102. See Muñoz, "Ephemera as Evidence"; Cvetkovich, *An Archive of Feelings*; Lee, *Producing the Archival Body*.
103. Monberg, "Like the Molave."
104. What Lee Edelman terms the "logic of meaning" in *No Future*.

to cultivate these fugitive knowledges, these archives act as sites of collaborative learning—modeling a *pedagogy* of relationality and mutual care.

In drawing attention to and centering the wisdoms of LGBTQ+ Asian Americans, *Constellating Home* makes the implicit argument that these stories are worthy of attention—of as many (re)readings and thoughtful deliberations as the other stories that compose canonical histories of the US. Author Viet Thanh Nguyen describes Asian Americans as living in "narrative scarcity"—that is, a dearth of characters who live and look like us, and even "when they [look] like us, [they are] not really human."[105] The answer, as Nguyen emphasizes, is not just one story. The reasons that recent minority-led films such as *Crazy Rich Asians* have come under such scrutiny is because they have borne the burden of narrative scarcity. Its foil, "narrative plentitude," requires an abundance of narratives, which not only stretches across (though can never fully grasp) the range and heterogeneity of Asian America but also disperses the burden of representation. Asian Americans need narrative plentitude so that our stories can be incomplete, imperfect, or even mediocre.

For as much as stories shape when, where, and how we notice race, gender, and other markers of identity, they—like all tools—have limitations. Storytelling has earned the justifiable suspicion of critical theorists and social activists for its ease of appropriation and its assimilability into neoliberal multiculturalism. Sociologist Sujatha Fernandes uses the term *curated storytelling* to describe the production of minority stories that distract from grassroots political organizing by endorsing myths of individual uplift. Likewise, Amy Shuman cautions that stories of individual tragedies might "serve as another's inspiration and preserve, rather than subvert, oppressive situations."[106] Activist-academic Yasmin Nair warns against the predominance of stories as political strategy, noting that one experience can always be countered by another, that dueling stories can become competitions of "[who] can be more melodramatically effective,"[107] and that stories are too often used as "a substitute for political analysis."[108] I am sympathetic to and, in many ways, share these concerns. Universities have been integral to the appropriation and commodification of minority narratives, using select tales as evidence of a diversified campus and/or curriculum without addressing the systemic and pervasive discrimination faced by minoritized students, faculty, and staff.[109] Still, even

---

105. Nguyen, "Asian-Americans Need More Movies."

106. Shuman, *Other People's Stories*, 5.

107. Nair quoted in Chávez, *Queer Migration Politics*, 62.

108. Nair, "The Politics of Storytelling."

109. Melamed, *Represent and Destroy*; Gutiérrez y Muhs et al., *Presumed Incompetent*; Ahmed, *On Being Included*; Ferguson, *The Reorder of Things*.

story's skeptics acknowledge its centrality to human meaning-making. Stories are so often appropriated *because* they are so powerful.

Rather than abandon narrative, I stress the need to engage with, and explore responses to, its complexities and flaws. Addressing Nair's repudiation of storytelling, Karma Chávez considers how this position might "miss an opportunity to retool narrative and emotion in productive ways."[110] As opposed to proscribing storytelling altogether, movement builders might "be better served by taking more seriously, or thinking more concretely, about what *moves* people into movement and activism generally and into coalitional subjectivities specifically."[111] For the LGBTQ+ Asian Americans whose voices fill these pages, that "what" is stories. The storytelling projects explored in these chapters function as community hubs—where QTAPI could hear others' stories and cultivate vocabularies that situate their own experiences in relation to others. In interviews, the organizers behind each of these archives called them "gathering spaces,"[112] platforms "for sustaining long-term relationships,"[113] and "a way to acknowledge and learn from the work that has been done before so that it can inform the work we want to do now."[114] An inversion of Fernandes's "curated stories," which individualize social issues, these homing stories are structured around consciousness-raising and building collective power.

The archives I study compile stories across genres and generations, employing a wide range of rhetorical tactics to explore Asian America's buried pasts and possible futures. Home is in practice and in constant flux. It is (re)made through dialogue, through resonant traumas and aspirations, and through a willingness to work through discordant needs and desires. The content and form of each archive invites rhetors and audiences to listen for relationships among stories. I map the relations I find into constellations that deconstruct normalizing imperatives of Asian American belonging, and that reimagine communities otherwise. To anchor my discussion, each chapter focuses on a specific archive and how it unpacks a particular theme of the model minority myth. The themes of the first three chapters are, respectively, *love, resilience,* and *ancestry.* The fourth and final body chapter connects these preceding discussions by exploring how their emergent themes inform QTAPI engagements with ideologies and sites of *home.*

110. Chávez, *Queer Migration Politics,* 77.
111. Chávez, 77.
112. Chan, personal interview.
113. Lin, personal interview.
114. Nakano, personal interview.

In classical rhetorical tradition, each of these topics could be considered a commonplace, or topos—ideological concepts so socially ingrained that their meanings might seem self-evident or taken for granted. Commonplaces in US national discourse, for example, include *equality, freedom,* and *democracy.* Precise definitions of these terms are elusive, and the policies through which to pursue those definitions are even more complex. Arguments about affirmative action might appeal to the commonplace value of *equality* but will differ dramatically depending on how, for whom, and from what point in history interlocutors define *equal.* Equality is thus invoked as a universal good, but it can be used to support, to oppose, or to nuance approaches to affirmative action. The power of commonplaces lies in this paradoxical nature—that they are accepted as shared truths but also shift according to context. For their rhetorical potency, Ralph Cintrón defines topoi as "storehouses of social energy" that organize, constitute, and help generate our social lives.[115] To capture their reiterative nature, Christa Olson describes them as "places of return" or "nodes of social value and common sense."[116] For the purposes of this study, it may also be helpful to keep in mind Aristotle's definition of topoi as "lines of argument." In the context of global diaspora, commonplaces can be seen as *storylines* that provide common understanding in the absence of physical common ground.[117] On this un/stable discursive terrain, queer diasporic subjects are able to challenge and reinvent the meanings, values, and practices that condition social belongings.

Centering my discussion of each archive around a particular commonplace, chapters 1 through 3 proceed in two parts. First, I establish the centrality of the topos in prominent narratives of Asian Americans, demonstrating how "commonsense" notions of love, resilience, and ancestry shape QTAPI experiences of, and journeys toward and away from home(s). Second, I listen across the archive's stories, tracing constellations that examine and redefine the values undergirding its topos. Because the power of topoi lies in their elasticity and ambivalence, I do not attempt singular, definitive explanations of their meaning. Rather, each chapter traces their affective contours—how love, resilience, ancestry, and notions of home *move* people and communities to particular actions and attitudes. Chapter 4 networks my own homing story with those of the archives and introduces *home* as an additional topos whose idealizations undergird imaginings of the previous three.

---

115. Cintrón, "Democracy and Its Limitations," 101–2.

116. Olson, *Constitutive Visions,* introduction.

117. The term *storylines* brings to mind Bonilla-Silva's usage, which he defines as "the socially shared tales that are fable-like and incorporate a common scheme and wording." *Racism without Racists,* 97.

My analysis throughout the book draws from the vocabulary of Chela Sandoval's *Methodology of the Oppressed,* which details a repertoire of discursive tactics through which oppositional movements decode languages of domination, cultivate coalitional subjectivities, and establish new meanings and relationalities.

Particularly relevant to my discussion are those tactics that act on "categories of meaning"[118] in order to transform them:

1. "Deconstruction"—challenging presumed truths in dominant ideological forms.
2. "Meta-ideologizing"—appropriating dominant ideological forms and assigning them new meanings.[119] In the following chapters, I often use the word *reappropriation.*
3. "Democratics"—channeling these analyses toward more equal futures.
4. "Differential movement"—strategic movement among these strategies and ideological positionings in order to apprehend and act upon structures of knowledge.

As queer practice, differential opposition does not aspire to correctness or consistency; rather, it forges knowledge and change through difference and dynamism. These QTAPI storytelling projects strategically (re)arrange divergent voices, genres, and rhetorical approaches to posit the archive as a crucible of insurgent knowledges. Through these differential tactics, they unpack the topoi of model minority and yellow peril mythologies. The resonances, dissonances, and harmonies across personal narratives track the fraught and contradictory positions that queer and trans Asian Americans occupy in the story of US American dominance.

Chapter 1 lays the groundwork by exploring the Dragon Fruit Project (DFP) as a site of "differential consciousness-raising"—the critical awareness through which one is able to enact differential movement. An ongoing oral history project, the DFP has involved hundreds of volunteers in collecting, coding, and disseminating personal accounts of QTAPI activism from the 1960s to the present. It pairs younger QTAPI volunteers with older QTAPI activists to conduct interviews about their experiences. This intergenerational engagement and reciprocity encourage the sort of relational reflexivity required for homing. I draw connections among these stories to consider

118. Sandoval, *Methodology of the Oppressed,* sec. "Semiotics and Languages of Emancipation."

119. Sandoval correlates this with Barthes's "revolutionary exnomination."

constellations of QTAPI love—how the language of love has structured relations within Asian American families, and the diverse ways that trans and
queer Asian Americans have redefined love. Through homing, these QTAPI
explore love as a practice that can (re)invent community within economies of
abandonment.[120]

Chapter 2 moves to the Visibility Project (VP), which began as a pho-
tographic collection and grew to include video interviews, a digital history
tour, and a biannual performance series. My listening practice focuses specifically on how notions of immigrant resilience delimit the conditions for
Asian American visibility. Through transformative applications of Eve Sedgwick's "nonce taxonomies"—that is, inventive terminologies that disrupt the
limited social categories into which we divide human identity—the rhetors
of the Visibility Project leverage their own experiences to challenge visibility
as a presumed good. The homing practices of the VP expose how controlling
images[121] of Asian femininity and masculinity participate in meritocratic fic-
tions of individual resilience. Through nonce taxonomies, these stories inno-
vate and circulate novel scripts around gender, race, (dis)ability, and sexuality
that explore and celebrate their interrelations. In so doing, the VP insists on
the contingent and relational nature of identity. Homing enables QTAPI to
(re)make the scripts through which we engage the world, emphasizing the role
of supportive communities that make space for and respond to our counterstories. This multimodal archive of photographs, videos, performances, and
other historical documents thus offers an alternative theory of resilience as
the practice of mutual care—a commitment to creating spaces that do not
replicate historic exclusions. From these models of collective uplift, I propose
a constellation of QTAPI resilience based in Mia Mingus's "crip solidarity"[122]—
that is, an ethics of interdependency that refuses to leave anyone behind.

Chapter 3 features the Queer Ancestors Project (QAP), an annual nine-
month multidisciplinary workshop focused on printmaking, writing, and
queer history. Students ages eighteen to twenty-six learn about the lives and
work of queer "ancestors"—both familial and figurative. They explore queer
and genderqueer lineages from non-Western histories as well as the lives and
productions of queer artists. Students print and write themselves into dialogue with these elders or other queer kin drawn from popular culture or
far-flung mythologies. Their homing practices are then documented in art

120. Povinelli, *Economies of Abandonment*.
121. A term and concept borrowed from Patricia Hill Collins, who explores controlling
images as racist and sexist ideological figurations of Black women (for example, mammies and
jezebels). Hill Collins, *Black Feminist Thought*.
122. Mingus, "Wherever You Are."

showcases and printed anthologies. Finding family in unlikely figures, these rhetors unpack the cultural essentialism embedded in notions of ancestry and genealogy. They expose the limitations of identity-based discourses that have narrativized a cisgender, heterosexual Asian America and an exclusively white queer community. In (re)claiming ancestors and inscribing new lineages through homing, QAP participants enact a "kuaer pedagogy." That is, a "race-conscious, womanist, and transnational"[123] *unknowing* of historical narratives that unsettle the foundations of family, community, and nation. I constellate their journeys to consider the lessons they provide about ancestry—about breaking restrictive bonds and discovering yet-inarticulable kinships and futures.

Finally, chapter 4 pulls the preceding discussions together with my own narrative. My body provides the archive for this chapter, and story functions as archival description. This, too, is a polyvocal collection. The theories and artistic innovations explored in previous chapters help make knowledge of my scars, migrations, and memories. Bodyminds,[124] I argue, record the impact of racism, cissexism, ableism, queerphobia, and other discriminatory forms. Narrative (re)negotiates the social meanings of those records. In conversation with the rhetors of the DFP, the VP, and the QAP, I offer my own experiences and redefinitions of love, resilience, and ancestry. These topics serve as common spaces where our stories converge. My exploration of these commonalities and divergences establishes a fourth commonplace: *home.* Reflecting on the fraught histories that diasporic and queer communities have with idealizations of *home,* I address how *love, resilience,* and *ancestry* have restricted, compelled, and/or empowered the migrations of queer diasporic subjects—departures from and journeys toward sites of belonging. My use of personal narrative not only participates in Asian American and Pacific Islander traditions of "talk story" as communal practice but also builds on legacies of scholar-activists who leverage their own stories to expose and transform the boundaries of academic knowledges and worldviews.[125] Storying my life in

123. Lee, "Kuaering Queer Theory," 312.

124. A term attributed to Margaret Price, marking the interrelations of mind and body. "The Bodymind Problem."

125. Texts that have been particularly meaningful in my own journey include Anzaldúa, *Borderlands*; Moraga and Anzaldúa, *This Bridge Called My Back*; Gutiérrez y Muhs et al., *Presumed Incompetent*; Kafer, *Feminist, Queer, Crip*; Patsavas, "Recovering a Cripistemology of Pain"; Price, "The Bodymind Problem"; King, Gubele, and Anderson, *Survivance, Sovereignty, and Story*; Bratta and Powell, "Entering the Cultural Rhetorics Conversations"; Del Hierro, Levy, and Price, "We Are Here"; Riley-Mukavetz, "On Working From or With Anger"; Ahmed, *On Being Included* and *Living a Feminist Life*; Clare, *Brilliant Imperfection*; Johnson and LeMaster, *Gender Futurity, Intersectional Autoethnography*.

concert with narratives from previous chapters, I join the QTAPI authors in queer diasporic homing.

The rhetors who fill these chapters include new im/migrants,[126] Native Hawaiians, and descendants of the Chinese railroad workers who built this nation's transcontinental backbone. Their stories traverse continents and generations. They identify as gay men, as lesbians, bisexual, queer, trans, and as genderqueer. It would be impossible—and pointless—to claim any universalizing, singular QTAPI worldview or experience. Rather, the genre of the archive is well suited for capturing "togetherness-in-difference,"[127] the term LuMing Mao assigns to amalgamated rhetorics that emerge from transnational migrations and cultural flows. In concert, these heterogenous voices map the myriad consequences of Asian Americans' trajectories in the US—a textured and prismatic history often elided in official accounts of the nation's past. Of particular interest to this book is what David Eng terms the "racialization of intimacy"[128]—the sociocultural mechanisms through which racial disparities are coded into idealized notions of family, intimacy, and citizenship. As intimate genres, the personal stories captured in interviews, photographs, poems, and performances offer thoughtful and felt insight into the entangled relations of individual experience and social power. While the particular configuration of theories, texts, and interpretations is uniquely mine, constellated into collective explorations of QTAPI commonplaces, my writing is made possible by the feminist of color, queer of color, critical trans, disability, and critical race theorists who have opened up new knowledges and given me community. Any mistakes I have made are mine, but I hope this book engages and extends their work and invites further explorations of the insights that come from the margins.

// In one of Writing Rainbow's *final writing experiments, we respond to a passage from Jade Snow Wong's* Fifth Chinese Daughter. *Wong writes: "Jade Snow made her own decisions. At no time did she consult her family about the various jobs; she simply told them when her mind was made up."[129] After we read a longer selection from the memoir, Nancy Au asks us to "write about a time your mind was*

---

126. For the most part, I follow Eithne Luibhéid's usage of *migrant* to refer to "anyone who has crossed an international border," de-emphasizing the categories delineated by state recognition. I do, however, use *immigrant* or *refugee* to refer to a specific rhetor when they have claimed that term as their own. I also use *immigrant* when specifically referring to state policies and stereotypes that reinforce these legal categories (Luibhéid and Cantú, *Queer Migrations*, xi).

127. Mao, *Reading Chinese Fortune Cookie.*

128. Eng, *The Feeling of Kinship.*

129. Wong, *Fifth Chinese Daughter,* 103.

made up." Recount a decision about which you felt strongly. Au begins by offering her own extemporaneous passage. She—or rather, her narrator—recalls storming out of her parents' house, wedging herself between the steering wheel and the shallow recline of a driver's seat, and sitting out in the cold until her sister comes to retrieve her. I don't know what car Au has in mind, but in my imagination, it is the 1997 beige Toyota Corolla in which I learned to drive. In my mind, we are parked in my high school's empty lot, windows open to the desert sky. In my mind, there is no sister because I have no siblings and I have driven too far from home for my parents to come in search of me. I also know that no one is looking. Trauma time is cyclical, a friend cautioned, and I responded: "Every experience of displacement becomes every other experience of displacement."

Exactly a week before my flight to San Francisco—a week before I met Celeste Chan on the rainy sidewalk outside The Flight Deck—my rented duplex caught fire. The apartment next door was hollowed out by the flames, and my unit was collateral damage. On a Saturday morning, I fled plumes of smoke with a dog leash in one hand and my laptop in another. For five nights, I slept on air mattresses and borrowed floors. Just before my flight, though, I turned down generous offerings of guest rooms and pull-out couches to slip back into my soot-stained rental. The fire marshal had declared it safe, though still smoky. I left the dog with a friend because she could not stand the smell. A tornado had touched down two hours away in Oklahoma, and the National Weather Service had issued a warning for our area. The surreal gray-green of the sky near dusk, the eerie, thick silence of the air felt like where I needed to be. Every experience of displacement becomes every other experience of displacement—every other night I had no place to call home. My mind was made up, though the decision was not really a decision. Hundreds of other decisions collapse into this one—a lifetime of stumbling on earth I was not made to settle, but the only foundation I knew.

Since my parents laid out sleeping bags in our first, unfurnished home, I have felt safest on the floor. Since I learned to run into the desert night, I have been soothed by open skies and cool dry breezes. Since I learned what I am as a betrayal, I have been most comfortable having no one to answer or come home to. My mother's and my father's stories are definitely not mine, though sometimes I wonder if I am the echo that lost its way back. My father has always loved stories and wordplay. I am told that he won a poetry contest in my first language, which now I can hardly read. My mother has an insatiable love of learning and is counting the years until she turns sixty-five, when colleges will waive tuition for the classes she never got to take. Neither of them had the privilege I did—to make learning and writing a vocation. I remembered this most of all when I cast my applications into a notoriously sparse academic job market. I remember it when senior colleagues (in kindness or coercion) invoke the specter of tenure in my decisions—how my father had told me that writing was a hobby but would not keep a roof over my head; how my mother insisted, with growing desperation, that it was not too late for me to pursue a more stable future. I wonder if they are haunted by their own parents' fears and longings.

My grandparents' lives are stories I have only heard secondhand—tales of living under Japanese occupation and fleeing Maoist persecution. I wonder if my parents can disentangle their own memories from the corollaries of war, colonialism, and trauma. The Sino-Japanese Wars and the Chinese Cultural Revolution were never taught in my history classes in American schools. These were lessons I pieced together between bits of conversation and eventually Google, tracing my bloodlines through the World Wide Web. The Japanese government, I learned, maintained control of its "model colony"[130] through public education, segregating students by ethnicity and shuttling Taiwanese children into vocational tracts to boost economic production. The roots of Japanese imperialism, however, are buried deep in an earth trammeled by Western expansion and the threat of exploitation under an industrialized world order.[131] I had to read these histories in translation—to reach across languages, through half a century and halfway around the world to imagine this experience that my grandmother lived. I have tried to tell a story that brings her life to mine but could find no plot that moves cleanly from Taiwan to the Arizona desert—no strong tether that holds me to this distant, muzzled past.

These are just a few tendrils in a rhizomatic history. In the infinite possible descriptions of my parents' lives, there must be stories of watching their child acculturate to a world that has defined them by their unbelonging. There must be stories (that I have never heard them tell) of raising that child in Mandarin and then surrendering to the forceful encroachment of English—the language through which they have been disparaged, discriminated against, and made "other" for most of their adult lives. These stories are not mine to tell, but I know with certainty that I too have brandished my adopted language to keep them at a distance. I have used it to deny their truths and the conditions that would impel them to enforce their child's conformity, and to fear for my safety if they did not.

It took me years to recognize memories of alienation and disenfranchisement in my father's distrust of Western values and my mother's search for Asian communities. For most of childhood, I heard only essentialist notions of identity in their reliance on shared ancestries. Much later, I realized that theirs wasn't a search for flat identification. It was a desire for belonging—a longing for modes of relation that did not exclude them as perpetual outsiders. In many ways, their trajectories

130. Ching, Becoming "Japanese"; Lin, "Political Indoctrination."
131. Suzuki, "Japan's Socialization into Janus-Faced European International Society"; Mishra, "Land and Blood."

have carried me to The Flight Deck, where we queer migrant children tell stories of intergenerational conflict and (dis)connection. I listen as our narratives inter-weave across oceans. I hear our memories diverging and converging in conflicted relations with home—the ones we lost or never knew, and the ones we found and are building, together. //

CHAPTER 1

Love in Constellation

The Dragon Fruit Project and Differential Consciousness-Raising

They could've given me a dishonorable discharge, so my investigating officer he was really nice and he said, "You're gonna have to write a letter. It's going to have to be this really cheesy letter saying you love your country and everything like that and you weren't gay before, because if they find out that you knew you were gay before and you misled the army, then we could put you in jail for misrepresenting yourself and trying to get the money."

—Kim Dang, Dragon Fruit Project (2012)[1]

Love and Its Imperatives

Kim Dang's interview for the Dragon Fruit Project (DFP) begins with her resignation from the US armed services. At a time when she was beginning to explore her sexual orientation, she was placed under investigation for "verbal initiative of being a homosexual."[2] Following instructions from her investigating officer, Dang successfully petitioned for an honorable discharge based on her love of her country and the claim that she had no prior knowledge of her homosexuality. The pairing of these two statements implies that queerness is a betrayal of the state—and, inversely, that loving one's nation is an exclusively heterosexual affair. "Fortunately," Dang recalls, "I was able to convince them, 'Look, I haven't done anything wrong according to your books, because I haven't even kissed anybody. So I haven't done anything, okay?'" In fact, while Dang was under investigation, she had a husband and a daughter. She was the wife/mother of the prototypical nuclear family. While Dang characterizes

---

1. Dang, interview.
2. Dang.

the marriage as one without connection—physical, emotional, or otherwise[3]—
she credits the marriage and the fact that she "could honestly say, 'Look, I
have never done anything'" for her honorable discharge. As Dang notes, the
terms of her discharge are critical: "Anything but honorable, you can't get a
job." Especially because she lost all her supportive networks after coming out,
her chances for survival depended on her ability to perform patriotism as
heteronormativity.

Dang's account offers one example of "love" as an ideological current that
channels nationalistic interests into the ostensibly private worlds of marriage
and family. Dang's love of her country was evidenced by her marriage and
child and by the (apparent) absence of queer relations. In Western countries,
this link between family, love, and national fortitude can be traced to the rise
of global capitalism. John D'Emilio's landmark essay, "Capitalism and Gay
Identity," identifies how free wage labor transitioned the family from an economic unit to an affective unit—in some ways, enabling (queer) intimacies
not directed toward reproduction. However, because capitalism itself relies on
heterosexual families for generating more workers, heterosexuality becomes a
matter of ideology. Through the language of intimacy and personal choice, the
nation ensures the familial units required for labor production. In this discursive environment, love is a commonplace that establishes patterns of behavior,
structures of relationality, and cultural values presumed "natural" such that
those outside its parameters are deemed amoral. That social deviance then
translates into unfitness for communal and national citizenship.

Sara Ahmed's *Cultural Politics of Emotion* adds a racialized dimension to
D'Emilio's analysis by identifying the nuclear family as a building block of
white nationalism. In Ahmed's explanation, "making the nation is tied to making love in the choice of an ideal other (different sex/same race)," which then
reproduces the national ideal "in the form of the future generation (the white
Aryan child)."[4] For example, the Creativity Movement enjoins "proud, white
women" to "lovingly work as devoted wives, mothers, Sisters, helpers, friends"
beside their male counterparts for the "purity" of the white race. The movement directly urges its followers to "be fruitful and multiply."[5] This strategy
can find antecedents throughout eugenicist rhetorics, for example in Theodore
Roosevelt's insistence that white Americans produce large families as a mat-

---

3. In her words, "I was just kind of going through the motions. This was what I'm supposed to do, but I didn't feel fulfilled."

4. Ahmed, *The Cultural Politics of Emotion*, 124.

5. These quotes are drawn directly from the organization's website in 2019, when this
passage was written. Sources: The Creativity Movement, "Declaration of the Women's Frontier"
and "The Sixteen Commandments."

ter of civic responsibility.[6] Love, in other words, becomes the embodiment of national allegiance through heterosexual reproduction and racial segregation. Queers, migrants, and racial "others,"—and their desires—are figured as threats to (white) love for family and nation.

This chapter establishes love as common ground where many QTAPI experiences converge and contend with broader social histories. I begin by exploring love as it has scripted Asian American racialization—how dominant narratives in both Western and Eastern cultures established heteronormativity and ableism as imperatives of Asian and Asian American belonging. Listening to the voices of the Dragon Fruit Project, I explore how these storytellers home in on the social scripts that constrained their experiences of love, as well as the forms of knowledge and community through which they redefine love. Homing, in these accounts, situates the narrator's lived experience in historical context to track the limitations and possibilities of love. As many DFP participants note, this relationally attuned storytelling also enables QTAPI to better understand their own memories of exclusion, unease, or injury. Meanwhile, diasporic listening equips me to connect their individual stories with one another's and with the historical patterns they invoke. The constellations I chart among DFP stories and related histories then outline a broad range of tactics through which love can be redefined toward intimate practices that maneuver across, along, and beyond cultural and geographical boundaries.

Lauren Berlant's deep dive into intimate affects helps articulate a theory through which to follow love's social circulations. In *Desire/Love,* Berlant defines desire as a state of attachment and love as "the embracing dream in which desire is reciprocated."[7] Put differently, love involves storytelling, which Berlant calls a "theatrical" and "scenic" structure that imagines a world in which desire endures.[8] While the possible fantasies through which desire finds longevity should be infinite, Berlant explores why love's expressions tend to be "so *conventional,* so bound up in institutions like marriage and family, property relations, and stock phrases and plots."[9] Through legal structures, entertainment industries, and journalism, the US has privileged a single "love plot" through which heterosexual couples provide familial continuity via "kinship chains."[10] Those who do not accede to this plot—including single or nonreproductive heterosexuals and LGBTQ+ folks—are subjected to shame

6. Roberts, *Killing the Black Body,* 60–61.
7. Berlant, *Desire/Love,* 6.
8. Berlant, 7.
9. Berlant, 7; emphasis original.
10. Berlant, 44.

or other forms of punishment by the carceral state and its rightful citizens. Valuations of love stories, expressed through state regulations and mass media depictions, then organize intimate practices into acceptable and unacceptable desires.

As a commonplace that scales from nation to household and back up again, *love* plays a crucial role in racializing Asian Americans. The perceived industriousness that made Chinese laborers indispensable to colonizing projects such as the transcontinental railroad also rendered them as threats to the white workforce—especially as labor markets diminished. Chinese Americans' willingness to perform life-threatening labor for low wages then flipped from a "model minority" trait to a foreign menace. In this light, Chinese assiduity was "'unhuman' and therefore barbaric and uncivilized."[11] The white heteronuclear family, as a disciplinary metric, served as a means of articulating that uncivility. Nayan Shah uses the term *queer domesticities* to describe the domestic configurations of San Francisco's Chinatown in the nineteenth century, which defied white middle-class norms.[12] These homes included households with multiple women, households dominated by women, communities of men in bunkhouses, and common-law marriages between Chinese men and white women—all of which were condemned by white politicians, physicians, and missionaries through the language of sickness. Predominantly male bachelor societies were regarded as sites of pestilence and moral perversion. Chinese women, perceived almost exclusively as prostitutes, bore the stigma of sex work and its attendant associations with disease and depravity. Put differently, Chinese Americans—for their violations of conventional love plots— were and still often are regarded as threats to the moral and physical health of the US nation-state.

By the mid-twentieth century, normative frames of Asian America shifted again in response to the civil rights movement. Frank Chin and Jeffrey Paul Chan famously used the phrase *racist love* to describe the model minority's subjugation as a beloved object of white America.[13] As opposed to the *racist hate* that produces more overt forms of exclusion, racist love disciplines Asian Americans into docile, uncomplaining, and white-proximal minorities. Love, in this case, names an interracial intimacy between whites and Asians that encourages aspirational whiteness. With the ascent of liberal ideologies through the rhetoric of equal rights, free trade, and individual uplift, Asians were (once again) marked as assimilable minorities. As a result of these

---

11. Sueyoshi, *Discriminating Sex*, 14.
12. Shah, *Contagious Divides.*
13. Chin, "Come All Ye Asian American Writers."

changing attitudes as well as the selective immigration laws that brought in more white-collar workers, perceived Asian American "achievement" fueled the nation's fantasies of itself as a beacon of multicultural inclusion.

Though *racist love* identifies Asian America's dangerous attachment to whiteness and the privileges of proximity, Chin and Chan's response still courts a similarly rigid, heteropatriarchal form of cultural nationalism. Along with collaborators Lawson Fusao Inada and Shawn Wong, Chin et al. pursue an Asian American identity built on hegemonic masculinity. In their introduction to *The Big Aiiieeeee!*—the follow-up companion to their germinal anthology of Asian American writing—Chin et al. lament the state of Chinese American masculinity: racist love, they postulate, has made Chinese men "the fulfillment of white homosexual fantasy."[14] They write: "It is an article of white liberal American faith today that Chinese men, at their best, are effeminate closet queens like Charlie Chan and, at worst, are homosexual menaces like Fu Manchu."[15] Chin, Chan, Inada, and Wong's solution is to return to "Confucian heroic tradition"[16] where "life is war [and] every human is born a soldier."[17] For Chin et al., "real" Asian American identity must begin with martial traditions in Asian history—ones that do counter particular Western fantasies of oriental softness while simultaneously endorsing the devaluation of femininity and queerness. As "founding fathers" of Asian American literary tradition, they advanced a "doctrine of compulsory heterosexuality"[18] and masculinity that replicates the gender hierarchy through which Asian American men are feminized, and through which femininity and homosexuality are denigrated and deemed shameful. The concatenation of these scripts—that of a *heterosexual* US patriotism, a *patriarchal* Asian tradition, and a nuclear family as the site where these values are cultivated—narrativizes a world where queer Asian Americans are ejected from nation, homeland, and family. To dream trans and queer desires—to imagine and realize defiant gender expressions and intimacies—sets LGBTQ+ people of color on narrative trajectories that remove them from the protection of traditional family structures. These departures, however, also carry them into novel figurations of family, nation, and home.

---

14. Chin et al., *The Big Aiiieeeee!*, xiii.

15. Chin et al., xiii.

16. While interpretations of Confucian texts vary and are subject to ongoing debate, Chin et al.'s open homophobia suggests that the editors are invoking conventional associations with Confucian values, including filial piety and traditional gender roles. Ironically, the conception of the East as a backward, antiqueer society also folds neatly into narratives of the West "liberating" other countries.

17. Chin et al., *The Big Aiiieeeee!*, xv.

18. Eng, *Racial Castration*, 21.

The remainder of this chapter responds to these heteropatriarchal histories with counternarratives from API Equality—Northern California (APIENC) and the community consciousness that this organization nurtures through the Dragon Fruit Project, an oral history archive of QTAPI activisms. I begin with a description of the Dragon Fruit Project itself and how its structure enables differential consciousness-raising. Its myriad narratives explore how discourses of love have foreclosed the possibility of queer Asian American existence as well as the heterogenous and divergent routes that QTAPI have taken to reimagine love. Listening diasporically, I hear love as QTAPI commonplace—as a site of affective intensity—where our experiences converge with commonalities and contradictions. I then constellate the homing stories of the DFP to expose the damage of normative scripts about love, and to trace their alternative intimacies and belongings.

Listening with the Dragon Fruit Project

By uplifting our queer API community histories, we're breaking through the silence that is a byproduct of systematic and institutionalized oppression. When community members engage with this work as interviewers, transcribers, cataloguers and archivists, we are actively resisting the systems that have isolated us from each other and keep us out of mainstream present-day and historical narratives. Not only are we active agents archiving our individual histories, we are also piecing together organizational, community, and movement histories that will contextualize our collective narrative. When we document our history we're also laying the groundwork for future work.

—The Dragon Fruit Project, API Equality—Northern California[19]

In 2012 historian Amy Sueyoshi looked into the GLBT Historical Society's archive of oral histories and found that only 2 (of 702) entries featured API women. While the Dragon Fruit Project does not contain *only* women's voices, it emerges from this discovery and offers alternative narratives through which the contributions of queer API women and nonbinary folks are restored as integral components of LGBTQ+ history. Sueyoshi, a groundbreaking scholar of queer Asian American studies, began interviewing queer Asian American elders about their involvement in LGBTQ+ and Asian American activism

---

19. API Equality—Northern California, "About."

from the 1960s to the present. At the start of the project, Sueyoshi focused specifically on the role of love in Asian Pacific lesbian activisms, inquiring into interviewees' experiences and definitions of love. Since then, the lines of questioning as well as the pool of interviewers and interviewees have diversified. While "love and activism" as a direct line of questioning drifts in and out of different interviews (designed and conducted by a wide array of interlocutors), love as concept and theme suffuses the archive in myriad, sometimes conflicting, definitions and enactments. Of course, radical practices of love have been critical for the survival of trans and queer and diasporic communities. However, as discussed above, "love" is also a freighted ideological concept affixed to state regulations of kinship and family. In its constellations of oral histories, the DFP explores how love is wielded for both punitive and liberatory ends, and it locates individual experiences within "a set of dominant institutions"[20] that determine the possibilities for complicity and rebellion.[21]

A year into her research, Sueyoshi passed the project on to APIENC, which was able to bring a much larger team to the work of collecting and archiving interviews. Since then, APIENC has involved over two hundred volunteers as "active agents" in producing QTAPI history. This work includes more than eighty narratives, interviews, and other movement-building materials. They have also created open-access content to distribute that knowledge, such as timelines of queer API history, Wikipedia entries, and a Dragon Fruit Project Zine.[22] In providing both space and time for intergenerational conversation, the DFP networks personal journeys into a collaborative (re)negotiation of communal identity and politics. These individual voices coalesce in a collective rhetoric that I term *differential consciousness-raising*, (re)naming the paradoxical experiences of queer diaspora as part of a communal past, present, and future.

Consciousness-raising, most often attributed to feminist movements of the 1960s, has been described by rhetorical scholar Tasha Dubriwny as "the process of giving individual experiences new meanings by moving them into the realm of social reality."[23] Even in the 1960s, however, when consciousness-raising was popularized by feminist organizations, the usage of the term and its practices varied widely. On a basic level, consciousness-raising provided the space for women to story those "personal" experiences that had been

---

20. Powell et al., "Act I."
21. To fold this into Tasha Dubriwny's language, consciousness-raising as collective rhetoric enables "oppressed groups [to] rename—and hence create new meaning from their experiences." "Consciousness-Raising as Collective Rhetoric," 396.
22. API Equality—Northern California, "Dragon Fruit Project Toolkit."
23. Dubriwny, "Consciousness-Raising as Collective Rhetoric," 401.

denied a public vocabulary. This form of shared vulnerability and open disclosure is the definition that has retained prominence in subsequent decades. When lacking an eye toward structural interventions, consciousness-raising could and sometimes has become a space for "unleash[ing] pent up hostility" without a direction for that rage and pain.[24]

Embedded in the work of consciousness-raising, however, was also "learning about patriarchy as a system of domination, how it became institutionalized and how it is perpetuated and maintained."[25] As bell hooks reminds her readers, revolutionary feminist consciousness—public and personal— required women to "confront their own sexism towards other women."[26] Put differently, consciousness-raising situated the personal within the political in ways that grappled with their reciprocity, and with the inevitable complicities of anyone entangled in these networks. It is this form of consciousness-raising that hooks insists on for the reinvigoration of feminist movements. It is this consciousness-raising that Gwendolyn Pough calls a "public pedagogy" capable of both situating issues in the public sphere and mobilizing action.[27] It is this consciousness-raising that the DFP cultivates through homing and multitudinous formations of queer diaspora. When viewed as a collective rhetoric, consciousness-raising amalgamates individual experiences into "novel public vocabularies" that transform audiences and challenge hegemonic ideologies.[28]

Queer archives, often built by the ephemera of LGBTQ+ experience, are poised to harness personal accounts toward consciousness-raising. As Jean Bessette demonstrates in her study of *Lesbian/Woman*—a collection of self-reported, written anecdotes by lesbians—identifying linkages among individual experiences can help (re)define "personal trauma not as a result of [individual] pathology, but rather the result of a world hostile to same-sex relations."[29] Similarly, contributors to the Dragon Fruit Project use homing to situate their experiences in a "web of relations,"[30] exposing the social grammars through which particular desires are stigmatized and punished. While any collection of heterogenous experiences will house contradictions, diasporic listening hears those tensions, discordances, and impossibilities as social critique and as collaborative unsettlings and reconstructions of home. The collective rhetoric that emerges from the Dragon Fruit Project, then, does

24. hooks, *Feminism Is for Everybody*, 7.
25. hooks, 7.
26. hooks, 10.
27. Pough, "Do the Ladies Run This?"
28. Dubriwny, "Consciousness-Raising as Collective Rhetoric," 396.
29. Bessette, *Retroactivism in the Lesbian Archives*, 42.
30. Powell et al., "Act I."

not posit a cohesive consciousness for QTAPI identity. Rather, it orchestrates something akin to Chela Sandoval's "differential consciousness," coalescing divergent perspectives within a polyvocal composition of LGBTQ+ Asian American and Pacific Islander (un)belongings.

As described in Sandoval's *Methodology of the Oppressed,* differential consciousness weaves between and among ideological positionings and builds from "correlations, intensities, junctures, crises."[31] Like the clutch in a car, differential consciousness permits one to "select, engage, and disengage" for the transmission of power.[32] As a diasporic archive, the DFP does not aspire to a seamless, unified articulation of Asian American experience or identity. Rather, it provides time and shelter for LGBTQ+ Asian Americans to learn about, dwell with, and respond to dominant and minor histories contiguous with their lives. The overall effect is a score of positionalities that compose a polyphonic account of what is and what could be. By converging on the topic of "love" and approaching it from myriad angles, the DFP's many narratives listen for and inscribe unanticipated intimacies. At the junctures, collisions, and confluences of these stories, the DFP both deconstructs social norms included in "love" and advances the imaginative possibilities enabled by queer love.

Archival Work as Homemaking

The structure of the Dragon Fruit Project itself embeds relationality in its practices. Though the oral histories foreground the voices of each narrator, they are also products of ongoing collaboration and knowledge-sharing. When Amy Sueyoshi first began collecting these histories, she conducted detailed (eight-hour) interviews with her subjects. Adapting academic research to communal praxis, APIENC reduced interview times to sixty to ninety minutes and involved teams of volunteers in creating accessible narratives that could be distributed online. Under APIENC's stewardship, the majority of DFP interviews pair a younger LGBTQ+ Asian American interviewer with an older interviewee, although some are group conversations and some take place between romantic partners or among friends. An audio file then gets passed to other volunteers who transcribe and code the interview for key

---

31. Sandoval, *Methodology of the Oppressed,* sec. II: The Theory and Method of Oppositional Consciousness.
32. Sandoval, sec. II.

terms.[33] Finally, someone curates quotes from the interview and drafts a one- to two-paragraph summary that serves as an informal archival description.

Throughout, one person's story passes through numerous hands. While volunteers work to honor the experience of the original storyteller, it is a product of shared labor and interpretations. Diasporic listening suffuses the process, attuning participants to potential resonances between this experience and others' histories. Transcription begins with a volunteer listening through a recording one tiny segment at a time, often rewinding to verify phrasings and to decipher particular words. That same volunteer or a separate coder will go through to identify "noteworthy themes" (e.g., Activism or Mental Health) that audiences might track across narratives.[34] This process of coding differentiates the DFP from a disinterested repository of oral histories. These narratives are actively curated; a team of QTAPI organizers have negotiated and identified themes that they have heard repeated throughout the interviews and that they regard as important to their communities. The themes then serve as connective tissue through which auditors can trace the varying contours of QTAPI experience.

After coding, the transcript goes to a quality control (QC) team member who must also dwell with the narrative, listening for missed connections, formatting the text, checking for consistency, and revising for readability. To make the transcript more reader-friendly, QC agents remove "false starts" or "extraneous remarks" and revise for clarity where appropriate.[35] Team members are instructed to "maintain the integrity and voice of the narrator,"[36] but this work requires them to impose their own judgment: Which words should be eliminated as extraneous? Which pauses become ellipses and which disappear altogether? Which sighs, gestures, or emphases should go down in history? As they make these decisions, the DFP team members leave comments or questions in the margins, which they pass on to a QC moderator. The moderator conducts still more proofreading, clarifications, and judgment calls, and eventually "locks" the transcription in its final iteration. The resultant interview, though a record of one particular conversation, results from myriad

---

33. The following are the codes provided in the Dragon Fruit Project Toolkit, though in practice, volunteers sometimes improvised with their own: Romantic Love; Activism; Immigration, Internalized Oppression, Discrimination, Familial Relationships, Post-War, Coming Out, Religion, Self-Identification, HIV/AIDS, Drugs/Alcohol, Mental Health, Childhood, Socioeconomic status, Gatherings, Friendship, Cultural Difference/Tension, Generational Differences/Gaps, Mentorship, Interracial Dating, Language Barriers, Influence of White Activism, Gender, Community.

34. API Equality—Northern California, "Dragon Fruit Project Toolkit," 14.

35. API Equality—Northern California, "Quality Control Checklist."

36. API Equality—Northern California, 3.

asynchronous negotiations over the defining elements of QTAPI experience and community. Among the infinite possible ways a life can be described, the "codes" serve as lodestars, directing volunteers toward notable patterns in QTAPI experiences. Homing, while based in and steered by one person's perspective, is, then, a shared practice—a way we maneuver toward and with one another to establish conditions for belonging.

When I accessed the archive in its developmental stages, I was able to see the conversations that volunteers left in the margins of each interview. Remarks include summaries of key points ("lacking words to describe trauma or violence"), copyediting remarks ("check spelling"), or simply reactions ("Really, really powerful quote!!"). Before they are cleaned up and "locked," these documents resemble a gathering space where the words of interviewers and interviewees commingle with highlights and marginalia from other volunteers. Describing the significance of APIENC's involvement, Sueyoshi says that the Dragon Fruit Project provided young queer Asian Americans a place to go where "folks [are] working on something instead of coming here just to drink or hook up or whatever."[37] As both spatial and rhetorical practice, homing constructed both physical and virtual settings for exploring imbricated lives.

DFP volunteer Jess Suarez describes the experience of working on the project as "groundbreaking because it [is] making history."[38] In fact, many members of the DFP echo this sense of *making* history together—of drawing a narrative arc between past queer API experiences and the present. Devika Ghai stresses that this particular archive illuminates "how much our lives today and our work today is really riding on the shoulders of people who dealt with those struggles [before]."[39] She adds: "Not that we don't still have struggles," but the DFP locates those struggles within a longer narrative. This historiography gives present-day LGBTQ+ API folks a legacy of resistance—what scholar and activist Glenn Omatsu called a "heritage of struggle."[40] For Reynaldo Culannay Jr., the DFP provides "the opportunity to learn so much of what history can do. You meet with so many different people. I would never have expected to be part of as big a community as I am now."[41] History, in Culannay's sentence, is the actor—not merely the memory of a more cohesive, better-organized community, but the very thing that makes community possible.

---

37. Sueyoshi, personal interview.
38. API Equality—Northern California, "About."
39. API Equality—Northern California.
40. Omatsu, "Four Prisons."
41. API Equality—Northern California, "About."

As an interviewee, Vince Crisotomo also describes the DFP in a way that compresses past and present. "I feel honored that this younger generation is looking back at the work that's been done," he says, "that validates your work. That validates your life, and that validates the choices that you make."[42] Crisotomo situates that validation in the present—when his life and his work are seen and acted upon by this younger generation. As in Dubriwny's definition of consciousness-raising, participants in the DFP rename individual experiences in pursuit of social analysis and communal understanding. Through this bidirectional engagement with time—writing from and onto the past—LGBTQ+ Asian American identity is reinscribed onto past social justice movements, and that past in turn becomes a channel through which present-day identities are articulated and set into motion. This is a collective rhetoric that then "raises" buried histories into individual and communal consciousness, cultivating narratives that (1) deconstruct presumed truths ("deconstruction"), (2) appropriate and redefine dominant terms and ideologies ("meta-ideologizing"), and (3) channel these knowledges toward more egalitarian futures ("democratics").

Even without Amy Sueyoshi's guiding questions about "love," the rituals of love—its social and ideological attachments—all pervade the DFP narratives. Over a century after British government officials engineered an Asian "middle class" through Christian marriage and reproduction, Christianity and the nuclear family remain touchstones of class mobility. It would be an oversimplification to draw a single line of causation across these hundred years, but the legacies of these colonial policies pervade the Dragon Fruit Project. The criteria through which Asian Americans were offered conditional recognition often haunt the narratives of the DFP. For LGBTQ+ Asian Americans, the benchmarks of middle-class respectability are often unachievable, not to mention undesirable. Through the experiences of these "impossible subjects,"[43] the Dragon Fruit Project tracks the myriad consequences of such social pressures. At times, the DFP's homing stories document the rupture of familial bonds and the ways that QTAPI folks are denied social stability and security. At others, these stories record and enact defiant networks of care. The archive serves as homing space, where intimacies are (re)negotiated, (re)defined, and choreographed into collective values and actions.

I draw from the DFP's coded themes to trace affinities and resonances among interviews. Guided by queer diaspora's attention to the entanglements of colonialism, ableism, and gender and racial norms, I listen for the DFP's

---

42. API Equality—Northern California.
43. Ngai, *Impossible Subjects*.

critiques and transformations of scripts surrounding national and familial love. I then write these connections into constellations of trans and queer API love. The multiplicity of the archive itself as well as the constellation as rhetorical form accounts for the particularity of each individual while exposing how transnational and transcultural flows (re)shape QTAPI experiences. My approach is at times associational, drawn by subtle affinities or felt resonances rather than direct correlations. Inspired by Gayatri Gopinath and Remi Yergeau, this narrative approach is calibrated to defy conventional categorizations, in search of vocabularies that open more intersectional and coalitional worldviews.[44] Linearity is the modus operandi of straight time; with home as practice, we chase more imaginative orientations.

Plotting New Courses for Love

Before Kim Dang joined the military, before she pledged her love of family and nation, before she denied any prior knowledge of her homosexuality, she was born in Vietnam and grew up in Massachusetts. She describes her family as working-class. They sent her to a private Catholic high school, where she was the only Asian student. Though her mother attended a Buddhist temple, Dang explains, "[my mother] wanted us to be able to assimilate. So my stepfather he was from this Irish-Italian family and they were Catholic, so my stepfather's mother wanted me to go to this Catholic high school, and so when I was a freshman in the Catholic high school, they had me baptized."[45] That high school was also where, Dang recalls, "it was really impressed upon me to do the right thing to marry a man you know what I mean." This narrative connects Dang's mother's assimilatory aspirations to their Irish-Italian stepfamily. Those intimate relations then impelled Dang's enrollment in a Catholic high school, immersing her in its "family values." Long before her military career, Dang experienced the nuclear family as a site where national ideals are cultivated, performed, and enforced through the guise of individual choice. This motif can be heard throughout the DFP, connecting Dang's experiences with those of other LGBTQ+ Asian Americans and Pacific Islanders.

Like many QTAPI, Dang found that her initial sites of community were bound by shared (and in this case, highly restrictive) fantasies of the "good" life. When Dang's personal longings departed from the (heteronormative) desires assigned to her, she lost her spaces of belonging. She says, "I had to

---

44. Gopinath, *Unruly Visions*; Yergeau, *Authoring Autism*.
45. Dang, interview.

take a huge leap and completely leave all of the people I associated with and talked to and hung out with and had activities with, even the activities I did, just none of them supported being gay. It was just like night and day."[46] After her military discharge, Dang found community in vastly different worlds. She worked in HIV advocacy and AIDS prevention, facilitated studies on queer women's sexual behavior, and collaborated with sex workers on safer-sex workshops. Retracing her journeys from and toward different homes, Dang investigates love's codification of heteronormative rituals as well as queer diaspora's ability to build alternative sites for survival and care.

Near the conversation's end, Dang's interviewer revisits the topic of love, asking, "Do you have any theories about love that goes into activism?"[47] Dang responds at a queer slant, recalling finding and fostering safe spaces for queer women of color. She says, "Back in the early days when we really were grassroots, I did have a really strong sense of community [. . .] one of the reasons why I was really involved and really active is I wanted as many women to be able to participate as possible." She then describes these actions—expanding safe spaces for queer women of color—as patriotism. Dang redefines the relationship between love and nation by declaring loyalty on her own terms: "I'm very patriotic (laughs). I have always felt the need to serve in some way because I feel like . . . You know, this country has given me a lot of opportunities. I went back to Viet Nam. People are really suffering, they're really poor. And that's why I don't feel like . . . I don't take this for granted. Do you know what I mean? I don't think romantic love is the only thing. I think helping your community and volunteering for things and um . . . is more important." This statement detaches patriotism from compulsory heterosexuality and instead redefines national pride and identity as giving one's time and attention to community care. Dang's homing disengages from a restrictive set of values and worldviews, and ventures toward cosmologies congruent with her needs. Dang's reimagined patriotism is driven by her attachment to queer community and desire to include "as many as possible." Deviating from the love plots that constrained her earlier life, Dang narrativizes a trajectory that orients desire toward the pursuit and preservation of community for queer women of color.

Readers might note that Dang's narrative, even in its critique of patriotic heteronormativity, also upholds notions of the US as the Western savior. This passage presents the US as a land of opportunity while relegating suffering to Vietnam, reinforcing the West/East divide in which Euro-American nations

46. Dang.
47. Dang.

"save" poor destitute citizens of backward countries. It would be misleading to discuss this element as just individual bias, and I refuse to speculate about the private beliefs or prejudices of individual QTAPI. Instead, I focus on how rhetorics reflect or oppose controlling scripts. The complicities of Dang's narrative are a reminder that hegemonic narratives pervade. In the absence of overt critique, individual stories fall into normalizing frames. Listening diasporically to the Dragon Fruit Project enables differential movement. I range through divergent narratives in search of patterns and disruptions that can facilitate QTAPI community and survival.

For example, because Dang's reappropriation of patriotism emerges from her discussion of love, the DFP flagged this section as pertaining to "romantic love"—in that she is disputing the common assumption that romantic love is the "only thing." If readers followed that code to other interviews, they would find Alma Beck's resonant skepticism of romantic love. Whereas Dang's discussion leads to a reinforcement of Western dominance, however, Beck identifies the focus on dyadic couples as a Western phenomenon. A first-generation Korean American, Beck says, "I think that the United States has a very very very narrow view on love, as 'romantic' love [. . .] Our [US] movies and our media, they're very focused on one person, [who] meets another person, and then you have, you know, a relationship and it involves sex and you're in love, and that's the answer to all your problems."[48] For contrast, Beck points to Korean media and its renditions of intimacies beyond sexual relationships. She adds, "Koreans, in our language, we talk about love and we have all these different words for it. So we don't just have the word 'love.' We have all these different kinds of forms of it that I think raise subtleties that we don't deal with in English right now." This linguistic variation on love, with multiplicity and nuance, provides the basis for Beck's theorization of love.

Like Dang, Beck views community activism as driven by love—but this is a prismatic affect, augmented by connections she has experienced through Korean culture. In contrast to the dichotomous views she attributes to Western philosophies, Beck regards positive and negative affects as deeply interwoven. She explains, "Love makes people angry, I guess. And it also makes people defensive, scared, happy and joyful."[49] For her, the strength of "lesbians and queer women and the trans folks that are related to us" is the ability to recognize the complexity and imbrications of their attachments—the ability not only to care and to fight but to identify and address the conflicting desires that compose a community and to prioritize interdependency. Notably, this

48. Beck, interview.
49. Beck.

emotional understanding that Beck describes as characteristic of the "queer community" is informed by Korean representations of love and its entanglements. In importing that definition to her experiences of community in the US, she avoids another polarized split between East and West, and refuses to reify Euro-American progressivism as the foil to Asian backwardness. Beck uses the first-person plural for US *and* Korean cultures, situating herself as an insider of both. In this space of cultural confluence, Beck arrives at a multitudinous, queer love where Korean cultural productions are complemented by her lived experience in the US.

Dang's and Beck's divergent perspectives offer distinct explorations of how prevailing "love plots" affect LGBTQ+ Asian Americans—whose individual, romantic, and/or sexual desires are more likely to be at odds with normative (and state-sanctioned) forms of intimacy. Because the Asian population in the US has risen by 72 percent since the year 2000, many of today's Asian Americans are, like Dang and Beck, recent arrivals.[50] Asian American families—the default unit for navigating capitalist societies—are more likely to span significant geographical and cultural distances. In the absence of global, national, and social structures supportive of transnationalism, the families of QTAPI youth encounter more challenges to establishing stable (economic and emotional) foundations. Every rupture in established foundations, however, is an opportunity to build anew. Dang and Beck, as specific individuals who offer glimpses into their distinct and convergent histories, come together in a resistive constellation that exposes the artificiality of social norms as well as the possibility of living and loving differently.

Love as Truth-Seeking

The tag "activism, love, and community" links Beck's story to that of Tita Aida, a leader in AIDS education and activism. As someone who built a career in speaking hard truths, Tita Aida approaches love, activism, and community with the imperative to seek suppressed knowledge about QTAPI histories and lives. Through a focus on truth-seeking, this section connects Tita Aida's story with that of Izzy Alvaran. A Methodist minister whose theorizations of love help reconcile his religion with his queer desires, Alvaran finds unlikely resonances with Tita Aida in their outspoken advocacy. Their truths expose the role of US imperialism in their own physical and cultural displacements, as well as the conflicted relationships they maintain with their adopted

---

50. López, Ruiz, and Patten, "Key Facts about Asian Americans."

country. These stories then (re)make home in the interstices of diaspora—in stolen spaces of refuge, in plotlines that tether personal histories to their geopolitical contexts, and in the promise of open conversation about submerged and difficult truths.

Tita Aida's very name is the product of radical honesty as mutual care. In the 1990s, when QTAPI communities had few HIV/AIDS resources, when the topic of AIDS "was very guarded, [and] not talked about,"[51] Tita Aida's voice came to the fore. Drawing from her background in Filipinx theater and show business, she became the character "Tita Aida," who responded to sex-based Dear Abby–style letters from queer and particularly MSM communities. She performed her responses as a stage show, under the name Tita Aida, which is Tagalog for "Auntie AIDS." Her goal, then and now, was to destigmatize and "[break] the silence surrounding the epidemic."[52] This chosen name created a persona that could demand more public conversations about LGBTQ+ health. Her DFP interview recounts this journey in a narrative of queer diaspora that crisscrosses national boundaries and refuses the easy distinction of East and West. The resultant definition of *love,* guided by bell hooks's voice, shuttled between Manila and the streets of San Francisco, pursues truth as the means to intimacy—seeking a radical honesty that connects individual needs to communal vulnerabilities and interdependent futures.

The opening of Tita Aida's story also evokes Kim Dang's through a discussion of Catholicism. The DFP links these two interviews through the tag "religion," though these stories highlight different social contexts. Born in the Philippines, Tita Aida attributes her choice to move to the US to her family's disapproval:

My family was the driving force that made me want to move to over here, because they were not accepting of my choices in life and how I would like to plan out the next 20, 30, 40 years of my life. I come from a very Catholic-oriented family and for them, at the time . . . I was myself searching. I think that was when the activism started in me because back in the Philippines you don't see transgender as a choice. If you are born male and act effeminate, you are gay. If you are born female and act butch, you're a lesbian. There is nothing in between.[53]

As in Dang's story, Catholicism provided an epistemological foundation in Tita Aida's early life and established the terms through which queerness

51. Aida, interview.
52. Tita Aida quoted in Ragas, "Tita Aida Honored as Woman of the Year."
53. Aida, interview.

became unspeakable. Also as with Dang's story, Tita Aida's search for more responsive terminologies carries her out of her communities of birth and into new spaces of connection. Despite these initial similarities, however, Dang's and Tita Aida's stories diverge in their views of the US.

Kim Dang's parents brought her to Catholic school, but Catholicism came to Tita Aida's home country, where it has remained a driving cultural force since the 1500s. The limited vocabulary for queerness and gender transitivity that Tita Aida experienced in the Philippines has been shaped by centuries of Spanish colonialism and fifty years of US governance. With each foreign government came social, linguistic, and educational structures imposed on Filipinx traditions and intimacies. It would be inaccurate to equate Western definitions of *transgender* and *queer* with precolonial Filipinx practices, but scholars have shown that a much wider range of gender diversity existed before colonial occupation and persists today.[54] The strict binaries that Tita Aida references in her oral history were entrenched by the religious and pseudomedical discourses of Euro-American settlers.[55] The myth of Western liberators in regressive Eastern countries requires the suppression of these encounters and their legacies.

To parse these histories, Tita Aida borrows from the language of bell hooks, whose *All about Love* Tita Aida references repeatedly in her interview. The opening chapters of *All about Love* provide meditations on parenting and the ways that families often pass practices of care, neglect, and/or abuse from one generation to the next. For Tita Aida, this discussion of inherited relationality enables a more compassionate view of her own childhood. She says, "[*All about Love*] change[d] my outlook on my parents and where they were when I was at that age. They brought me and my sister up the way they knew how."[56] Building from hooks's exploration of love as a *practice* of critical reflection and mutual care, Tita Aida traces her own experiences through her parents' life trajectories and to the larger familial and social histories that surround them. This is a definition of love committed to "truth telling [as] the groundwork for the openness and honesty that is the heartbeat of love."[57] For Tita Aida, this groundwork also laid the foundation for reconceptualizing her initial home life. These truths are not about individual confessions but require

---

54. Manalansan, *Global Divas*; Garcia, *Philippine Gay Culture* and "Nativism or Universalism." For a polyvocal exploration of gender and sexual diversity in the Pacific Islands more broadly, see Besnier and Alexeyeff, *Gender on the Edge*.

55. Garcia, "Nativism or Universalism," 53.

56. Aida, interview.

57. hooks, *All about Love*, 53.

excavating buried histories as well as the seeds of internalized oppression—much like the mission of early consciousness-raising sessions.

Whereas Dang's account focused on the US as a land of opportunities, Tita Aida provides a rather different lens on her adopted country. Tita Aida's displacement continued after her move to San Francisco, where she struggled with housing insecurity: "If I see a homeless person on the street, I would see myself in them."[58] Her compassion for similar outcasts impelled her work with HIV/AIDS. She says: "I saw firsthand discrimination and oppression. These were folks who were treated so badly." Tita Aida's journey follows the multiple displacements familiar to many LGBTQ+ Asian Americans, and she credits this shared experience for her activism: "I can stand up for people. I didn't have much to lose at the time because I didn't have too much [. . .] I didn't have a home to go to or anything." The instability of her own home emboldened Tita Aida to create shelter for others. Her oral history, which names this decision to enter HIV/AIDS activism as "an awakening," then also marks advocacy work as an integral part of her own journey—how she built a life for herself in relation with others.

Like Tita Aida, Izzy Alvaran established his advocacy by speaking submerged truths. His oral history builds from hers with a direct critique of US colonialism and its continuing effects on the Philippines. A political asylee, Alvaran identifies as a polyamorous, queer/gay clergyman who works with API, LGBTQ+, and social justice communities. Considering the twisted paradox of having to apply for US citizenship, he embeds his own experience within the histories and social structures that have shaped it:

> It's most unfortunate that I have to stay here as an asylee and seek the protection of the country that conquered my own, you know [. . .] Ironically, US citizenship would protect me from persecution back home. [. . .] You know, we were a colony of the United States for 50 years. My grandparents had to speak English in school and were fined for every Tagalog word they had to speak [. . .] We learned English from the Americans that conquered us. [. . .] But I believe that Americans like any other people, are human beings. You know, we're struggling. But it's the system that's pervasive, not just in the US, but in my country. It's capitalism, it's colonialism, you know? It's religion in general. [It's] systems that oppress us. So I was conscious of that. That's why I think my life in the United States, especially if I am to become a citizen, is to really struggle with justice.[59]

---

58. Aida, interview.
59. Alvaran, interview.

Alvaran deconstructs the notion of the West as an innocent harbor for refugees, connecting this typically decontextualized façade of benevolence with the histories through which the US has perpetuated and benefited from global instability. Tacking out, though, he refuses to focus narrowly on individual blame, instead pointing to the ideological underpinnings of global inequity.

For Alvaran, this history also complicates the meaning and desirability of US citizenship. While national inclusion is so often the presumed goal of asylum-seekers, Alvaran points out that "you're renouncing a lot" when you take that oath.[60] For him the primary appeal of US citizenship is actually the additional protections it would give him for political agitation. When he applied for asylum, he was asked whether he would "do the rabble rousing that you were doing in the Philippines," to which Alvaran's answer is a resounding *yes*. He says, "I will take full advantage of American democracy [. . .] I will be a rabble rouser." Alvaran shifts through multiple definitional gears in this interview, considering first how American ascendency required the exploitation of non-Western resources and then how American citizenship can provide shelter for active dissent. "America" (as the US) in this formation is both the source of global instability and a potential refuge for redistributive organizing. This trajectory moves through the contradictions of queer diasporic life—that apparatuses of oppression and resistance are intimately entwined.

Alvaran delves further into the contradictory, oppositional forces of queer diaspora when he explains the motivations for all his advocacy work. As a minister of the United Methodist Church, Alvaran traces his activism to his religious faith, which he defines in terms of "love." Of his profession, he says: "My work as a clergy person right now is to advocate for LGBTQ rights."[61] Alvaran describes his faith as one "rooted in love." He explains:

> A God of love is so contrary to what I was hearing spoken against me and my people [. . .] the Jesus that I know is somebody who would hang out with the people that I wanna hang out with! Jesus was hanging out with prostituted people, Jesus was hanging out with the tax collectors, people that others hated, he was there. Jesus had parties with them, ate with them, and sat with them, and hugged them, and ministered them. It's that idea of a God who loves me, you know, from religion, is also the same that gave me resilience against religion itself. So I believe that, you know, this institution can change and will change. It will repent of its sins of discrimination.

---

60. Alvaran.
61. Alvaran.

The faith that Alvaran describes seems to be a belief in queer love—in the worldmaking potential of defiant and unsanctioned intimacies. He attributes his survival to his ability to imagine and foster a faith independent from the prevailing, homophobic biblical interpretations that pervade his church. His own denomination is one that he sees as "still homophobic" and one that "shuns" LGBTQ+ folks. Rather than abandon the church, though, Alvaran insists, "I am doing my very best to share my story"—to make queers and queer relationality possible in his religious circles.

Alvaran's narrative offers one instance of working through and forging pathways from entangled legacies of queer diaspora. He grew up generations removed from US control of the Philippines, inheriting the English that his grandparents were forced to learn. He speaks and prays in the language that colonial authorities selected for him before he had a name. As he describes them, English and Christianity are both mechanisms of colonization *and* tools that have been wielded and (re)shaped by dissenting communities. While acknowledging and grappling with the violent histories through which English and Christianity arrived in his home country, Alvaran has also experienced these as discursive realms through which to critique and combat the ideological bases of discrimination and disenfranchisement. As in Dang's story, Alvaran's narrative reappropriates components of US belonging (imperfectly, incompletely) and repurposes them to foster queer community.

As a queer diasporic archive, the Dragon Fruit Project is able to connect these disparate experiences without claiming equivalence. Alvaran's critique of US colonialism contradicts Dang's easy division of East and West. Meanwhile, Tita Aida's isolation through Catholicism refuses Alvaran's faith in Jesus as queer savior. These are not direct assertions and negations; the interlocutors are not engaged in debate for *the* defining queer Asian American experience. Rather, I read them as constellation—as distinct parts whose collective meaning emerges from their connections and contrasts.

Love as the Means for Activism

Whereas Alvaran deconstructs and redefines Western traditions through QTAPI experience, Steve Lew's interview augments Chinese language practices with queer diasporic meaning. Lew and his interviewer, Yifan Mai, connect the reticence of their families to the Chinese concept of "saving face," which remains integral to relationality in Chinese tradition. As LuMing Mao defines it in his foundational study of Chinese American rhetoric, Chinese face signifies "a public image" that one cultivates in relation to others and to sociocultural influences.[62] This is a conception of self that stresses "the interconnectedness between self and public"—one that Mao contrasts with Euro-American individualism.[63] Lew's and Mai's experiences of *face,* however, are situated within American upbringings. In dialogue with Mai, Lew reassesses *face* at a queercrip slant, and redefines it through his experience as a gay Chinese American man living with HIV. Their conversation then reappropriates the phrase to consider how intimate ties create the conditions for social change.

Yifan Mai, who also identifies as Chinese American and gay, begins with a traditional definition of *face.* He attributes his parents' misgivings about queerness to the "Chinese face concept where [. . .] their identity is sort of linked to mine."[64] Mai explains:

> They in part measure their worth as Chinese parents as how well they bring up their kids to be Chinese, respectable, and successful, and things like that [. . .] part of my parents' metric of their own success and then my success is like how much I look like a middle-class person who's financially responsible, who eventually, you know, becomes the head of a family, a traditional nuclear family.

In Mai's experience, *face* binds his parents to masculinist, heteronormative notions of respectability and shames them for raising a gay son. Lew responds with a resonant experience, but as the conversation develops, *face* takes on a transnational context.

Though Mai describes *face* as a set of "Chinese" values, the discussion decouples "Chinese" from any clear linguistic or continental boundaries. Both men recall childhoods surrounded by Chinese communities and identify as Chinese American, but Mai grew up in Singapore and Lew in Sacramento. Lew offers his Chinese name at the beginning of the interview, appending, "I actually don't know much more about or even how to write that name."[65] His grandparents and great uncle were US civil rights activists. Lew's father is a US military veteran and retired postal worker, and in another DFP interview, Lew describes his parents' aspirations for him as shaped by "Western" concepts "that we take for granted: that parents want you to have a good education and a good family and a good job."[66] In other words, the class anxieties and

---

62. Mao, *Reading Chinese Fortune Cookie,* 39.
63. Mao, 43.
64. Lew, interview, September 2015.
65. Lew.
66. Lew, interview, May 2, 2014.

respectability politics that Mai and Lew attribute to Chinese *face* are bound by global histories and exchanges. The fact that Lew and his parents still identify as Chinese despite not speaking the language and being born and raised in the US simultaneously captures the "perpetual foreigner" position of Asian Americans while also insisting on the particularity of Chinese (US) *American* experiences (shaped in part by that perpetual foreignness).

As Lew expands on his story, he offers a redefinition of *face* rooted in Chinese communities on US soil and shaped by his embodiment. Both Steve Lew and his brother identify as gay men, and Lew recalls his father's initial discomfort and reticence as "a similar kind of face or saving face."[67] In Lew's story, however, HIV/AIDS imposes an immediacy that connects cultural biases to lived consequences. As someone who works in HIV/AIDS advocacy, and who is HIV-positive, Lew experiences directly the ways that illness exceeds individual responsibility. While mainstream conversations have more recently recognized the ways that governmental and societal misconduct weaponizes HIV/AIDS against minoritized communities,[68] Lew and his parents witnessed firsthand how attitudes within their local communities impact the survival of LGBTQ+ Chinese Americans.

Noting the influence of Chinese newspapers and other cultural institutions—especially Chinese health clinics—Lew and his parents "thought it was really important to at least try to start changing some of the attitudes in the Chinese community and all the other Asian Pacific Islander communities."[69] Lew recalls:

[My parents] came and they spoke as Chinese parents and talked about how they had two gay sons, one of them is HIV positive, and how proud they are of both of us and my sister. It just really felt like, despite those things they decided that this was important enough. And, it became the part of the beginning of their careers like, parents who are gonna be talking to other Chinese families about, you know, that it's fine to have—and it's actually a good thing to have—queer LGBT kids.

Lew goes on to discuss how his parents formed an API "P-flag type group" and facilitated reunions among other Asian American families. In fact, younger LGBTQ+ folks even contacted his parents in search of that relationality. In advocating for LGBTQ+ families and for those living with HIV/AIDS,

67. Lew, interview, September 2015.
68. Sontag, *Illness as Metaphor*; Shilts, *And the Band Played On*; France, *How to Survive a Plague*; Chávez, *The Borders of AIDS*.
69. Lew, interview, September 2015.

Lew's parents became a public face for queer families—in multiple senses. Not only did they model parental support for their own children; they played the role of chosen family for others. Despite their initial discomfort, Lew's parents eventually participated in and facilitated the sorts of queer kinship that have sustained so many LGBTQ+ and disabled lives.

These supportive networks are necessitated by a world where heterosexual reproduction provides the limited social foundation for individual striving—where queer and disabled folks are often isolated from others with similar experiences. In fact, crip theorist Robert McRuer identifies that isolation as "the most frequently cited connection between disability and LGBT movements."[70] In calling on a broader Asian American community to confront and redress this alienation, Lew and his parents refuse "compulsory individualism"[71] in favor of communities of care. If *face* is (as Yifan Mai proposes) measured by the ways Chinese parents bring up their children, then Lew's parents forge a different paradigm for Chinese American families—one in which parenting can encompass relations beyond biological lineage. We might hear within this story the practice of bell hooks's (and Tita Aida's) definition of love as "the will to nurture our own and another's spiritual growth"[72] as well as Izzy Alvaran's belief in love as queer and disruptive intimacy.

Just as his position *within* the church enables Alvaran to story new possibilities for Christian faith and embodiment, Lew's identity as a gay, HIV-positive Chinese American allows him and his parents to reimagine possibilities for Chinese American familial relations. Lew recalls his parents' willingness to be *public* as particularly significant:

> One of the things that has really helped me through the years has been knowing that my parents were going to be there. They thought for a long time that I would end up dying before them, so they had to come to terms with that as well as me. But, I think just experiencing them during that time as being willing to play that role, being public, talking to other Chinese parents, risking whatever fears they had about being public about this with their family really just was a source of . . . I don't know . . . strength for me as a person who was working [with] HIV. I think it was also just really heartening to know that I could count on my family to be a part of that work.[73]

---

70. McRuer, *Crip Theory*, 88.
71. McRuer, 49.
72. hooks, *All about Love*, 6.
73. Lew, interview, September 2015.

In this section of Lew's story, his family's expressions of love *are* activism. In "being public" as Chinese American parents who support their gay son, Lew's mother and father helped shift narratives surrounding homosexuality, HIV/AIDS, and Chinese American belonging. In contrast to dominant narrativizations of HIV/AIDS as an individual moral failure, Lew's parents responded to his status as a call for communal action. They highlighted the ways social neglect had constructed the precarity of folks with HIV/AIDS. They also modeled inclusivity by addressing illness as an experience that—in the words of crip scholar Alyson Patsavas—"flows through, across, and between"[74] relationships.

Akin to the sort of work Alvaran does in his communities, Lew and his parents build on extant networks of care and open them to LGBTQ+ inclusion. Both Alvaran and the Lew family enact distinctly communal practices of love—interpersonal desires and attachments removed from dyadic heteronormative couplings. The activism they do is possible because these communities already see them as integral to their collective past and future—because the people around them are willing to listen to the futures they envision and to see themselves as part of those worlds. This sort of love, a love predicated on imagining and pursuing worlds where all members of your community can belong, provides the conditions for diasporic listening, for discovering constellated relations, and for reconfiguring home in ways that embrace those relations.

At the end of the interview, Lew and Mai draw their stories together, emplacing them in a longer arc of Asian American worldmaking. Lew begins by comparing the work he did with the scope and resources of the Dragon Fruit Project, reflecting that "it's nice to see how the work and struggles that we were doing in the late 80's and 90's has helped it to be where younger Asian and all sort of queer youth could really choose to be out in public in high school."[75] Mai responds with gratitude—a common gesture for the volunteer interviewers of the DFP: "We are always really grateful to start on the foundation of work that you guys [built]." Whereas Lew's and Mai's experiences of homosexuality and Chinese American families might have been seen as isolated accounts—as mere accidents of history—the Dragon Fruit Project situates them within a purposeful, tightly bound cord of QTAPI heritage.

The DFP's many stories, converging and diverging through dialogue, enact a togetherness-in-difference[76] attentive to the heterogeneity of Asian America. This comingling of perspectives destabilizes any universalizing claim

74. Patsavas, "Recovering a Cripistemology of Pain," 213.
75. Lew, interview, September 2015.
76. Mao, *Reading Chinese Fortune Cookie.*

about Asian Americans. Meanwhile, diasporic listening attunes audiences to connections forged through displacement. As in Tita Aida's story, the standards of white middle-class respectability haunt Lew's and Mai's families and remind them of their precarity in the US. Lew recalls "feeling very much like both wanting to be a part of the so-called 'American Dream' and also continually coming up against reminders that we could be a part of it but there was a cost."[77] For many of the trans and queer Asian Americans in the Dragon Fruit Project, the imperatives of US American belonging compound with the pressures of racial/class-based/disability/gender marginality to wedge communicative divides between generations—between parents concerned for their children's safety and children for whom the cost of assimilation is too great. Over and over again, the speakers of the DFP narrate their ejection from "model minority" trajectories—from Dang's military discharge to Tita Aida's isolation from her blood relations. As Lew demonstrates with his account of home-(re)making, however, that rupture also opens space for resistive forms of love and kinship.

Though DFP interviews do not adhere to a uniform script, Amy Sueyoshi's founding question appears in many of them, serving as a philosophical bedrock: "What is the relationship between love and activism?" Normative conceptions of love haunt many accounts of oppression, but the DFP also abounds with divergent, imaginative, and courageous forms of love that consociate interpersonal connection with truth-telling, truth-seeking, and responding to communal needs and vulnerabilities. Willy Wilkinson, for example, discusses how his partner's love establishes the foundation from which he has built his prolific career in HIV/AIDS advocacy, law and policy reform, and health services trainings. He recalls how his relationship with Georgia coincided with his growing engagement with the transgender community. Their first date was a trans event, and her support "gave me that feeling of home to do the work that I had done over the years."[78] For Gisele Pohan, that sense of home comes more from community than from individuals. She centers her discussion on community love, defined as "compassion" and "generosity, without expectation."[79] That compassion fuels her work in prison abolition and in forging alliances among other communities of color. Reverend Izzy Alvaran's love-based faith inspires his work in social and economic justice. He explains: "How can I have a fabulous wedding as a gay man if I am unemployed? Or I was fired from my job for being gay? Or I was evicted from my house for being gay? Or I was deported because I am undocumented? You know, all of

---

77. Lew, interview, September 2015.
78. Wilkinson, interview.
79. Pohan, interview.

these issues come together."[80] Economic justice, prison abolition, immigration policy, LGBTQ+ liberation, and racial justice all converge in the stories of the Dragon Fruit Project. Loving someone and/or a community requires an active commitment to their possibilities—and to establishing the material conditions in which they can build their lives. Love as nurturing practice is a willful belief in a world that can house more inclusive and imaginary intimacies, and a faith in one another to conspire together toward that possibility.

Love without Words

Steve Lew's story models an overt queering of Asian American family, as do many others in the DFP, but the archive also provides more nimble vocabularies for capturing the ephemerality of queer experience. This section rounds out my discussion of the Dragon Fruit Project with Lotus Dao's and Alice Hom's interviews, which apply insight about the cultural tensions of diaspora to re-envision their own familial histories. My constelled reading bridges their two interviews to consider how Western "coming out" narratives might reinforce queer alienation and silence in migrant families. Alternatively, Dao and Hom offer reflexive, nonverbal, affective grammars for exploring and embracing LGBTQ+ members of Asian American families.

Like many DFP interviewees, Lotus Dao (all pronouns) begins his story with the trouble of language(s). Both Dao and his interviewer, Avery Nguyen, are in their twenties and identify as Vietnamese, queer, and trans. Dao's mother came to the US as a refugee, along with Dao's two older brothers. Dao grew up in Little Saigon near Westminster, California, where he was surrounded by Vietnamese folks. Gender and sexual orientation "just wasn't part of the conversation."[81] When Dao first came out to his mother, he used the only term at his disposal: "bê đê," which he equates with "faggot." Both Dao and Nguyen reflect on having assumed that this was the *only* available term in Vietnamese for queerness—that to be Vietnamese and queer was to embody a slur.

Despite her initial discomfort, Dao's mother gave him a different phrase for homosexuality—"Đồng Tính," meaning *same-gender loving,* which opened the door to a Vietnamese culture that could coincide with queerness. Dao began "learning the language and meeting other Vietnamese and queer people"[82] and eventually traveled to Vietnam to explore what queerness felt like in his

---

80. Alvaran, interview.
81. Dao, interview.
82. Dao.

mother's country. Thinking through the disparate communicative styles that have shaped his family, Dao reflects:

> I think for me when I came out as a teenager, I came out modeling the narrative that I saw online. I was like, "I'm a lesbian." I'm being very direct about it, like, "Take it or leave it. This is who I am." My mom was so overwhelmed. She didn't know what to do, and I would actually consider that a pretty Western way to come out.

Compared with how Dao describes his usual exchanges with his mother—"very modest and humble"—the declarative, unilateral nature of the traditional "coming out" reads as unintelligible aggression. The only scripts Dao had for discussing his sexual orientation defied the communicative terms he shared with his mother. This dialogue was written for a family that had little in common with theirs.

After this strained coming-out, Dao was estranged from his mother for a few years. They reconnected only after a drug overdose placed him in rehab; his parents were called as his emergency contact. Dao explained to his mother that he had distanced himself "because you're homophobic and I'm queer."[83] His mother replied that she wasn't concerned about his sexual orientation in and of itself. Rather, "I have a problem with the fact that it makes your life harder [. . .] We're already immigrants, we're already poor." In Dao's words, his mother is responding to "systems of oppression or violence or colonialism" and their consequences. Though she may not name them directly, she knows how sociopolitical structures have disadvantaged her and her family. Her actions have been shaped by their imprint on her life, and her fears for her children are based in experiential knowledge of discriminatory violence. By reflecting on his mother's concerns and connecting them to operations of dominance, Dao rejects the compartmentalization of social responsibility within nuclear families and instead points to the ways that queer precarity is connected to and affected by other forms of racial and class-based inequities.

With this understanding, Dao builds a resistive vocabulary *from* the silence that had distanced him from his family. When he decided to come out to his mother as trans, he began by reflecting on the means through which they communicated. Speaking to the DFP, he says:

> I was like, "Okay, how does my mom normally communicate? By not talking." So that's how she normally talks and she shows love. She doesn't say

---

83. Dao.

I love you, you know what I mean? She doesn't hug me, she doesn't say "I love you" but she cooks and she's taken care of me and she shows it in other ways. And so I was like, "Okay, how can I come out to my mom that would actually make sense to her and be accessible to her?"[84]

Rather than announcing himself as transgender—a term already overladen with imposed stigma—Dao told his story through action, in a language closer to home. Accompanying his mother on a trip to Vietnam, he brought his hormones and his binder. Instead of concealing these elements of his life or initiating an argument about transphobia, Dao explained that these things helped him "feel better." Likewise, he consistently used men's restrooms, simply telling his mother, "No, mom, this one" when she tried to redirect him to the women's room.

Dao recalls his mother accepting these moments with the same matter-of-fact tone with which he approached them. When she repeated her concerns about the ways that gender transition might make his life "harder," Dao framed this aspect of his identity in terms of his own well-being:

I was super casual about [taking hormones], I focused on my health and happiness and never used the word trans actually and she was just like, "Okay, that makes sense! Like you should stay on it if you're happy!" and I'm like, "Yeah!"[85]

While wordlessness—the lack of a shared vocabulary for queerness—initially served as a limitation, Dao eventually found a way to move *with* that silence. He chose to discard the terminologies that would alienate his mother and instead spoke in terms of her values—in this case, his own health and happiness. Through this negotiated grammar of affect and action, Dao and his mother forge a language that bridges (however flawed) the distance cleaved by migration and conquest.

As a narrative of queer diaspora, Dao's story takes audiences through the paradoxical, impossible tensions of LGBTQ+ (im)migrant life. The indirectness with which he and his mother approach trans and queer identity has limitations, but it also refuses the cultural and generational distance designed and enforced by US empire. Historian Erika Lee describes the history of Southeast Asian refugees in America as "a story of contradictions and unfinished journeys."[86] US interventions in Vietnam, Cambodia, and Laos, fueled

---

84. Dao.
85. Dao.
86. Lee, *The Making of Asian America*, 314. See also Nguyen, *The Gift of Freedom*.

by aggressive post–World War II anticommunist policies, "helped produce the very conditions that forced people to flee."[87] Of the 1.6 million refugees that left Vietnam between 1975 and 1997, the largest percentage were resettled in the US, "but there were often strings attached."[88] (In Steve Lew's words: "There was a cost."[89]) Immigration officials favored married couples and young families, applying heteronormativity as a yardstick for deserving citizens. The growing population of Southeast Asians in the States stoked anti-immigrant anxieties, subjecting them to increased discrimination and violence.[90] Lotus Dao's mother built a life for her family under these conditions, and her view of his life chances are inevitably shaded by these interceding narratives. The love that returns Dao to his mother appears to be a mutual desire to remain in each other's lives, enabling this unspoken resolution to prioritize connection over correctness.

Alice Hom offers an even more explicit reflection on the strategies through which LGBTQ+ Asian American families traverse the communicative distance of diaspora. She describes her parents as working-class immigrants and herself as a Chinese American, queer, gender-nonconforming academic, activist, and cultural worker. Bringing together the multitudinous communities that have shaped her worldview, Hom's DFP interview bridges critical discourses with the vernacular grammars of lived experience. Like many other interviews, hers begins with the cultural and linguistic disjunctures of diaspora. Hom's Taishanese is limited, as is her mother's English, so they do not rely on verbal communication. When the interviewer, Sine Hwang Jensen, asks Hom how she connects with her mom outside of language, Hom explains: "It's always about eating and driving. I live in LA so it's always about driving anyways. So I take her places. If she wants to go somewhere, I will drop everything and just take her."[91] As in Lotus Dao's story, action fills the space between spoken words.

Language, however, has also been a powerful resource in Hom's life. As a path-breaking scholar of queer Asian American studies, Hom credits ethnic studies and women of color feminism for illuminating the cultural imperatives that have shaped her family. These fields provided vocabularies for examining the interrelations of gender and race. They also connected Hom to histories of communal solidarity and mutual uplift among queer women of color. Hom went on to co-edit *Q&A: Queer in Asian America,* a foundational anthology

87. Lee, *The Making of Asian America,* 314.
88. Lee, 314.
89. Lew, interview, September 2015.
90. Lee, *The Making of Asian America,* 339.
91. Hom, [169].

of queer Asian American voices, and she completed a doctoral dissertation on communal organizing by lesbians of color. The narratives Hom studied and helped uncover also provided context through which to (re)interpret her interactions with her family, their expectations, and their forms of expression. Like Lotus Dao, Hom narrates extraverbal exchanges where she and her family worked through her refusal to conform.

With the rise of her academic career, Hom was "out" in her public life, giving campus talks and publishing on queer activisms while identifying as a Chinese American lesbian. Still, Hom was not explicitly "out" to her parents—a fact that was possible because they did not read her academic work or the publicity around it. Explaining further, Hom says, "They knew but I didn't actually tell them [. . .] I think there's a way where the telling doesn't have to be verbal."[92] In those years, Hom brought her girlfriends home without explicitly naming their relationship. She continued to dress in "men's" suits and ties. Like Dao, she lived her identity without prescribing labels, and Hom's mother responded in kind—by giving Hom the time (and food) characteristic of their mother–daughter exchanges.

Hom concludes her interview by sharing two tremendous gestures of acceptance that also defy verbal boundaries. When Hom graduated with her PhD, her mother hosted a banquet, which was attended not only by Hom's friends but also by her mother's friends. Hom describes the magnitude of the celebration like this: "I think my mom knew that I was never going to have a wedding banquet so to speak. My graduation party was my wedding banquet."[93] Her mother queers an otherwise heteronormative milestone. This ceremony, which usually marks heterosexual union as one of life's major events, is repurposed to celebrate Hom's achievement as the first member of their family to receive a graduate education.

Later, Hom discovered that her mother had placed a copy of Q&A and Hom's dissertation on the mantle, across from the family altar that honors those who have passed. Of the significance of this gesture, Hom says:

> I don't need her to go to gay pride. I don't need to her to go to PFLAG. I don't need her to say I'm proud of my daughter and I'm going to wave a rainbow flag. Those things mean nothing to her, and it wouldn't have enough meaning for me if she did that because that's not a way to express love. I like sharing that story because I think there's other ways that people from other cultural backgrounds can show their love and affection for their queer chil-

92. Hom.
93. Hom.

dren, which doesn't have to be in a Western, verbal methodology because it doesn't resonate with her. So why would I want her to do something that doesn't resonate with her. That's how I know my mom loves me.[94]

Like Dao, Hom explains how traditional "coming out" narratives are antithetical to her family's understandings of intimacy. She refuses to interpret her mother's response through normative scripts. Instead, Hom listens for love in the language of her mother's actions. For Hom's mother, marching with Pride parades or attending PFLAG meetings would bear no personal symbolism. The scripts for "coming out" and family acceptance hold little significance in the context of this family and its histories. Instead, Hom and her mother find a way to script queerness into the traditions that they share—and that have been presumed antiqueer by Western paradigms. Hom's mother's placement of Hom's dissertation on the family mantle and her reappropriation of a wedding banquet capture a desire not only to celebrate Hom's achievements as a queer scholar but to make those achievements legible within their own family traditions. This is a diasporic love—with friction, contradictions, and attachments so strong that they traverse generations and hemispheres to dream up connections that will hold.

De-coupling Love: Transforming at/as Home

Like the participants of the DFP, APIENC itself has benefited and grown from its intimate relations. As an organization that has fought for prison abolition, environmental justice, and the depolicing of Pride, APIENC's origins in marriage equality may seem surprising—given the many critiques of marriage equality in queer politics.[95] It would be possible to dismiss APIENC's early involvement in California's Proposition 8 controversy as only an example of David Eng's "queer liberalism"—a project that extends the "right of privacy" to particular (usually white, cisgender, middle-class) gay and lesbian couples.[96] However, closer attention to APIENC's engagement with Asian American histories reveals the role of homing—narrativizing unlikely affinities and belongings that defy presumed borders—in moving both queer and antiqueer Asian Americans toward more transformative Asian American politics.

94. Hom.
95. Eng, *The Feeling of Kinship*; Spade, "Toward a Critical Trans Politics" and *Normal Life*; Alexander and Rhodes, "Queer Rhetoric and the Pleasures of the Archive."
96. Eng, *The Feeling of Kinship*, chap. 1.

Both branches of API Equality (Northern California and Los Angeles) were founded in 2004, in direct response to rising homophobia within Asian American communities. That year, when San Francisco began granting marriage licenses to same-sex couples, Asian American voices filled a forceful contingent of the conservative backlash. Chinese migrant churches in particular "attracted thousands of Chinese Americans—and mainstream media attention—in San Francisco and Los Angeles."[97] The challenges to these short-lived marriage licenses coincided with (and fueled support for) California's notorious Proposition 8, which eventually banned same-sex marriage until a federal court ruling in 2010. APIENC and its sibling organization, API Equality—LA, trace their origins directly to the exigence generated by anti-LGBTQ+ action among Chinese migrant communities.

Reflecting on these early days of queer Asian American organizing, Karin Wang, co-founder of API Equality—LA, focuses on the intersections of "public education and community organizing."[98] She says, "We wanted to lift up California's shameful history of racist marriage restrictions targeting Asian immigrants. We hoped that by highlighting how anti-miscegenation laws—along with governmental restrictions on immigration, citizenship, and other rights—had isolated and excluded Asian immigrants for decades from mainstream American society, more Asian Americans would understand and support the LGBT community's fight for the freedom to marry."[99] API Equality narrativized the continuity between anti-LGBT ideologies, the anti-immigrant policies of the 1800s and 1900s, and the ways that normative (white, heteropatriarchal) models of family and kinship have delimited and continue to delimit civic belonging. From its inception, API Equality deployed storytelling as a means of public pedagogy, constellating seemingly distinct histories to nurture community relations.

Establishing this link between queer exclusion and ongoing anxieties about racial minorities corrupting the white family/nation helps counter one of the central components of queer liberalism: the separation of queer politics from racial politics. David Eng's *The Feeling of Kinship* traces this history through which queer politics was articulated as that which follows racial liberation, establishing queer rights as a "politics of the present"[100] and racial equality as an achievement of the past. Through such a narrative, the possibility of reading queerness and race "as constitutive, as intersectional, as politically and

---

97. Wang, "Parallel Journeys through Discrimination," 157.
98. Wang, 158.
99. Wang, 158.
100. Eng, *The Feeling of Kinship*, chap. 1.

temporally coeval is foreclosed."[101] API Equality's storytelling campaigns leading up to Proposition 8 established an alternative temporality through which the exclusion of Asian migrants extends into prohibition of same-sex marriage. Sharing their own stories as LGBTQ+ Asian Americans, API Equality's organizers restored LGBTQ+ folks as part of the Asian American community. They are living, embodied proof that queer politics is inextricably bound to Asian American, migrant, and racial politics.

This strategy culled support from sixty-three Asian American organizations, which threw their collective weight behind an amicus brief submitted to the California Supreme Court in 2007. While Prop 8 still passed (narrowly), this collaborative action prompted many Asian American groups to "come out" as LGBTQ+ allies. Following the passage of Proposition 8, the brief also provided a foundation for future LGBTQ+ advocacy, having established the relationships and the knowledge for future action. In fact, Wang identifies the "biggest legacy" of this period as the rapid shift in Asian American attitudes toward marriage equality. Whereas 68 percent of Asian Americans had supported a ballot measure banning same-sex marriage in 2000, that contingent dropped to 54 percent in 2008—a shift that outpaced the attitudes of the general population. Numerous factors undoubtedly affected this change, but Wang credits the storytelling efforts for "drawing a direct line" between Asian migrant experiences and the exclusion of queer couples from US public life.[102]

Although access to marriage itself grants recognition and access to particular couples, broader visions of queer justice necessitate more expansive conceptions of intimacy, communion, and mutual care. Questions that might preclude the pursuit of marriage equality include: To whom is this form of recognition available? What rights, permissions, and privileges do we attach to this form of recognition, and why is it bound to this particular form of relationality? How can we decouple basic human needs and resources from dyadic unions that are not accessible or desirable for all? After the struggle against Proposition 8 (which was deemed unconstitutional by a federal court ruling two years later), both API Equality organizations pursued such inquiries. The conversations among their expanding membership steered attention

101. Eng.

102. Storytelling has been a critical strategy throughout queer activism—for example, see Son Vivienne's work on digital storytelling and gender and sexual diversity in *Digital Identity and Everyday Activism* and "Little Islands of Empathy." Storytelling also remains an integral component of many Asian American trans and queer organizations. In addition to the archives explored in this book, there's API Equality—LA's "Pioneers Project" and "Q&A Space"; NQAPIA's "Family Is Still Family" and "Queer Asian & Proud" campaigns; numerous narrative archives compiled by the *Asian Pride Project*; and still others being conceptualized and developed as I write.

beyond state recognition, focusing instead on interpersonal relations and mutual aid. In Southern California, API Equality—LA identifies their current emphasis as one of "community care," including but not limited to increasing access to LGBTQ-affirming and culturally responsive mental health care and cultivating community spaces for LGBTQ API folks in general.[103] Northern California's APIENC describes their focus as building "real solutions that are centered in our communities, build self-determination, and promote healing and restoration for the land and the people."[104]

For APIENC, the Dragon Fruit Project became a crucial means of outreach and of identifying community-driven goals. APIENC's Community Organizer, M. Lin,[105] describes the project as an "entry point" through which the organization engages most of its two-hundred-plus volunteers.[106] As APIENC's most visible program, the DFP is often the first point of contact for new volunteers. LGBTQ+ API folks often find APIENC through the DFP's materials—including a 2018 exhibit at the GLBT History Museum, where Sueyoshi's project began. APIENC then works to ensure that those who partake in the project are "not just one-timers."[107] The narratives exchanged through these conversations become discursive channels that map the priorities of community members. M. Lin describes this in terms of physical movement: "We want to align in the direction of where you're going as well."[108] Storytelling, as homing practice, enables APIENC to follow the leads and desires of their members.

Tuning in to LGBTQ+ API folks across generations, the Dragon Fruit Project does more than distribute their stories—it builds on them. To quote M. Lin again: "The overall vision of Dragon Fruit Project is that one conversation or interview is much bigger than itself. It's not just a Q&A. It's a conversation where people are getting to know each other and hopefully getting to know each other for the long term."[109] The DFP provides an infrastructure through which to query "What are our elders and our youth voicing out now? How can a system of reciprocity and genuine care be built from the ground up in which we're meeting each other's needs through the things that we can do and the skills that we can gather as opposed to relying on institutions?"[110]

103. API Equality—LA, "Mission."
104. API Equality—Northern California, "Building."
105. M. Lin has since transitioned out of this role for APIENC but worked with me extensively at the start of this book and served as Community Organizer throughout 2015–18.
106. Baik et al., "Beyond Survival, Toward Resistance & Alliance Building."
107. Lin, personal interview.
108. Lin.
109. Lin.
110. Lin.

At the core of these questions is APIENC's investment in one another's desires as organizational strategy. They are oriented by community members' aspirations and toward reciprocal structures that can pursue their visions. These communicative exchanges thus recognize and respond to trans and queer API experiences and affects as *knowledge* that can then inform and shape collective action.

When M. Lin considers the limitations of APIENC, they say, "We don't have capacity to cover social services, day-to-day essential needs, but we do have the capacity to imagine and initiate the relational needs of our community."[111] In Muñoz's theorizations, such queer relationality enables the imagining and pursuit of radical futures. In practice, APIENC leverages the connections of the DFP into other major projects, including leadership development programs, trainings for more trans-inclusive workplaces and organizations, and environmental justice initiatives focused on BIPOC.[112] The oral histories of the DFP serve as primary texts for many of these programs, often providing insight into QTAPI history and survival strategies, as well as inviting further explorations of resonant experiences.

Toward these priorities, and to further the organizational capacity of racial, gender, disabled, and sexual minorities, APIENC works regularly with other QTPOC organizations and other Asian American and Pacific Islander groups. Their connections model solidarity as mutual vulnerability and ongoing communication across difference. APIENC also retains the openness of its early years—the willingness to be changed by members old and new and by the relations they form. APIENC's continued evolution—the expansion of its membership, its agendas, and its alliances—evidences the transformative love discussed throughout the Dragon Fruit Project, how we are changed by those for whom we care. Here contradictions are not necessarily impediments but catalysts for growth. The borderland where you and I meet is not a boundary but the grounds for transformation.

Love as Democratics

While the narratives of the Dragon Fruit Project undoubtedly have personal significance for both interviewees and interviewers (and the interlocutors say as much), the archive itself does important rhetorical work by providing public access to counterstories of Asian American identity, family, and belong-

111. Lin.
112. API Equality—Northern California, "Building."

ing. As oral histories, they are less about memorializing a past than about proffering possible futures. In this chapter, I proposed constellated readings of the DFP that examine normalizing imperatives surrounding love, nation, and family while also exploring defiant reconfigurations of those social forms. Christian churches appear both as controlling forces and as sites for cultivating allies and resistive relationalities. Religion draws from both the West and the East, and dissertations are given places of honor beside ancestral altars. A military veteran finds communion among sex workers, and an oral historian eschews spoken language to connect with her family.

The messages here are at times contradictory. While Dao and Hom offer means of (re)building or revising familial relationships without naming their queerness, the archive itself is also about the power of identifying and narrativizing queerness where it was deemed impossible. The polyvocal nature of the archive enables it to hold these paradoxes in balance. Lotus Dao's account offers one familial configuration around queerness, and Steve Lew's, another. Some QTAPI folks choose to build LGBTQ+ resistance within conventionally normalizing spaces, as Izzy Alvaran does with his historically antiqueer church. By contrast, Kim Dang leaves both her Christian and her military communities and finds family among HIV/AIDS and safer-sex advocates. The divergent experiences take audiences through a differential mode of consciousness—generating not one counternarrative but many, for folks who were denied any place in the US American story.

Following Chela Sandoval's methodology of the oppressed, these QTAPI narratives move among deconstructive analyses and visionary embodiments of family, love, and citizenship. Like the Third World feminists of Sandoval's study—in fact, many of the DFP interviewees cite Third World feminists among their inspirations—the storytellers of the DFP speak in and of communicative forms typically denied academic or state recognition. Vanessa Coe, a Lead Organizer for APIENC, describes the work of such stories as forging access and "communal healing"—making legible these experiences "in languages that our mothers know."[113] Explaining further, Coe also invokes the language of "saving face": "I can tell my mom something that she will not understand, but if I say it another way . . . like 'saving face,' which is a common theme in our cultures, she'll understand that right away." In the combinatory languages and embodied rhetorics of diaspora, the Dragon Fruit Project archives innovative expressions of solidarity, identity, and love. These fusion and fugitive tongues animate the tensions and contradictions of queer Asian migration, dreaming up mobile sites of belonging that maneuver across generational and cultural distance.

---

113. Coe, interview.

// *A month after my first visit to the Dragon Fruit Project—after I sit across from Amy Sueyoshi at her desk, sharing popcorn and green tea—I am in a conference hotel in Minneapolis. Far from the squishy embrace of Amy's office chairs, I find myself instead sitting stiff-backed at the end of a partitioned ballroom. The projection screen reads "An Absent Presence in Rhetorical Studies: Asian/American Rhetoric as Case Study." This roundtable discussion is the first time I see my name situated beside those of scholars whose careers paved the way for my own—who defined Asian American rhetorical studies and insisted on our experiences and communicative innovations as topics worth studying. My body feels too small for the excitement humming beneath my ribs. I have so much that I want to say to this audience, in both gratitude and frustration. A year before this conference, the Asian / Asian American Caucus published a history of our field, titled* Building a Community, Having a Home. *For all I pored over its pages, I could find no evidence that trans and queer Asian Americans existed—let alone that Asian American racialization is ensnarled with cissexism and homophobia.*

"16% of people in the US say that they have personally met a trans person," I begin, "So, hello." This wasn't how I planned to begin a broader, more impersonal discussion of how Asian American rhetorical studies has often utilized the prefix "trans-" without engaging the transgender Asian Americans whose experiences of border-crossing illuminate critical elements of Asian American racialization. But in that room, in a too-big jacket and tie I had just purchased, in this body that I was still (re)learning how to dress, I wanted this audience to see me. More, I wanted them to listen to the courage and imagination of Tita Aida and the world made possible by Amy Sueyoshi's community-based research and M. Lin's careful stewardship. I wanted them to know that "our" legacies derived from a lineage that is (gender)queer and crip, and that continued erasures of those histories conspired with the mythologies that render Asian Americans passive subjects in US politics past and present.

I wanted the people in that room to know—to feel as I did—the stakes of what we said in these conference rooms in four-star hotels, in the papers we go back to write and the syllabi we design. I wanted them to see our articulations of the field(s) as acts of intimacy and as declarations of whom we call into community and whom we do not. I wanted them to see the myriad people left out of disciplinary histories and therefore our present—how many we have chased out of universities by centering conversations they could not or would not want to engage. I still don't know if this is the best course of action. I don't know whether any amount of "inclusion" can transform spaces designed for exclusivity.

Classrooms and heady, theoretical conversations gave me refuge when I did not know where else to run, but I also know how often LGBTQ+ folks and people of color and disabled people have had our stories stolen to "diversify" academic spaces with no will for change. I have too often been the body invited for orna-mentation rather than substance. I don't know that it's possible to revolutionize the university. I don't know that disciplines built on white elitism and theft can be entirely redeemed. I do know, however, that compassionate educators have saved lives, including my own. I know that before ethnic studies became institutional-ized, they were dreamt by organizers striving to give their communities a fighting chance. These activists demanded community-accountable educations in concert with housing rights, labor unions, and transnational coalitions. I know that it is impossible to be born into and grow up in the US without inheriting and being entangled in mechanisms of colonization. I know that, from its inception, Asian American identity blurred, crossed, and renegotiated the presumed boundaries of campus and community. I know that the Dragon Fruit Project itself is a product of this border-crossing, shifting from Sueyoshi's research to APIENC's "entry point," demonstrating that knowledge grows and transforms with its keepers. I hold on to that promise and responsibility as I carry these stories with me—as I share them with you. I hope the connections and divergences you find become still more com-mon ground on which we can gather, deliberate, and build. //

CHAPTER 2

Resilience as/in Homing

The Visibility Project and
Transformative Taxonomies

Mia Nakano's *Visible Resilience* is the largest single collection of images and stories focused on "queer Asian American women, trans and gender non-conforming" folks in the US.[1] Nakano traveled coast to coast, meeting, photographing, and recording interviews with LGBTQ+ Asian Americans and Pacific Islanders. The portraits were compiled in a full-color book published in 2017, titled *Visible Resilience*. Page after glossy page, AAPI stand in their power, their creativity, and their whimsy and defiance. They wear three-piece suits, tank tops, suspenders, or beanies. They hold family portraits or walking canes. Their own words caption their photos, naming a galaxy of genders, ethnicities, sexual identities, and orientations to home/land. On page 31, Alice Hom smiles from behind thick-rimmed tortoise shell glasses. Amy Sueyoshi and Celeste Chan face one another on pages 19 and 20, the former in a plain gray sweater and the latter with bold red lipstick, and a matching rose pinned to her hair. Chan's hand rests atop her head, palm up, wrist exposed to reveal a four-letter tattoo: *hope*. *Visible Resilience*'s 140 pages traverse generational and national boundaries, tracing an outspread array of stories that constitute the multiplicity of QTAPI experiences.

Among these, Kay Ulanday Barrett's entry captures the resilience made visible by this collection. In their portrait, the thirty-year-old sick, disabled, queer (SDQ) Pinoy American folds their hands over the handle of their

---

1. Nakano, *Visible Resilience*, 2.

cane—a companion made ever-memorable in their poetry with the assertion "Every cane is a drum calling into the earth."[2] On the opposite page, Barrett answers Nakano's query:

> *How do you react to being mispronounced? How do you choose to say something or not?*
>
> I think it's a question of safety. Am I going to get jumped, am I not? Is there going to be some sort of verbal altercation or am I in a community loving space where people can have a dialogue about what multiplicity in gender means. What does queer pinoy mean? What does mixed race transgenderness mean? I pick and choose my fights, you kinda have to in order to survive.[3]

Whether Barrett confronts an act of misidentification depends on their safety, which in turn depends on whether this space is open to dialogue about "the multiplicity of gender." In other words, active challenges of harmful social scripts require community—others willing to witness Barrett and affirm their truths.

As I explore throughout this chapter, this community-based definition of strength and empowerment pushes against common applications of resilience, most popularly defined through neoliberal individualist terms. I begin first by tracing the social contours of resilience as it has shaped Asian American racialization. Essayist Wesley Yang provides a case study for how resilience and its attachments to white masculinity are leveraged to exclude trans, queer, and disabled Asian Americans from the possibility of resilience. The Visibility Project (VP)—which includes *Visible Resilience,* the *Resilience Archives,* and *Performing Resilience*—then offers transformative reconstructions of this commonplace. Listening for these rhetors' attachments to and departures from understandings of resilience, I constellate their stories to explore enactments of resilience that critique its racialized, gendered, and ableist histories, and that embrace interdependence-in-difference. Homing—in this case enacted through portraits and interviews, virtual history tours, and live performances—enables QTAPI rhetors to track the narratives of resilience that have rendered particular harms il/legible, and to co-create spaces that affirm one another's experiences and paths toward healing.

---

2. Barrett, "To Be Underwater & Holy," 67.
3. Nakano, *Visible Resilience,* 104.

Resilient Topos

As Elizabeth A. Flynn, Patricia Sotirin, and Ann Brady observe, resilience has become an exceedingly popular concept in therapeutic, corporate, educational, and popular contexts—with overwhelming focus on heroic individualism and self-sufficiency.[4] Corporations, for example, have turned to "resilience training" programs to boost employee productivity through supposed resistance to physical and mental illness.[5] In *Resilience: The Science of Mastering Life's Greatest Challenges*, psychiatrists Steven Southwick and Dennis S. Charney examine the resilient strategies of Vietnam POWs, Special Forces instructors, and civilian trauma survivors and find that resilient people "accepted, to an impressive degree, responsibility for their own emotional well-being, and many used their traumatic experiences as a platform for personal growth."[6] In these contexts, resilience is most frequently "the ability of the *individual* to cope, adapt, or mobilize protective resources in the face of adversity."[7] Congruent with Flynn et al.'s findings, these applications of resilience valorize individual strengths over systemic analysis and transformation. Independent "toughening up" is valued over communicating needs and sharing resources. This individualistic emphasis, reiterated across contexts, congeals into a stock story, establishing particular events as recognizable trauma (e.g., war, physical assault, interpersonal abuse) and particular responses as resilient (e.g., physical and emotional discipline, acquiring professional and social prestige).

Medical researchers Emily Hutcheon and Gregor Wolbring have criticized the ableism embedded in these understandings of resilience. They describe *resilience* as a discursive technology that "provide[s] an understanding of how individuals ought to function—understandings that are found in culturally sanctioned ways of functioning and in the fulfillment of similarly sanctioned roles."[8] While scientific and social scientific fields lack a clear consensus about what constitutes resilience, most researchers overemphasize individual strength.[9] Hutcheon and Wolbring find that "one popular criterion for 'resilient' living is the accomplishment of life's tasks independently,"[10] eliding the

4. Flynn et al., "Introduction."

5. Kohll, "How You Can Build a More Resilient Workforce"; Gerdeman, "Distressed Employees?"

6. Southwick and Charney, *Resilience,* chap. 1.

7. Hutcheon and Lashewicz, "Theorizing Resilience," 1; emphasis added.

8. Hutcheon and Lashewicz, 4.

9. Hutcheon and Lashewicz, 5.

10. Hutcheon and Wolbring, "'Cripping' Resilience."

sorts of mutual care networks characteristic of crip, queer, poor, and migrant communities. This definitional bias means that any survival strategies *outside* of sanctioned narratives (ones built on, for instance, reciprocity and communion) are read as *not* resilient. Likewise, harms inflicted through systemic means (for example, institutionalized ableism) are less legible as sources of trauma. Such conversations, as well as the more explicit "resilience trainings" throughout higher education, corporate, and health care settings, serve to align human behavior with ableist, sexist, colonial, neoliberal, and other normative interests.

Diasporic listening hears in these accounts the scripts for pain and recovery that have predominated Asian American history. This listening departs from popular and disciplinary definitions of resilience as individual character trait, instead considering it through racialized plots that orient individual and social relations to hardship and recovery. Commonly understood as "the capacity to recover quickly from difficulty; toughness,"[11] resilience is at the core of Asian American racialization. For example, William Petersen's 1966 article begins with a plot that embeds neoliberal striving in model citizenship: Japanese Americans, despite maltreatment, "undertook menial tasks with such perseverance" that they achieved modest economic success.[12] As with "love," the possible approaches to challenges and recovery are myriad, but certain scripts dominate popular imagination. These narratives establish which experiences are publicly acknowledged as adversity and which survival tactics and outcomes are worthy of recognition. Following Berlant's approach to *Desire/Love,* I will not attempt an essential definition of "resilience." Rather, I trace its patterns and expectations when attached to different bodies and social contexts. What emerges is an understanding of resilience as an orientation to events and people—a commonplace that is operationalized both to contain available reactions to hardship and to defy those scripts.

Undistinguishable Faces, Un/Resilient Asians, and Aggrieved Masculinity

Let's return to the matter of faces—a specific face this time. In 2008 the literary magazine *n+1* asked Wesley Yang to write a piece about the shooting at Virginia Tech, which was described at the time as one of the deadliest mass

---

11. Stevenson, "Resilience." This is the definition with which the *Performing Resilience* workshops begin—before participants offer their own innovative definitions.

12. Petersen, "Success Story, Japanese-American Style," 21.

murders in US history.[13] The piece that Yang published, "The Face of Seung-Hui Cho," helped establish him as "one of the preeminent Asian-American essayists in the country."[14] As the title suggests, Yang spends a significant portion of the ten-thousand-word essay contemplating the face of the Korean American man who killed thirty-two of his fellow students at Virginia Tech. He writes: "Those lugubrious eyes, that elongated face behind wire-frame glasses: He looks like me."[15] Rather, to Yang, Cho looks like all Asian American men. Cho becomes a synecdoche for Yang's argument that "as the bearer of an Asian face in America [. . .] you were presumptively a nobody, a mute and servile figure."[16] This presumed servility then becomes the open wound of Asian American masculinity on which Yang fixates throughout his writing.

Throughout *The Souls of Yellow Folk*, Yang empathizes with Cho's "peculiar burden of nonrecognition, of invisibility, that is a condition of being an Asian man in America."[17] Speaking "as a bearer of an Asian face in America," Yang laments the fact that Asian faces are "by default unloveable and unloved."[18] More specifically, this is "a face that has nothing to do with the desires of women in this country."[19] As several other writers have pointed out, Yang seems to be working with one very particular definition of love—one that can only be satisfied by women's sexual interests and one that often confuses sex with intimacy. Dana Goldstein observed in *The American Prospect*, "you can't help but take away from the essay that, if only one kind girl had taken the trouble to love Cho, to relieve him of his virginity, 32 people would be alive today."[20] To fold back in the language of resilience: Yang suggests that the sexual denial of the "aggrieved Asian Man"[21] is a hardship deserving of violent retribution, and that this hardship can only be overcome through (hetero)sexual dominance.

---

13. While competitions of pain are not beneficial, it must be noted that these taxonomies also exclude mass killings executed by military forces even in the case of surrender—notably the many massacres of Native Americans that reportings have separated from "modern U.S. history." See Revesz, "Orlando Is Not the Deadliest Mass Shooting in US History"; Peralta, "Putting 'Deadliest Mass Shooting in U.S. History' into Some Historical Context."

14. Chang, "The Familiar Defiance of Wesley Yang."

15. Yang, *The Souls of Yellow Folk*, 10.

16. Yang, xii.

17. Yang, xi.

18. Yang, xi.

19. Yang, 11.

20. Goldstein, "Race, Sex, and the Virginia Tech Killer."

21. Yang, *The Souls of Yellow Folk*, 17.

"The Face of Seung-Hui Cho"—described as "remarkable" in the *New York Times*[22] and the "best thing I've read in a good long while" in *The Atlantic*,[23] and selected for volume 3 of *The Best of Creative Nonfiction*—establishes some of the central themes in Yang's 2018 collection, *The Souls of Yellow Folk*. The book aggregates some of his landmark essays on Asian American identity and has been lauded for probing "the identity crises of Asian American men."[24] By fixating on white heteropatriarchal visions of the good life, Yang sells normative views of Asian America and Asian American pain. Not only does Yang reiterate many of the restrictive assumptions around love explored in the previous chapter; his arguments reinforce forms of resilience that elevate white hegemonic masculinity at the expense of Asian Americans and other POC, women, and other marginalized peoples. Revisiting Yang's writing through diasporic listening reveals how prominent narratives about and even *by* Asian Americans reinforce racial, gender, and other hierarchies through normalizing approaches to adversity and overcoming.

The second essay of *The Souls of Yellow Folk*, "Paper Tigers," directly blames Asian culture for the emasculation of Asian men and their "barely distinguishable" faces.[25] First published as a *New York Magazine* cover story, "Paper Tigers" responds to Amy Chua's *Battle Hymn of the Tiger Mother*, simultaneously praising Chua's boldness in writing the memoir and condemning the strict parenting methods for which she is now famous. While much of the publicity around Chua's book emphasized her "brute-force Chinese education"[26] as a driver of child success, Yang concludes that these parenting tactics render Asians "products of a timid culture, easily pushed around by more assertive people, and thus basically invisible."[27] What Chua describes as traditional Chinese values—"be modest, be humble, be simple . . . never complain or make excuses"[28]—Yang extends into a pan-Asian work ethic that disciplines Asian America into a complaisant and invisible workforce. If the "crisis" is Asian America emasculation, then Yang identifies the cause as Asian culture itself.

As in "The Face of Seung-Hui Cho," Yang's discussion of invisibility circles quickly back to Asian men's perceived sexual impotence. The yellow peril / model minority tract that hones Asian Americans into "conformist quasi-

---

22. Schuessler, "Writing Dangerously."
23. Yglesias, "The Face of Seung-Hui Cho."
24. *O Magazine* quoted by the publisher. "The Souls of Yellow Folk."
25. Yang, *The Souls of Yellow Folk*, 31.
26. Yang, 59.
27. Yang, 33.
28. Chua quoted in Yang, 59.

robots," performing "earnest, striving, middle-class servility," also constrains Asian American men in the dating market.[29] Or, phrased in Yang's rhetorical questions: "What if you missed out on the lessons in masculinity taught in the gyms and locker rooms of America's high schools? What if life has failed to make you a socially dominant alpha male who runs the American board-room and prevails in the American bedroom?"[30] Drawing a direct route from locker room to boardroom to bedroom, Yang revealingly interlaces the ritu-als of white masculinity, capitalism, and compulsory heterosexuality. In this trajectory, social dominance requires being seen as the physically dominant "alpha male" who conquers corporate ladders and white American women. These metrics have continually positioned Asian American men as meek, sec-ondary players in white America; they created the very problem that haunts Yang's writing. Yang, however, not only is compelled to meet these standards but blames a caricature of Asian culture for his inability to do so. As in con-ventional models of resilience, Yang approaches social inequities as personal responsibility and enjoins individuals to work harder to meet the very stan-dards that have conditioned their subjection.

Following the roadmap laid out by Petersen's 1966 article, Yang encour-ages Asian Americans to pursue aggressive individualism and capital gain. He writes, "If the Bamboo Ceiling is ever going to break,"[31] it will be through models such as "Silicon Valley hotshots" or the irreverent chef Eddie Huang, whom he quotes: "What I've learned is that America is about money, and if you can make your culture commodifiable, then you're relevant."[32] One of Yang's most extended examples of Asian American "defiance" is J. T. Tran. Also known as "the Asian Playboy," Tran founded and runs a business that teaches Asian men to pick up women. In Yang's laudatory description:

> The story [Tran] tells is one of Asian-American disadvantage in the sexual marketplace, a disadvantage that he has devoted his life to overturning. Yes, it is about picking up women. Yes, it is about picking up white women. Yes, it is about attracting those women whose hair is the color of the midday sun and eyes are the color of the ocean, and it is about having sex with them. He is not going to apologize for the images of blonde women plastered all over his website. This is what he prefers, what he stands for, and what he is selling: the courage to pursue anyone you want, and the skills to make the

29. Yang, 30–31.
30. Yang, 47.
31. Yang, 53.
32. Huang quoted in Yang, 54.

person you desire desire you back. White guys do what they want; he is going to do the same.[33]

Yang sees this as Tran "dar[ing] to be interesting" and calls for more Asian Americans to similarly "push themselves into the spotlight and to make some noise, to beat people up, to seduce women, to make mistakes, to become entrepreneurs."[34] In this articulation of Asian American liberation, a homogenously weak Asian culture is the oppressor and women are a prop for male conquest. Yang's vision of Asian America is composed of and *for* cisgender men and courts the recognition of white men and women.

Ironically, Tran's pickup tactics are very much embedded in the model minority tradition; participants study, memorize, and then emulate the patterns of "alpha male" behavior. Yang recounts an exercise from one of Tran's classes where students rehearse an iconic line from Arnold Schwarzenegger's 1982 *Conan the Barbarian*. Tran shouts, "What is good in life?" and students respond, "in the loudest, most emphatic" voices they can muster: "To crush my enemies, see them driven before me, and to hear the lamentation of their women—in my bed!"[35] The primary difference between Tran's supposed individuality and the behavior of Yang's "barely distinguishable" Asians is that the former aligns Asian Americans with stereotypes of white masculinity rather than those of Asian men. Yang's discussion upholds a racial dichotomy that contrasts quiet, striving Asian bodies with the "social dominance" of white Americans. These are allied mythologies that uphold racial hegemony in the US. As this story goes, "good" immigrants work hard, keep their heads down, and do not question authority. Meanwhile, (cisgender, heterosexual, white) alpha males (and, occasionally, white women) become leaders, entrepreneurs, and lotharios through a radical "individualism" that can nevertheless be formulated and taught in Tran's classes.

Yang does not use the term *resilience,* but his arguments build from its topical centrality in the formation of US racialized identities. He expresses resentment for stereotypes about immigrant resilience but does not attack the stereotypes themselves, suggesting instead that Asians have actually created cultures of quiet servility. Yang's argument echoes the racial logics through which model minority narratives have been weaponized against nonconforming Asians and other racial minorities. The assumption is that if Petersen's model Japanese Americans or, more recently, Andrew Sullivan's "prosperous, well-educated, and successful" Asian Americans could thrive by

33. Yang, 49.
34. Yang, 60.
35. Yang, 50.

"maintain[ing] solid two-parent structures" and "[emphasizing] education and hard work,"[36] then POC who fail to do so are limited by cultural or constitutional inferiority rather than by racist conditions. Similarly, Yang does not question the racial scripts that stereotype Asian American men as weak and effeminate and that objectify Asian American women. An exemplar of Berlant's "cruel optimism,"[37] Yang presses harder into the very standards designed for his degradation.

Yang's narrative reveals the paradox of Asian American resilience. The model minority myth posits Asian Americans as resilient in their ability to work their way out of adversity and thereby disprove the existence of racism. At the same time, the model minority is *un*resilient in their softness and deference—in accepting the place that white supremacy assigned them. The striving for which Asian Americans are celebrated as model citizens also casts them as obsequious foils to Schwarzenegger's Conan, as "passive, obedient, submissive, a hardworking nonentity, a nobody, a nullity, one of those mute, lugubrious bespectacled glum-faced inscrutable spiky-haired presences haunting the library behind a stack of books."[38] Yang ignores the double standard at work: that Asian American bootstraps-ism is attributed to cultures of quiet obedience while white achievement belongs to independent hotshots. Asian striving is "good enough" for nameless, foreign laborers, but never good enough to compete with white exceptionalism. This distinction is not about any innate character of Asian or white people but about the scripts assigned to them. Our actions are drawn into the interpretive orbits of stock stories, which in turn center and shield whiteness. Asian alienness is an inherent feature of this narrative, and while *some* individuals might achieve marginal acceptance by mimicking the postures of white masculinity, no amount of Schwarzenegger lines or entrepreneurial spirit will result in equal treatment for Asian Americans as a whole.

Understood as a taxonomy that distinguishes acceptable conduct from "fragility"—that separates the hyperarticulate, crucible-forged from the coddled and weak—"resilience" designates certain events as harm and particular responses as commendable. These designations are unavoidably shaded by circulating narratives about race, gender, sexuality, ability, and other vectors of identity. When Yang proposes that Asian Americans' "burden of nonrecognition, of invisibility" can only be cast off by becoming a major player in "the scrimmage of American appetite,"[39] he endorses whiteness as the unnamed

---

36. Sullivan, "Why Do Democrats Feel Sorry for Hillary Clinton?"
37. Berlant, *Cruel Optimism*.
38. Yang, *The Souls of Yellow Folk*, 193–94.
39. Yang, 47.

standard by which all others are measured. Echoing the resilience trainings that pervade health care, workplace, and educational settings, Yang's individualist focus cannot address the racialized gender expectations through which conventional resilience is judged. He does not have to individually expound on these values in order to endorse them. They have the gravity of stock stories; they are so much the established norm that their pull is ambient—a fact of everyday living. Through these common understandings, "resilience" enforces a value system that designates particular people as deserving of success and thriving, and others as too lazy, incompetent, or weak to do the same.

On Taxonomies

Asian Americans are no strangers to the potency and problems of taxonomies. A notoriously incohesive group, Asian America aggregates over twenty different countries of origin and even more languages and cultures. With its political origins, Asian America named a strategic alliance to agitate for better living, working, and learning conditions.[40] More recent work in Asian American studies has paid particular attention to how multiracial Asian Americans challenge the stability of racial categories while still mobilizing them for community-consciousness and antiracist interventions. LeiLani Nishime's *Undercover Asian,* for example, explores how representations of multiracial Asian Americans are used to naturalize or counter racial essentialism.[41] Nicole Rabin, though more expressly suspicious of (multi)racial labels, discusses how Kip Fulbeck's *The Hapa Project* destabilizes identity by spotlighting the range of identifications among mixed-race APIs. Like the multiracial subjects of Nishime's and Rabin's studies, the participants of the Visibility Project confound identity categories while reclaiming them in meaningful ways. Through this taxonomic dexterity, the VP itself exposes the hegemonic usages of "resilience" while also reinventing it as a foundation for communal strength and healing.

To better understand the role of taxonomies in shaping human interactions, I turn to philosopher Ásta's "conferralist framework," which regards social categories as properties *conferred* on people with the authority either of an institution (such as being legally married) or of social norms (being engaged).[42] These properties come with constraints and enablements. For example, legally married partners are protected from testifying against one

40. Omatsu, "'Four Prisons'"; Lee, *The Making of Asian America*, 301–5.
41. Nishime, *Undercover Asian.*
42. Ásta, *Categories We Live By.*

another in court, or wedding bands often signal to others that an individual is "taken." Ásta's conferralist framework accounts for both the social construction of human categories and their reliance on circulations of power. A couple cannot proclaim themselves legally married if they do not meet the requirements set by state authorities, and an engagement necklace would not achieve the same widespread understanding as a ring.[43] In other words, conferred categories are socially constructed not as a matter of individual whim but through ongoing circulation and the authority of institutional policy and narrative accumulation.[44]

As a conferred property, "resilience" is most commonly correlated with white masculinist norms not by coincidence but because cisgender, heterosexual white men both established and benefit most from US political and cultural systems. Their successes are more likely to resemble individual uplift because current social arrangements provide them unmarked privileges and support systems. Those without such privileges (without, for example, generational wealth, ready access to education, presumed authority or good will) are more likely to require mutual aid in the form of other people. These survival strategies are in turn less likely to be celebrated and rewarded as resilience, creating a cycle of unrecognition that continues to conceal the wounds and triumphs of LGBTQ+ folks, disabled folks, and people of color.

Categories, however, can also be reappropriated and repurposed by those they were meant to control, as in the histories of both *queer* and *crip*. Because the labels deployed by the Visibility Project do not aspire to the permanence of queer or crip, they function more as Eve Sedgwick's "nonce taxonomies"— novel terms and concepts "fashioned against social norms for a particular purpose, which are to be discarded or redesigned as utility dictates."[45] *Nonce,* meaning "for a particular occasion, temporarily,"[46] creates locally specific, contingent categorizations always subject to revision. As Sedgwick's answer to the *un*queer rigidity of dominant categories, nonce taxonomies enable "the making and unmaking and remaking of and redissolution of hundreds of old and new categorical imaginings concerning all the kinds it may take to make up the world."[47] The participants of the VP practice this collaborative world(re)making through reparative taxonomies. On their tongues, extant terminologies splinter into novel understandings of gender, ethnicity, and sexuality—into countless possible journeys.

---

43. Speaking for a US-based context.
44. See also Butler, *Excitable Speech.*
45. Sedgwick paraphrased in Singer, "The Profusion of Things," 71.
46. *Oxford English Dictionary Online,* s.v. "nonce, n.1."
47. Sedgwick, *Epistemology of the Closet,* 23.

For example, when Kay Ulanday Barrett emphasizes their identity as one of "mixed race transgenderness," they refuse a homogenizing trans experience. They point to the effects of their own mixed heritage on their safety, insisting on race as integral to how different trans people encounter public spaces. Throughout the VP, nonce categories such as this one function as homing devices, naming the speaker's experiences in ways that connect them with lands, histories, and communities while also critiquing the conditions for belonging. With resilience as commonplace, I listen for resonances among these accounts, situating them within national and global histories. Diasporic listening takes me not just through materials directly housed in the VP but also to the trove of public materials created by the VP's participants—many of whom, like Barrett, are activists and QTAPI leaders in their own right. Differential movement enables me to maneuver among these perspectives to deconstruct presumed truths. The resulting constellations not only expose the plasticity—and, well, resilience—of this topos but also reappropriate resilience as strength-in-interdependence, in direct opposition to fantasies of individual dominance.

The Visibility Project

A photographer, activist, and archivist, Mia Nakano has grown the Visibility Project well beyond the initial portrait series that formed *Visible Resilience*. By now, the VP is composed of three allied components, all of which unmake and remake notions of resilience:

> *Visible Resilience*: A photo portrait and video collection focused on queer Asian American women and trans and gender-nonconforming folks. The book, *Visible Resilience,* is accompanied by video interviews, which readers can access on the Visibility Project website: https://www.visibilityproject.org/.

> *The Resilience Archives*: A community-sourced digital history tour of Bay Area Queer Asian Pacific American history. Nakano describes it as "Pinterest meets Google maps."[48] Visitors can click on different locations to access documentation of events that happened at each site, and they can also upload and contribute their own materials at https://www.resiliencearchives.com/.

---

48. Nakano, personal interview.

Performing Resilience: A biannual ten-week storytelling and performance workshop that culminates in a performance showcase and photography exhibition. Workshop participants build their performances from materials in the archives, and the showcases take place alongside exhibits of the Visible Resilience portraits: https://www.resiliencearchives.com/our-work/performing-resilience/.

In naming its undertakings visible resilience, archiving resilience, and performing resilience, the VP exercises the (re)definitional power of archives. As Caswell et al. put it in their introduction to critical archival studies: "Naming is a form of legitimating. Naming is power. Naming is a way of demarcating and defining and delineating and harnessing."[49] Nakano's deliberate naming challenges normative definitions of resilience and centers the actual resilient practices of her communities.

An expansive, multiplatform undertaking, the Visibility Project responds to a conundrum adjacent to, if not aligned with Yang's own exigence: the invisibility of Asian Americans. In the words of Mia Nakano: "I grew up not seeing images that looked like my family in the media. In school, the only thing I learned about my cultural history was that my family was stripped of almost everything they owned, except for two suitcases, and forced into incarceration for over two years."[50] Like many migrant family stories, Nakano's begins in struggle. This is not a tale of individual triumph, however. In contrast to Yang, who seems attached to one particular version of Asian American success, Nakano is concerned with the limitations of any one story standing in for QTAPI experience. Hardship, in her formulation, is to be overcome not by individual determination but by working on and through the stories and structures that enable it. This working-through requires *both* self-definition *and* listening to and connecting with the stories of others. While the Visibility Project is replete with examples of personal hardship and of overcoming, it is itself a model of interdependent resilience as home-building—an example of how communities can create the conditions for one another's survival.

The VP's sprawling, multimodal nature results in part from Nakano's view of (in)visibility as a corollary of accessibility. It is not that trans and queer Asian Americans do not exist; it is that their voices and stories often do not have public platforms. When Nakano began the VP, not only was she one of very few openly queer Asian Americans in her circles, but she had a difficult time even "find[ing] images of my community."[51] Because internet searches

49. Caswell, Punzalan, and Sangwand, "Critical Archival Studies," 3.
50. Nakano, *Visible Resilience*, 1.
51. Nakano, 2.

turned up few results, she set Google alerts to notify her any time new material appeared with keywords relating to LGBTQ+ Asian Americans. All she found was porn—often framed through exoticizing and fetishizing lenses.[52] This meant that, prior to the VP, trans and queer Asian Americans could find very little public representation—and what little they did find was not intended for them. As a queer Japanese American woman living in the San Francisco Bay Area, Nakano wondered, "If I felt so alone [. . .] what was happening in the rest of the country?"[53] The Visibility Project emerged from this curiosity and desire for her findings to reach QTAPI folks dispersed around the country and the world.

Building from Nakano's background in photography, Visible Resilience was the first component of the VP. With over two hundred participants, this is still the largest single collection of images focused on queer Asian American women and trans and gender-nonconforming folks. In the *Visible Resilience* book, the images are sorted by geography, beginning in Hawai'i and moving through the continental US. Participants' ages span eighteen through sixty-three, and they claim an inventive universe of gender identities and ethnicities. Because Nakano's goal was to create an unedited platform for other QTAPI folks to tell their stories, the words that accompany the photos were all directly written or spoken by the participants. Now, when you run internet searches for LGBTQ+ Asian Americans, not only does the Visibility Project feature prominently among the results, but Nakano herself appears among the early images. Through the lens of her camera, QTAPI appear as they wish to be seen. As a reflexive and growing project, the VP not only documents the challenges of QTAPI visibility; it has worked toward community-driven solutions. It has provided the grounds for QTAPI to write, speak, and otherwise story ourselves in relation to one another and to the values and responsibilities that move us. If home is not a place we can ever lay claim to, platforms like the VP give us home as collaborative making—creating and sustaining the conditions for one another to be fully present, seen, heard, and felt.

Visible Resilience and Taxonomic Reappropriation

Visible Resilience compiles Nakano's portrait collection alongside each participant's self-descriptions. Nakano asked them seven simple questions: "(1) What is your name? (2) Where do you live? (3) What is your age at the time of this

---

52. Nakano, personal interview.

53. Nakano.

photo? (4) What is your ethnicity, race, and/or cultural identity? (5) Your gender identity? (6) Pronouns? (7) Sexual orientation/identity?"[54] Their answers
appear as single words or phrases beneath their images, at times accompanied by longer quotes from their conversation with Nakano. Because they
self-identify without predetermined labels, their answers do not adhere to
any fixed taxonomy. Rather, the terminologies selected by participants are as
original as each of their histories. This particularization reveals the reductions
and erasures of dominant categories for race/ethnicity, gender, and sexuality—what Sedgwick calls the "inconceivably coarse axes of categorization"
that dominate critical and political discourse.[55] As nonce—temporary, con-
textually dependent—taxonomies, each speaker's self-identifications pinpoint
how the (in)visibility of personal experiences can highlight historical and contemporary patterns of exclusion, erasure, and emergence. In a polyphony of
queer and Asian Pacific American experiences, contributors to *Visible Resilience* inquire—both explicitly and implicitly—What are the consequences of
being grouped together in homogenizing categories and identities? How do
we access the power of such collectivities without ignoring and obscuring
intragroup conflict and difference? What terminologies can capture previously
unseen histories and experiences without subjecting them to surveillance and/
or fetishization? Through homing, they navigate these precarious discursive
conditions, leveraging nonce taxonomies to foreground particularized insights
and needs, evade the normative gaze, and pursue pathways oriented by shared
politics.

   Visible Resilience's stories are told through a combination of portraits,
nonce-taxonomic labels, longer anecdotes, and video interviews, situating
individual voices within larger constellations that re-envision "what it means
to be queer and AAPI."[56] Holding the specific in tension with the general,
these stories trouble the boundedness of social categories and instead posit
identities as relational, dynamic formulations. Those who appear East Asian
might trace their roots to other parts of the continent; those who look traditionally feminine do not necessarily use feminine pronouns or nouns; and
their sexual orientations expand well beyond the letters of *LGBTQ*—or sometimes remix once-familiar terms into novel combinatory formations. The
book, and the broader archives that follow, build from this work to explore
the power of naming—the ability to claim, discard, and redefine one's identifications in dialogue with others. Through this discursive maneuvering, the
Visibility Project facilitates differential movement among the multitudinous

---

54. Nakano, *Visible Resilience*, 1.
55. Sedgwick, *Epistemology of the Closet*, 22.
56. Nakano, *Visible Resilience*, 1.

identifications that compose Asian America. It explores how racial and ethnic identities modify experiences of gender, sexuality, and disability, as well as how naming the specificity of those experiences can critique and revise US cultural norms. The resilience that it captures is less about individual healing than about creating the conditions for interpersonal care and mutual uplift.

In an inversion of the "perpetual foreigner / always (im)migrant" narrative of Asian America, *Visible Resilience* begins in Hawai'i, centering experiences of Pacific Islanders, who are often overlooked in the expansive category of "API." The first portrait of the book features Moana, whose self-identification reads "Hawaiian, Chinese, German. Female most times (gay boy inside). Queer lesbian alien chick."[57] In her photo, she is wearing jeans and a pink tank top with a boldly patterned jacket. She has accessorized with multiple long, beaded necklaces, one of which ends in a large cross. Sunglasses sit atop her head—on stylishly cropped, short gray hair. She is grinning at the camera and holding both hands in shaka signs. On the opposite page are her words: "Hawaii is a spiritual place. Our people are spiritual people. Our land today [and what happened to it], it's terrible. Our people were a million plus, and by the time they got done with us we were down to fifty thousand."[58] The "invisibility" that begins this collection is communal and historical rather than simply individual—it is the erasure of colonial incursions and the obscuring of Pacific Islanders beneath the Asian American umbrella.

Notably, the "we" with which Moana begins is specifically Native Hawaiians, calling attention to how Hawaiian experience and futures may differ from or even conflict with Asian American trajectories. Early Western settlers (initially, Germans) who established sugar plantations on the islands imported Chinese, Japanese, and Filipinx workers and situated them in competition with Native Hawaiians.[59] Once again, Asian laborers were praised for their willingness to work for lower pay while being "prompt at the call of the bell, steady in their work, and quick to learn."[60] By 1890 Chinese people composed almost 19 percent of Hawai'i's total population, actively replacing Indigenous peoples on their own land.[61] In fact, people of Asian ethnicity are now nearly 40 percent of Hawai'i's population, making them the largest demographic on the islands and one that has frequently acted against the interests of Native Hawaiians.[62] In pursuing legitimacy through state recognition and power,

57. Nakano, 5.
58. Nakano, 6.
59. Fleischman and Tyson, "The Interface of Race and Accounting."
60. Lee, *The Making of Asian America*, 74.
61. Fujikane and Okamura, *Asian Settler Colonialism*.
62. Saranillio, "Why Asian Settler Colonialism Matters"; Day et al., "Settler Colonial Studies, Asian Diasporic Questions."

Asian Americans were integral to—and continue to benefit from—Hawaiian dispossession.[63] Moana's decision to disaggregate Hawaiian experience from Asian America's participation in settler colonialism begins the Visibility Project with this difficult tension of "API" identity.

With its range of perspectives, the Visibility Project is able to explore and even highlight the frictions among QTAPI histories without presenting a seamless, settled multiculturalism. Rather, in compiling these voices as integral components of "Asian Pacific American" experience, the project asks auditors to dwell with the unresolved discord and open wounds of Asian Pacific American identity. At the same time, by naming itself an archive of APA stories, the Visibility Project invests a cautious optimism in the coalitional potential of the limited but potentially generative categories. Moana's quote, for example, is situated alongside that of Keiva—a Native Hawaiian trans woman who was born and raised outside of Hawai'i. Moving from the historical to the personal, Keiva's story begins with the dispersal that emerges from the colonial disruption of communal ecologies.

Though she identifies first as Native Hawaiian, Keiva was born and raised off the islands. Her first experience of acceptance was in the Mission District of San Francisco, where she found transgender community. As a high-profile transgender and HIV/AIDS activist, Keiva has described the San Francisco Mission District as the first place where she felt she could "live freely in my skin," and where she forged genuine, lasting connections.[64] When she needed to begin antiretroviral therapy, however, Keiva also knew that the pace of life and lifestyle she had forged in SF was unsustainable. It was then that she returned to Hawai'i, where she has now been for over twenty years, and where she facilitates culturally informed care for transgender folks living with HIV/AIDS. Bridging her experiences in California with her Hawaiian roots, she works with community service providers to design outreach and other programming sensitive to the distrust and anxieties many trans folks have with medical institutions, to the financial constraints of many trans people, and to the discomfort many Polynesians feel around Western medicine.[65] The community that Keiva builds with this work, then, is centered in Hawaiian cultures, situated on Hawaiian land, but also informed by and attuned to the other communities she has found in her life.

While not a decolonial undertaking, the Visibility Project takes on Asian America's often dissonant relationship with the Native peoples of this land—

---

63. Trask, "Settlers of Color and 'Immigrant' Hegemony"; Fujikane and Okamura, *Asian Settler Colonialism.*

64. Cadena, *Positively Trans.*

65. Cadena, "A Day Just for Us."

one on which Asian Americans have often fought for state recognition and its attendant protections. Like Izzy Alvaran in the Dragon Fruit Project, many subjects in the Visibility Project renounce the desire for belonging on normative terms, whether through US citizenship or through inclusion in the majoritarian story of Asian America. Instead, participants like Stephanie Camba augment identity categories to position their stories within, and as critiques of, American militarism and forced migration. In Camba's portrait, they wear a bright yellow shirt and a patterned blue-and-yellow loop scarf. Their hair is styled in a mid-length, asymmetrical haircut, and their bangs sweep across a youthful, smiling face. On the opposite page, their words read:

> I was born in the Philippines, but I grew up in the Marshall Islands near Hawaii. They tested atomic bombs there, on Bikini Atoll. That's all it's known for. As a result, there's been a lot of migration to the United States and a small amount of money they distributed to the elite class and government. Everyone else was left to suffer through nuclear related diseases. There's such a high rate of disease in Pacific Islands. That's a result of colonialism and shifting the way that Native people live. This has only started coming up over the decades. Not many people are doing the research or correlating these diseases with nuclear fallout.[66]

In the caption to their photograph, Camba notes that they are "Filipina, Asian" but that their nationality is "Marshallese, Islander."[67] They insert a new category to supplement Nakano's query about "ethnicity/race." In doing so, they declare an allegiance established through experience rather than blood or birth. They separate ethnicity and race from nationality, acknowledging how personal histories and intimate relations modify one's means and places of belonging. While Camba is a settler of color (or "alien" or "arrivant")[68]— and they acknowledge such in their racial and ethnic identification—they also align themself with Marshallese struggles. They use their nationality to call attention to the plight of Marshallese peoples, whose lands and bodies were bartered for US nuclear arms development—a history that gets buried within broader statistics about Asian American success and health outcomes.

Like the above examples, Suzanne Presard also pressures the presumed fixity of racial categories while challenging the dominant voices within those categories to cede narrative control. In her portrait, Presard's hair falls in long

---

66. Nakano, *Visible Resilience*, 56.

67. Nakano, 55.

68. Byrd, *The Transit of Empire*; Day, *Alien Capital*; Day et al., "Settler Colonial Studies, Asian Diasporic Questions."

dark curls as she grins at the camera. She is wearing a red tank top, featuring Marvel comic book heroes Thor and Spider-Man. The caption reads simply "The Bronx, NY. Indo-Caribbean." On the opposite page, Presard elaborates:

> Identifying as Asian American isn't something that resonates with me. What's problematic in this country is that people who are Indo-Caribbean or Indo-Jamaican have to choose. One of the reasons why I wanted to participate in this project is because we get pigeonholed into many labels, boxes, categories. This has a homogenizing effect on our identities. In college I had to check the Asian American box, because I wasn't Black. There was no Caribbean American or Indo-Caribbean. You are ethnically of Indian descent from South Asia, so you end up checking that box. [. . .] What's important to me is representation among the diaspora. I think there is value in doing projects where people can identify under a certain heading. That's a way of building solidarity. I also think it's important to recognize all the people left out.[69]

Here, in a collection of "queer AAPI (Asian American Pacific Islander) women, trans, and gender nonconforming"[70] individuals, we encounter a speaker who actively *disidentifies* with the category of Asian American—in both the colloquial and the Muñozian sense. Presard's decision to claim *just* "Indo-Caribbean" among myriad possible self-identifications foregrounds the significance of this term and its absence from most racial and ethnic taxonomies.

Defined by Muñoz as "recycling and rethinking encoded meaning,"[71] disidentification can be understood as a tactic resonant with Sandoval's meta-ideologizing—as the strategic resignification of a dominant sign. Presard disidentifies with dominant narratives of Asian America through her nonce taxonomies—through her temporary claim to both Indo-Caribbean and Asian American identity. Her caption stands out as uncommonly minimalist among other, more colorful self-descriptions. In choosing to describe herself as Indo-Caribbean, without any other modifiers, she spotlights multiple erasures in the broad categorization of "Asian American / Pacific Islander." Indo-Caribbean, itself an umbrella term, still signals a heterogenous, transnational collective, encompassing Indian and South Asian diasporas in Guyana, Trinidad and Tobago, Jamaica, Barbados, and other islands, as well as those who have since moved to the US—particularly, New York City. Both Presard's words and her

69. Nakano, *Visible Resilience*, 114.
70. Nakano, 1.
71. Muñoz, *Disidentifications*, 31.

very presence in this archive work to redefine AAPI as a strategic umbrella that might be better attuned to those it has historically ignored. While actively rejecting homogenizing scripts of Asian America, Presard also leaves room for movement within that social identification. This is a critique she has found that she can make effectively *within* Asian American projects, using her (un)belonging to establish these categories as contingent and changeable.

Nakano herself builds from Presard's play on taxonomies by spotlighting Presard as the first speaker in a demo video for the Visibility Project. The four-and-a-half-minute clip devotes two full minutes to Presard and her relationship with Asian American identity. Presard says, "I thought even though I might not necessarily identify as Asian American, society often pegs me as that—because of that labeling system."[72] She goes on to offer the insights repeated in the book—that she sees potential in projects where many can gather beneath a strategic heading, but that those projects must simultaneously recognize the inevitable limitations of that heading as well as the fact that people necessarily belong in "multiple boxes."[73] Nakano, by foregrounding this critique of Asian America on a project *about* "the queer Asian Pacific American women and transgender community,"[74] re-envisions QTAPA community through Presard's story of unbelonging. In naming this project one of Asian Pacific American resilience, Nakano redefines QTAPA community as one responsive to, and made stronger by addressing, the ways it has silenced others. Nakano's answer to the struggles of Asian American invisibility is, then, necessarily collaborative. She provides the platform, the remixing, and the amplification, but this crowdsourced resilience is driven by journeys like Presard's and the myriad experiences they introduce to Asian America in their own terms.

As with the Dragon Fruit Project, the rhetorical agility of *Visible Resilience* lies in its polyvocality. Other profiles in *Visible Resilience* answer Presard's call for thoughtful and coalitional identifications through much more elaborate nonce taxonomies. In fact, many of the participants describe themselves in ways that bind ethnicity/race, gender, and sexuality into inseparable phrases. For example, in Moana's "lesbian alien chick," lesbian and alien modify the way she inhabits "chick." For Tara Shuai, ethnicity and region inform her embodiment as a "Chinese, Taiwanese. Russian, Jewish southern belle. High femme bonvivant."[75] Joy Messinger identifies as "sick, disabled" before "cis

72. Nakano and Visibility Project, *Visibility Project + Resilience Archives Work Sample.*
73. Nakano and Visibility Project.
74. Visibility Project, "About."
75. Nakano, *Visible Resilience,* 123.

female."[76] Bex Ahuja chooses to list no pronouns but in their video identifies as someone who is "butch female-bodied transmasculine" and whose friends switch between pronouns as "a term of endearment."[77] These gender identifications are journeys more than labels, calling attention to how our "coarse axes" of social belonging are inevitably intersectional and subject to change. Belonging, in other words, is a transient, unsettled practice.

"Masculinity-in-Disability" and Revising Resilience

Kay Ulanday Barrett's photo is accompanied by an eight-part video interview, in which they offer an in-depth exploration of how gender, race, and disability interlace and necessitate redefinitions of resilience. In their portrait, Barrett wears a plain gray T-shirt. Their short hair lifts up from their scalp in a thick fauxhawk. Their accessories—a black watch, four bracelets, a bone necklace, and square glasses—all have a minimalist, stocky aesthetic. Against their grayscale wardrobe, the red of their cane stands out, centered in front of their body. The caption reads "New Jersey. 30. Mixed Race Pinoy American. Transgender and Gender Nonconforming. K, ne, they, pogi. Queer. Genderqueer."[78] In contrast to Presard's singular approach, Barrett uses their entry to explore how all these identities fold into one another. In their story—and on their body—disability, gender, race, and ethnicity entangle to expose the constraints of normative expectations.

Masculinity serves as the anchor that grounds Barrett's wide-ranging discussion. As Barrett explains in their video, their chronic pain made starkly apparent the bounds of conventional masculinity. They say, "You're supposed to lift shit. You're supposed to be strong . . . and that's just not how my masculinity strolls these days."[79] Barrett sustained lasting nerve damage when they were working with homeless LGBTQ+ youth; an altercation broke out, and they were injured when trying to intervene. Since then, Barrett says, they have been growing their community through "trying to understand, you know, what does it mean in my queer, brown, mixed masculinity to be disabled and to work in a disability justice framework?"[80] Met with a gender paradigm that rendered them inherently inadequate, Barrett chose to reimagine masculinity rather than contort to fit predetermined standards. Learning to inhabit

76. Nakano, 46.
77. Ahuja, "Bex (Rough Cut)."
78. Nakano, *Visible Resilience*, 103.
79. Barrett, "Kay Ulanday Barrett—New York."
80. Barrett.

their body in its "makeshifts, and changes, and limitations,"[81] Barrett claims a bespoke masculinity suited to their experience and needs, simultaneously creating room for others to join in this remaking.

Barrett achieves this redefinition through naming. Their story detaches masculinity from individual grit and imports it to reflexive and communal forms of crip resilience. Whereas Barrett, who identifies as nonbinary, used to bind their chest to appear more conventionally masculine, they say, "now I'm a grumpy old man and that shit hurts me." In this statement, *man* functions as a nonce-taxonomic label that asserts Barrett's masculinity even as they deny masculine norms and binary gender. Barrett goes on to explain the reasons they decided against hormone therapy: "I'm in the worker's comp system, and as a disabled person. What are the negative ramifications about shifting gender presentation in that space? I'd have to think about that—the element of safety."[82] Safety and self-preservation are not the makings of traditional masculinity—not in the sense of Yang's "tough, brassy, risk-taking, street-smart entrepreneurs"[83]—but in orienting their own gender expression toward feelings of safety, Barrett models a masculinity attuned to the strength and freedom of supportive community.

Similarly, while Barrett's younger self once defined even queer gender expressions with rigidity ("This is what butch is"[84]), they have found that their own gender presentation shifts depending on "where I am, how safe I am, how much in community I am, how comfortable I am, how *joyful* I am."[85] In adapting their gender expression to feelings of safety and joy, Barrett not only highlights how gender is relational and intersectional but also reveals how social arrangements protect some forms of masculinity and femininity while exposing others to potential violence. This orientation to visibility, like the VP as a whole, does not pursue visibility as an inevitable good. Barrett's willingness to be seen in their "multiplicity in gender"[86] depends on whether they feel safe with the people around them. The contingency and contextual specificity of Barrett's gender expression is true for everyone. We are able to express and to be recognized as masculine, feminine, or wherever we see ourselves in the galaxy of gender, better in some settings than in others. Those who live in social environments that affirm their self-perception are simply spared such continual self-reflection and adaptability.

---

81. Barrett.
82. Barrett.
83. Yang, *The Souls of Yellow Folk*, 52.
84. Barrett, "Kay Ulanday Barrett—New York."
85. Barrett.
86. Nakano, *Visible Resilience*, 104.

Without romanticizing or diminishing their ongoing struggle with chronic pain, Barrett narrativizes the ways that crip experience has necessitated and afforded them other approaches to inhabiting their body. When Barrett walks into worker's comp ("looking the way I do"), they are "sized up"[87] based on appearance—based on their visible difference. They are measured by gendered, racialized, heterosexist, ageist, and ableist standards that plague "any other governmental system."[88] Because they are more likely to be met with confusion (at best) than with empathy, they are also more vulnerable to dismissal or neglect. In listening to and building knowledge from this experience, Barrett demonstrates how bodily histories document the intricate relations of gender, race, sexuality, and disability. Barrett's masculinity is shaped by the ways they navigate their disability. Their experience of disability is also conditioned by how people see (or fail to see) their brown, queer, genderqueer body.

Barrett's "masculinity in disability"[89]—and the vibrantly queer gender expressions of the many participants in *Visible Resilience*—functions as survival work, as community- and home-building, and as activism. Throughout their career as a public figure, Barrett has remarked on the ways that trans masculinity in mainstream media approximates white, ableist bodily norms. This is a masculinity that "feels cut and paste"[90]—the parade of able-bodied, thin white men whose images monopolize hashtags such as #ftm #transmen, and #selfmademan. Even when there is room for men of color, Barrett notes, "it feels closer to colonial conceptions of brown cis binary masculinity."[91] Under white supremacy, brown masculinity "is only worthy if it can achieve labor and physical laborious tasks for white capital."[92] Barrett provides a racialized analysis of gender, noting how the physical norms imposed on men of color derive from the exploitation of their bodies for white material gain. By contrast, learning to inhabit a disabled body has impelled Barrett to make room for other forms of masculinity—for one that strolls with a cane and without a binder, one that builds community around the multiplicity and possibilities of gender, and one that pursues worlds embracive of disability justice.

Barrett's story cuts through the reductive formula driving popular understandings of resilience. Their struggles for self-expression and community

---

87. Barrett, "Kay Ulanday Barrett—New York."
88. Barrett.
89. Barrett.
90. Barrett quoted in Leibowitz, "Dapper Crip."
91. Barrett quoted in Leibowitz.
92. Barrett quoted in Leibowitz.

could not be realized through individual overcoming—and in fact are worsened by the cultural elevation of rugged independence. Barrett responds not by replicating this restrictive paradigm but by facilitating altogether different ways of surviving. Their story and their career as organizer and poet highlight resilience-through-interdependence—how those relegated to the margins create conditions for one another's thriving. The goal is, then, not to be visible on the terms they have been given but to create myriad ways for being seen and heard that respond to the needs and circumstances of community members.

Visibility as Vulnerability

Nakano's conscientious space-holding echoes Barrett's nuanced approach to visibility, calling attention to the ways that context affects one's ability or desire to be seen. Each entry in *Visible Resilience* is formatted to suit the speaker, instead of the other way around. Notably, the section for Tennessee features just one individual who is listed without a name or descriptors. The full quote reads as follows:

> My parents are very against homosexuality, my entire family is. Last night at dinner, we were talking about it, they were saying that gays were lazy, gross, and dirty. I spoke up. I don't usually speak up, but I said they had to have compassion. Those kinds of comments, people have to hear those types of comments every single day. It's painful to sit there and take it. I can see why queer folks try to kill themselves. It's hard. Then I started crying and it got really awkward.[93]

In place of a full-color photo, this page has only black text on a blank page. The speaker's inability to be named or seen is striking amid so many other elaborate self-portraits. The brevity of their statement replicates the silencing of their family's judgment, while their anonymity calls attention to the vulnerability and/or loss that often attends LGBTQ+ visibility.

Tennessee's presentation of in/visibility stands in contrast to Yang's pursuit of social and sexual conquest. For this unnamed contributor, the gaze that lionizes "the socially dominant alpha male"[94]—this narrow vision of the good life—censures queerness as a failure of masculine dominance. In other words, the visibility that Yang and his compatriots pursue for a limited sector of Asian

93. Nakano, *Visible Resilience*, 76.
94. Yang, *The Souls of Yellow Folk*, 47.

America renders *invisible* the broad range of embodiments that others need and desire. Rather than offer one perspective or one unitary objective, *Visible Resilience* convenes a diversity of experiences at the myriad intersections of gender, race, nationality, Indigeneity, migration, and disability. Among these many participants, those who can share their stories in depth illustrate the range and dynamism of queer API lives, while those who necessarily withhold parts of their journey remind readers of the many barriers that remain for QTAPI to live more fully as themselves.

Keeping in mind the risks of visibility, the closing section of *Visible Resilience* provides a toolkit for those who may use the VP's content in their classrooms. These materials serve not only a pedagogical role but a rhetorical one as well. Nakano makes visible the thought, labor, and empathy required to foster these communal exchanges—the safety needed to make a home. Anticipating how minority stories are often misread, Nakano and the VP's curriculum team offer guiding principles, lesson plans, and lists of resources for further learning. Nakano notes that all participants were provided release forms that outlined how these images and videos could be used and seen, and she urges educators to conduct their own classroom discussions with similar care:

> It is crucial to think about the potential ramifications of what would happen if someone were unintentionally "outed" during this process. It is also important to think about "outing" someone not just in terms of their gender or sexuality, but religious beliefs, being undocumented, perceptions of class, parental rights, and much more.[95]

In other words, visibility is also often an act of faith. Interviewees or students who give us their stories are also gifting us their trust. In its careful approach to visibility, *Visible Resilience* reminds readers that bonds are both built and broken by how we tender these truths and their concomitant vulnerabilities.

To prepare instructors for the potentially sensitive conversations prompted by this material, Nakano provides guidelines for discursive care as well as a list of potential conflicts that may arise. For example: "Create prefaces for the topics. Let participants take the time to leave the room and come back if needed."[96] She offers discussion questions that move from individual ("How do you identify?"[97]) to structural (How would a loved one coming out as LGBTQ impact "any social, political, or economic decisions that you would

---

95. Nakano, *Visible Resilience*, 131.
96. Nakano, 132.
97. Nakano, 136.

make in the future?"[98]). Some questions build from the portraits and oral histories of *Visible Resilience,* while others refer instructors to the Dragon Fruit Project and other QTAPI media productions such as the API Pride Project and the Dari Project. The curriculum thus posits this material as ever-expanding—a launchpad for future connections and networks of care.

By narrativizing the thought that went into curating and presenting these materials, *Visible Resilience* rejects the illusion of visibility as a straightforward or untroubled process.[99] Instead, this rich compilation of counterstories unpacks and redefines (or, in Sandoval's terms, "deconstructs" and "meta-ideologizes") the prevailing terminologies through which Asian Americans have been made visible. The VP's manifold taxonomies explore the innumerable possibilities through which people can be grouped, and the promise and limitations of claiming different labels. In place of a single "overly broad umbrella," *Visible Resilience* moves through alternative scripts, noting how deliberate self-categorizations might highlight internal inequities among API, declare strategic coalitions, or reimagine gender norms. In narrativizing the thought and care that go into collecting and distributing these stories, Nakano also disidentifies with the notion of resilience as unflinching persistence through individual will. Rather, she has created a homespace for communal resilience based in empathy and mutual respect—where Barrett's "multiplicity in gender" can be explored in its unbounded possibilities. This is a project built on trust, which Nakano extends to participants through her assiduous care, and which they return to her through their stories.

Archiving Resilience through Communal Curation

While working on *Visible Resilience,* Nakano established the connections that made possible the *Resilience Archives* and *Performing Resilience,* which adopt two contrasting approaches to visibility. While the former compiles "personal and organizational ephemera" into a widely accessible, lasting digital archive, the latter produces fleeting encounters that resist documentation and preservation. This section focuses on the collaborative history-making (and keeping) of the *Resilience Archives.* Building on *Visible Resilience*'s exploration of reparative taxonomies, the *Resilience Archives* is structured so that contributors

---

98. Nakano, 137.

99. Criticisms of visibility and its limitations and risks are also very prominent in critical race studies, trans studies, queer studies, and disability studies—see, for example, McRuer, *Crip Theory*; Samuels, *Fantasies of Identification*; Nishime, *Undercover Asian*; Gossett and Huxtable, "Existing in the World"; Beauchamp, *Going Stealth*; Benjamin, *Race after Technology*.

and visitors can name and explore the elements they wish to bring into the broader narrative of QTAPI history. The community-sourced curation enables QTAPI to shape the sites and terms of their belonging, and the adaptive format of the digital archives encourages each visitor to find their own journeys and constellations of meaning in the collection. With this customizability, the archives enable resilience through the knowledge and stories its people find most meaningful, and through the caretaking of this shared wisdom.

Much like the organizers of the Dragon Fruit Project, Nakano met many QTAPI movement elders who had rooms full of historical materials (and the memories attached to them) and no way of making them public. The *Resilience Archives* arose from Nakano's desire to further democratize this knowledge along with her commitment to accessibility, resulting in a web-based, interactive map that continues to collect and digitize materials from anyone willing to donate. In sourcing and incorporating materials from community members, the *Resilience Archives* inverts the top-down model of traditional archives, through which authorities select and curate materials to preserve and present to the public. Instead, contributors to the *Resilience Archives* can designate subject tags for their items, determining the themes and categories that will tether these items to other people and events. Through this particular approach to acquiring and arranging artifacts, the *Resilience Archives* defers to the expertise of each text's original owners, acknowledging the wisdom that comes with direct experience.

Like *Visible Resilience,* the *Resilience Archives'* reliance on contributors' self-definitions results in categories otherwise elided in dominant archives. For example, the terms *pinoy/pinay/pin@y* are used for and by people from the Philippines, or the acronym QCC stands for the Queer Cultural Center, which has been home to many Bay Area QTAPI events and exhibits. This preference for insider terminologies marks the *Resilience Archives* as one both curated by and intended for QTAPI. It prioritizes LGBTQ+ Asian Americans as the producers and caretakers of this material, with the authority to decide the terms of its circulation.

Not only do archives document communal terminologies, however, they also participate in the ongoing renegotiation of shared meanings.[100] In the VP, a photo from the first conference of overseas Chinese gays and lesbians is tagged *tongzhi,* a transliteration of the Chinese 同志, meaning literally *same will.* While tongzhi is commonly translated to *gay* or *queer* in many Western contexts, writers from China, Hong Kong, and Taiwan have explored its much

---

100. Caswell, Punzalan, and Sangwand, "Critical Archival Studies"; Lee, *Producing the Archival Body.*

more expansive meanings in local contexts.[101] As Chou Wah-Shan explains, "Unlike 'homo' or 'hetero,' tongzhi is not defined by the gender of one's erotic object choice but connotes an entire range of alternative practices and sensitivities in a way that 'lesbian,' 'gay,' or 'bisexual' does not."[102] Carried across the Pacific, tongzhi continues to transform alongside its communities.

Already a transnational phenomenon, tongzhi has distinct formations in HK, Taiwan, China, and now diasporic Asian communities around the world. The term originated in Hong Kong, where homosexuality was both criminalized and then decriminalized by the British colonial government. It then circulated to Taiwan and China, where Western influences *and* Sinophone traditions centered the heteronuclear family as the site of social and financial capital. In the US, tongzhi links LGBTQ+ Chinese, Hong Kong, and Taiwanese US-Americans with communities of gender and sexual variance influenced by but also distinct from US/American contexts. As an archival tag and homing coordinate, tongzhi claims a diasporic identity circumscribed by disparate histories and geographies. The *Resilience Archives* thus adds to the continued expansion of this community and its evolution across global contexts.

With this collaborative and adaptive approach to documenting history, the *Resilience Archives* invites users into the co-construction of meaning. The archive itself is organized into an interactive map with no predetermined routes. True to Nakano's description, the interface resembles a mash-up between Google Maps and Pinterest. On the left side, there is a map with "pins" marking interest points across the Bay Area. On the right side are thumbnail images from each of these locations. Users can move through the collection by selecting thumbnails, points on the map, or tags that pull up related entries. While users may narrow their search by locale or by year, they are free to navigate as they please—to find and forge connections among entries that interest them. Clicking on either the image or the pin will bring up an anecdote or longer story about that particular location/event. Users can contribute text or video comments, and they can suggest corrections to the date and location of the artifact. The interactive features—what digital rhetorics scholar James Purdy describes as the integrative properties of digital archives—make visible the fact that meaning-making is always negotiated and contextual.[103] By opening channels for discursive exchange, *Visible Resilience* makes that process more transparent and interactive. While I trace one pos-

---

101. Lim, "How to Be Queer in Taiwan"; Engebretsen, Schroeder, and Bao, *Queer/Tongzhi China*.

102. Chou, *Tongzhi*, 3.

103. Purdy, "Three Gifts of Digital Archives."

sible journey through the archives, its format invites visitors to find their own constellations.

For example, selecting Compton's Cafeteria, a black pin at the corner of Taylor and Turk Streets, launches a photograph of the 2006 commemorative plaque installed at that location. Below, a quote from transgender rights activist Tamara Ching recalls, "Everybody that lived in the Tenderloin ate at Compton."[104] A sex worker and activist, Ching partook in the 1966 riots, which preceded the Stonewall riots of New York. Trans scholars—including Susan Stryker, who is quoted in this pin—have since established the Compton Cafeteria riots as "the first known instance of collective militant queer resistance to police harassment in United States history."[105] The *Resilience Archives* entry also includes a black-and-gray photograph of the eatery from 1966, which links to NPR's account of the uprising. By foregrounding Ching's voice in their entry, the *Resilience Archives* situates Asian American history in connection with trans history and queer history—threads that are too often discussed in isolation.

From Compton's Cafeteria, a visitor can move just down the street and around the corner to Market Street, where Trikone (one of the oldest South Asian Gay and Lesbian organizations) marched in San Francisco Pride for the first time. Clicking this pin will bring up a photo from 1986, featuring South Asians standing behind a purple banner with "GAY SOUTH ASIANS" in rectangular, cut-out lettering.[106] Another block away, on Mason Street, is the famous I-Hotel, a landmark in Asian American history and literature.[107] This pin pulls up a sepia-toned photograph of protestors standing with linked arms before the International Hotel, fighting the eviction of (primarily Filipinx and Chinese) tenants in 1977.[108] Two blocks south will take the visitor to Mission Street, where the *Performing Resilience* workshops began in 2017. The grayscale photo, taken as a selfie, features workshop leader Kat Evasco and participants Nancy Phalom, Un Jung Lim, Mia Nakano, and Cesar Cadabe.[109] Even with just these three points in the archive—spanning two square miles and five decades—the *Resilience Archives* gathers landmarks of "LGBTQ+" history and "Asian American" history into a narrative of "LGBTQ+ Asian American" history, emplacing QTAPI activists as intrinsic components of these often distinct lineages and geographies.

---

104. Hahm, "Compton's Cafeteria."
105. Stryker quoted in Hahm.
106. Hahm, "Trikone Marches."
107. For example, Yamashita, *I Hotel*; Lee, *The Making of Asian America*, 307–8.
108. Resilience Archives, "International Hotel."
109. Resilience Archives, "Performing Resilience Workshops Begin."

A visitor to the archives, however, does not need to maneuver geographically. One might choose instead to move thematically or temporally. Each pin is tagged with keywords that may note the ethnic or sexual identities of the subjects, the medium of the artifact, the genre of the event, and/or the period from which it emerges. Mission Street's *Performing Resilience* entry, for example, has the following tags: "performance; arts; Japanese; Korean; Filipino; 2010s; lesbian; Laotian; Resilience Archives; Visibility Project; Mia Nakano; Kat Evasco." The tag "2010s" cross-references this entry with other events from the decade. Through that tag, a visitor might encounter the Valencia Lesbian Stroll, created by queer disabled Sri Lankan artist-activist Leah Lakshmi Piepzna-Samarasinha. Piepzna-Samarasinha led over eighty people down Valencia Street in a physical history tour, sharing stories about the landmarks they passed.[110] From here, the tag "disabled" might take the archival explorer to a flyer for the debut performance of Peacock Rebellion, a Bay Area QTPOC collective. Or, the visitor may choose instead the photo of Mia Mingus posing with Alice Wong, both API disability activists.[111] The entry links to Mingus's three-part interview for Wong's Disability Visibility Project, in which Mingus discusses "how do we build access, when under capitalist system, access is always about money now?"[112]

For Mingus, the answer is partly captured by the title of her blog, *Leaving Evidence*. Wong quotes directly from it in the interview:

> We must leave evidence, evidence that we were here, that we existed, that we survived and loved and ate. Evidence of the wholeness we never felt. An immense sense of fullness we gave to each other. Evidence of who we were, who we thought we were, who we never should have been. Evidence of each other, and there are other ways to live past survival, past isolation.[113]

Discussing this passage, Mingus and Wong narrate a desire resonant with those articulated by creators of the Dragon Fruit Project and the Visibility Project: the need to see themselves as characters in a story longer than their own—to have predecessors who dreamt of and worked for the ways they live and love, and to have successors who will inherit this knowledge. In naming her collections *Resilience*, Nakano marks this continuity as crucial to one's capacity for responding to adversity—the ability to see oneself in a past, present, and future with others. The *Resilience Archives* calls attention to history

110. Resilience Archives, "Valencia Lesbian Stroll."
111. Resilience Archives, "Mia Mingus in the Disability Visibility Project."
112. Wong, "Mia Mingus, Part 1."
113. Wong, "Mia Mingus, Part 3," 3.

as actionable knowledge; those who have models of others' survival tactics and organizing methods are also more likely to rebound from new challenges.

The *Resilience Archives* provides some of that intracommunal durability by rendering queer ephemera more accessible while working to minimize the disempowerment that usually attends formal archives. Contributors can mail their texts to the *Resilience Archives* along with item descriptions, at which time volunteers will digitize them and return both originals and copies of the electronic files. Those who have large collections can work directly with Nakano and Sine Hwang Jensen, a UC Berkeley librarian, to determine archival guidelines suited to the content. As with *Visible Resilience,* the *Resilience Archives* makes extensive use of release forms that detail permissions for usage. In addition to release forms signed by each contributor, images taken in private spaces must be accompanied by "model release forms" from all individuals in the photograph. The website itself then has a brief guide for finding the copyright holder for each document. In providing this transparency, the Visibility Project not only builds a structure for its own accountability but also models that thoughtfulness for visitors to the archive and any who may use it for their own projects.

For those familiar with digital archives, some features of the *Resilience Archives* likely evoke qualities that have been explored in other digital archives. James Purdy, in particular, identifies three major "gifts" of digital archives: integration, customization, and accessibility.[114] Integrative components that allow visitors to comment on entries, for example, facilitate collaborative interpretations and effect collective memory-making. Meanwhile, user experiences are indefinitely customizable through different navigational and classificatory strategies. In addition to broadening access in ways expected of digitization and web-based distribution, however, the *Resilience Archives* draws attention to the consequences of inviting others to witness and interpret these stories. While Nakano and her team describe their values as centering "accessibility" and "sharing knowledge," they are equally careful about protecting those who have opened their histories and personal details. As with *Visible Resilience*'s conscientious approach to visibility, the archives broaden access to QTAPI narratives while reminding audiences that these stories are attached to people whose lives and/or loved ones are affected by their circulation. The final branch of the Visibility Project, *Performing Resilience,* then provides an extended, embodied meditation on what it means to connect with and pass on these stories.

---

114. Purdy, "Three Gifts of Digital Archives."

Performing In/Visible Resilience

The newest component of the Visibility Project, *Performing Resilience* is a ten-week performance workshop offered once or twice a year to LGBTQ+ Asian Americans and Pacific Islanders. Facilitators lead classes in writing personal narratives and performances. Each workshop series begins by introducing students to materials in the *Resilience Archives* as well as other collections of QTAPI history. From these texts, participants build performance pieces that connect their own experiences to their archival findings. These stories are often deeply personal, at times whimsical, at others traumatic. Though the resulting performance is one person's view of their own story, it is also clearly a collaborative production—composed in conversation with QTAPI archives, nurtured by a workshop of QTAPI peers, and eventually shared with a primarily QTAPI audience. As a practice of communal pedagogy and witnessing, *Performing Resilience* helps participants find and forge the discursive and physical environments they need to feel at home. This project then rounds out the VP by grounding resilience in the conditions to be present for and support one another.

The performance showcase that concludes each workshop season is the culmination of the Visibility Project's three branches. At the biannual "Performing Visible Resilience Showcase + Exhibition," portraits from *Visible Resilience* limn the performance space in large-scale, high-quality prints. Often, *Visible Resilience* interviewees are also in the audience. At a 2019 showcase, Alice Y. Hom posed for a photo beside her own larger-than-life portrait, which had been reproduced as a tintype. On the same wall was a photo of Lenore Chinn, who also sat in the front row, taking pictures. Two portraits over from Chinn's was that of Un Jung Lim, who now co-facilitates the *Performing Resilience* workshops. Movement elders are scattered among the audience, watching another generation of QTAPI take up these histories and channel them into their own. With so many of the Visibility Project's collaborators and collaborations in one setting, the *Performing Resilience* showcase feels like a communal hearth—one, like Celeste Chan's Writing Rainbow, built in borrowed space.

Before the performances begin, Nakano frames this gathering with the same care that guides her other projects. She asks the audience to refrain from taking photographs or videos of the actual performances, noting the risks performers take with sharing their stories. Her precaution, in addition to safeguarding sensitive material, draws attention to the concomitant power and elusiveness of performance. This is a genre that evades capture—made to be experienced in the moment. Unlike reading a text or watching a film, attending a performance necessitates sharing time and space with other people. The stage/staging generates a live "negotiation of meanings" across performers and attendees.[115] The knowledges and affects that emerge are particular to this moment, this shared commitment to being together and believing in these stories. There is no way to completely replicate the experience.

As an extension of the *Resilience Archives,* the performance series evidences that memory is, in the words of Thomas Dunn, "the very opposite of history."[116] Unsettled and ever-evolving, memory "can be found and celebrated in the everyday and, as such, connects people to their past in ways wildly distinct from history."[117] *Performing Resilience* makes it abundantly clear that the archives from which it draws are living documents—ones that grow and flex with the lives and stories of the communities they serve. As dynamic texts that respond to their authors and audiences, the components of the Visibility Project evoke KJ Rawson's description of queer archival practices, which "challenge normative conceptions of archives as document repositories."[118] In rendering the past as a generative resource for the present and future, the Visibility Project *makes visible* the generous intergenerational and interpersonal connections that have enabled QTAPI resilience. This trio of platforms, taken together, theorizes resilience as the product of collective imagining. Their community-driven resilience requires shared trust and vulnerability—the will to listen across distant experiences to care for one another and build structures inclusive of one another's thriving.

Democratics through Transformative Access

Involving the audience in these thoughtful explorations of *what* we make visible and *how,* the Visibility Project challenges uncritical pursuits of visibility for its own sake. The gaze on the other end of that pursuit, after all, belongs to a worldview that normalized extant inequalities. Wesley Yang, for all his love of iconoclasts, often conflates success with one's ability to draw that gaze. In his profile of irreverent chef Eddie Huang, Yang writes, "[Huang] doesn't want to purchase mainstream accessibility at the expense of the distinctiveness of his lived experiences."[119] Despite Huang's unorthodoxy, Yang describes him as

---

115. Pérez, "Staging the Family Unfamiliar," 374.
116. Dunn, *Queerly Remembered,* 6.
117. Dunn, 7.
118. Rawson, "Archive This! Queering the Archive," 238.
119. Yang, *The Souls of Yellow Folk,* 64.

exceptional *because* he achieves mainstream acclaim.[120] Absent is a consideration of whether the "mainstream" is something worth accessing—worth affirming in one's pursuit, let alone whether it is even capable of accepting outsiders beyond superficial recognition. Even Huang says himself: "I don't believe anybody agrees with what I say or supports what I do because they truly want to love Asian people. They like my fucking pork buns, and I don't get it twisted."[121]

This limited inclusion evokes Jay Dolmage's definition of *retrofitting,* which provides reactive additions to existing structures and practices. Under such practices, those deemed "misfits" will never fully belong and will always need to request accommodations to spaces that never anticipated them. They will always be positioned as the problem. Retrofitting, in other words, grants small concessions to particular needs without ever changing the mechanisms that created the inequities in the first place. In contrast, Brewer, Selfe, and Yergeau propose "transformative access." Whereas dominant forms of access are made to absorb difference—to allow particular people into a space or text, transformative access requires "[rethinking] the very construct of allowing."[122] Rather than merely inviting "others" to join a structure designed for their exclusion, transformative access co-creates something—someplace—new. While inevitably imperfect, the VP's many strategies for sharing authority and renegotiating the terms of engagement model such collaborative reimagination.

Like any grassroots undertaking, the Visibility Project could use more resources. Some archival entries await tagging and more detailed entries, and the performance showcases—for as careful as they are about accessibility within the space—are of course inaccessible to those who cannot be in the Bay Area or who have difficulty traveling outside of their residences. Any undertaking will be limited by its medium(s) and geographic and temporal setting(s). More, there is no such thing as universal access. Disability justice collectives have long recognized and navigated conflicting access needs. Rather than pursuing that impossible universality, the Visibility Project emphasizes specificity and adaptability, positing access as situationally negotiated rather than a predetermined process.

This ground-up approach is most evident in the evolution of the project as a whole, expanding with the material that participants were willing to share with Nakano and project leaders. What started as a portrait series extended into video interviews because subjects' stories could not be contained in images alone. The conversations led Nakano to archival materials

120. Yang, 65.
121. Yang, 55.
122. Brewer, Selfe, and Yergeau, "Creating a Culture," 154.

that were buried in people's houses, for which she created a platform through the Resilience Archives. The archives themselves then inspired present-day conversations and narrations that found homes in Performing Resilience. The showcase is shaped by the audience members, who are provided accessibility information and queried for any further needs when they register to attend. Each of these initiatives emerged from seeking out and co-creating with community members. The Visibility Project itself, with its sprawling media, is difficult to describe succinctly because it does not fit extant genres. Rather, it was an organic response to the experiences of LGBTQ+ Asian Americans whom Nakano met throughout her work.

This approach to accessibility brings to mind Mia Mingus's "crip solidarity," which she captures in the phrase "wherever you are is where I want to be."[123] In other words, if a space is physically or emotionally inaccessible to one of us, it is inaccessible to all of us. We will build the space where we can be together. Crip solidarity pursues access by beginning with the *people* we want to call into—and keep in—community, rather than the structures that were never designed for us in the first place. Accordingly, the Visibility Project builds linguistic and material vocabularies around the participants: establishing novel terms by which each individual would like to be hailed; creating taxonomies divergent from conventional usage; and connecting present experiences with archival memory and a durable lineage of QTAPI survival. Defined in this way, resilience is not an individual property or character trait. It is communal praxis, made by caring about one another enough to imagine and create a space where those we call into community are all valued.

The VP's spaces may be small on the global scale, but they offer shelter for utopian dreaming. Resilience is reimagined as a communicative exchange where participants take shared responsibility for one another's vulnerabilities, fears, and desires. On a practical level, Mingus's maxim translates into collective strength. If we *all* care enough to refuse places where one of us is not allowed to enter, then our social and physical architectures necessarily change. If Asian American resilience is understood not as that which positions us closer to white patriarchy but as a communal empathy that refuses to leave one another behind, then we are able to revolutionize structures of exclusion rather than simply enter them. Through this sort of ongoing reflexivity, the Visibility Project channels individual stories into negotiations of communal needs. In doing so, it empowers trans and queer Asian Americans to (re)compose themselves as co-conspirators at the fore of a transformational American story.

---

123. Mingus, "Wherever You Are."

// *For the 2019 showcase, Nakano reproduced images from her Visible Resilience photoshoots as tintypes—a grayscale method of printing used throughout the American Civil War. The technique enabled faster and cheaper production than its predecessor, which made it popular among soldiers, migrants, and the working class. The resulting aesthetic—dark and smoky, as if shot through coal dust—is one I associate with photos of Abraham Lincoln, dusky shots of Union officers, and cowboys of the Old West. Before the show starts, I marvel at these larger-than-life images of trans and queer Asian Americans—a style of classic Americana reinvented through Bex Ahuja's sly smirk, Un Jung Lim's sideways glower, and Suzanne Presard's knowing smile. Before this backdrop, the Performing Resilience cohort delivered their stories, which I will not repeat for you. Imagine, though, their bodies in quiet synchronicity, swapping roles between sets: performers, stage managers, lighting and sound technicians, and audience members who applaud and weep and roar with joy.*

Dorinne Kondo explains that performance requires a "reflexive estrangement from common sense"[124] shared by performers and audience alike. The performer takes us into another world—a memory, a dream, a vision for the future. For this to work, we must collectively suspend disbelief. We must agree that other realities are possible. Overhead lights flash as lightning. Thunder growls from computer speakers. A dance floor blooms in the aisle between rows of chairs; we are in New York. Vietnam. In the '80s. The '90s. We are traveling companions bound by our willingness to be here together, right now.

When the showcase ends, Un Jung Lim finds me in the audience. We have exchanged emails, texted about the best places to get boba and pandan waffles, but we only met in person a day ago. "I want to introduce you to Alice," Lim says before interrupting a conversation between Alice Hom and Willy Wilkinson. As she sums up their lives and activisms for me, I fight the urge to join in the storytelling—to say I have spent hours listening to Hom's APIENC interviews. I have pored over her words, overlaid her stories with mine until they mapped us both onto a topography of API queer (un)belonging. I have read Wilkinson's autobiography and watched him recite spoken word on YouTube. I have listened to his voice drop with the decision to start testosterone therapy at age fifty, watched him make poetry of his scars at the San Francisco Trans March in 2015. I have clung to his narratives of chronic illness, of gender nonconformity, of hardening his flesh on the edges of our social vocabularies. I am self-conscious about this one-way intimacy, though. Knowing someone's writing is not the same as knowing them; being familiar with the parts of themselves they chose to make public is a far cry from being in genuine community. I want more than the former.

---

124. Kondo, *Worldmaking*, 27.

I am fearful of becoming the detached researcher, extracting blood from sub-jects the academy has historically regarded as object. A question that haunts this project: How do I bridge these worlds without replicating the voyeurism of the ivory tower? How do I write for our discipline(s) without contorting these sto-ries into something unrecognizable to those who lived them? The Visibility Proj-ect reminds me that the goal is not uncritical exposure, stripping someone else's truths naked for critical analysis. Rather, I am searching for precise language that can render QTAPI folks as they desire and need to be seen—that can situate them in broader narrative arcs as forceful actors and innovators, and as richly varie-gated and whole humans worthy of nuance and care. //

CHAPTER 3

Tendering Kin

Constellating Relations with the
Queer Ancestors Project

For the 2020–21 Queer Ancestors Project (QAP), Cairo Mo created four lino-cut prints that "[seek] to honour their queer ancestors and revitalize the lost queer history in Chinese folklore."[1] In "The Ballad of Mulan," the titular character stands waist-high in a pool of water, a full moon at her back. Mulan holds a sword in one hand and grips her hair with the other. She has already sliced partway through her hair, the frayed locks depicted mid-fall. A magnolia tree stretches toward her from the left side of the frame. On the right, above her head, Mo has etched the words 扑朔迷离, meaning *impossible to unravel.*

With this image, Mo reappropriates one of the more recognizable Chinese figures in the West—made perhaps even more mainstream by Mulan's canonization as a Disney princess. Capturing Mulan at the moment of transformation—as she dons a masculine disguise to join the army—Mo situates the heroine as a fellow border-crosser. Returning to the original Chinese text, Mo quotes from the poem in their artist's statement:

> "The buck bounds here and there, Whilst the doe has narrow eyes. But when the two rabbits run side by side, How can you tell the female from the male?" What if those lines meant Mulan rejected a false gender binary?[2]

---

1. Mo, "About the Artist."
2. Mo, "The Queer Ancestors Project 2021 Exhibition."

Like most QAP participants, Mo makes no claim about their chosen ancestor's specific identity. Instead, they posit Mulan's gender as "impossible to unravel" within her time and within retrospective transcultural and translinguistic interpretations. By placing her among "trans ancestors of the Chinese diaspora,"[3] Mo instead situates Mulan in a constellation of gender variance that provides precedent and grounding for their own embodiment.

Throughout the QAP—an annual nine-month printmaking and writing workshop—LGBTQ+ youth explore, reclaim, and story themselves into community with such ancestors. Like Mo, many draw inspiration from fiction or legends. Some give fictive lives to historical figures, others script imagined conversations with past relatives, and still others write to and for living kin. This search for durable lineages arises from the trouble of family that queer studies has long explored.[4] For queer diasporic subjects, whose experiences of family are often stretched or sundered across physical and cultural displacement(s), traditional kin can be even more difficult to locate or identify. With the (interdependent) resilience of queer family, QAP students listen for submerged relations and story them into far-reaching genealogies that can carry the "strength, power, and determination of our trans ancestors."[5]

In this chapter, I begin by discussing how the topos of ancestry shapes many LGBTQ+ Asian American experiences of family and belonging, journeying through the recent popularity of genetic ancestry tests (GATs) as well as ancestral traditions in Asian American cultures. These initial touchstones establish ancestry's grounding in particular stories often used to essentialize Asian and Asian American identities and cultures. I then delve into the first two QAP anthologies, published in 2018 and 2019. I constellate these stories with the mythologies, films, and historical and contemporary events they invoke. Through homing, chronicled through linocut prints, short stories, poems, and personal essays, QAP students find, name, and tend to chosen familial bonds. Their artistry provides approaches to ancestry that deconstruct normative assumptions of where we come from and how those lineages matter. Their differential perspectives reconceptualize ancestry as an array of stories through which QTAPI place themselves in longer traditions of resistance, courage, and care. Like Nakano's collaborative resilience, this view of ancestry is based in reciprocity and accountability—in seeing themselves as inheritors of longer traditions and as forerunners for future generations of trans and queer kin.

---

3. Mo.

4. Weston, *Families We Choose*; Muñoz, *Cruising Utopia*; Nicolazzo, *Trans* in College*; Shange, "Play Aunties and Dyke Bitches."

5. Mo, "The Queer Ancestors Project 2021 Exhibition."

Defining Ancestry

Characteristic of most commonplaces, *ancestry* contains multitudes. In everyday usage, ancestry might refer to someone's geographic roots, ethnic heritage, and/or religious or other cultural communities. The term garnered renewed attention in 2017, when purchases of direct-to-consumer GATs began to surge. By 2019 over 26 million people had purchased GATs, which promise to "connect you to the places in the world where your story started."[6] By the reasoning of these companies, DNA encodes indelible truths about who you are and "what makes you unique."[7] The science that informs GATs emerged from the 1991 Human Genome Diversity Project (HGDP), which attempted to collect and categorize genetic data to explore histories of human migration. The project never fully took off, meeting resistance from scientific communities as well as the Indigenous communities from which researchers hoped to collect initial data. While the founders of the HGDP saw themselves as antiracist, critics noted how the HGDP's mission to identify and categorize human difference veered dangerously close to the race science that fueled eugenics. HGDP's germinal ideas, however, found new life in the highly lucrative market of at-home GATs, which retain the HGDP's usage of "ancestry" and "human variation" as an approximation of race.

While HGDP and GAT companies are careful to avoid the word *race*, they rely on continent-based taxonomies (Native American, European, Asian, Oceania, and Africa) that map easily onto racial stereotypes—so much so that white supremacist groups have flocked to GATs for "evidence" of their whiteness.[8] As the preceding chapter demonstrates, the very usage of these categories suggests that they are in themselves meaningful—worth seeking, quantifying, and recording as a part of one's identity. Though GATs emerged from opposing scientific motives, scientific racism established the primary terminologies through which we narrativize new data. What results is, in the words of historian Aviva Chomsky, "a cheerful, Disneyfied wrapping" around "antiquated ideas about the biological origins of race."[9] Regardless of original intent, this "it's-a-small-world-after-all multiculturalism"[10] papers over histories of conquest and exploitation with biological determinism.

---

6. "AncestryDNA."
7. 23andMe, "DNA Genetic Testing & Analysis."
8. Panofsky and Donovan, "Genetic Ancestry Testing among White Nationalists."
9. Chomsky, "DNA Tests."
10. Chomsky.

The recent and stratospheric popularity of GATs captures the durability and adaptability of "ancestry" as topos. As an "elastic symbolic tool,"[11] ancestry can implicitly stand in for race while explicitly signaling something distinct from race. At the same time, it can carry enough cultural value to mean something *more than* race. The appeal of tracing one's ancestry—whether through cutting-edge biotechnologies or in the tradition of drawing one's family tree— is the story it enables of where one came from, and presumably who one is or may become. Marketing for these tests promises to "connect [you] with your people in new ways";[12] "get more of your inside story";[13] and "help [you] find new relatives"[14] and discover "the places your ancestors called home."[15] As Alexis Pauline Gumbs puts it, language around genetics reflects "who we think we are, what we believe at a gut level about our kinship loyalty and our perceived survival needs," but genes are only one approach to that story.[16] This chapter joins Gumbs in querying how we can conceive of familial lineages in ways that disrupt, challenge, and reinvent the categories that have isolated and harmed queer diasporic subjects. Listening to the innovations of the Queer Ancestors Project, I explore storylines and taxonomies that trace the legacies of colonialism, capitalism, and their effects on human and nonhuman lives.

In an essay for *Salon,* writer Nicole Karlis examined genetic ancestry tests as "a particularly American phenomenon," asking why US consumers compose the overwhelming majority of the GAT market.[17] Karlis proposes two possible factors—first, that "America is a young country and full of immigrants" searching for a sense of culture and identity; and second, that the US's particular emphasis on personal independence has created widespread loneliness. She writes that North American culture is "a sort of isolated anti-culture, a synthesis of capitalism and individualism." While Karlis's points are valid and significant—many folks in the US are geographically removed from personal and familial histories, and capitalism continues to stoke alienation throughout a globalizing economy—the US has also actively concealed its own histories in ways that impede reconciliation and reparation. What sort of national pride emerges from stolen land and stolen labor? What stories does

---

11. Olson, *Constitutive Visions,* introduction.
12. "AncestryDNA."
13. "AncestryDNA."
14. "MyHeritage DNA."
15. "MyHeritage DNA."
16. Gumbs, *Dub,* "a note."
17. Karlis, "Amid Growing Feelings of Isolation, Americans Flock to DNA Testing Services."

one tell of a "nation" that has no territory of its own but instead maintains a political economy through indefinite colonial occupation?

As with the preceding topoi, Asian American approaches to ancestry draw from transcultural influences. In North America, Asian ancestry has been narrativized to exclude peoples from the possibility of US belonging—even those who stewarded the land prior to European settlement. Colonial manipulation of Asian racialization becomes particularly apparent in Alaskan history, where (in tandem with gender norms) Asian ancestry serves both to rob Alaska Natives of their homeland and to deny Asian migrants state or social inclusion. As Juliana Hu Pegues explains, US government officials "conceived of Alaska Native peoples as separate from American Indians through a common Asian ancestry."[18] That is to say, "the sign of the Asian other"[19] is so indelibly foreign that US officials were able to deny Alaskan Natives' claims to Indigeneity by attaching them to Asian descent. At the same time, actual Asian laborers who were foundational to the economic development of Alaska were dismissed as inherently inassimilable. The almost exclusively male demographic of Asian workers—and the racism that prohibited racial intermixing—meant that Asian laborers had no access to the nuclear family unit emblematic of US national belonging.

Doubling down on this contradiction, missionaries praised Alaskan Natives for their Christian assimilability "based on perceived Asian cultural traits" while consistently ignoring the presence of Asian migrants.[20] In Pegues's analysis, "settler colonial time and space"[21] conceptualized both groups as always already outside the nation-state. By colonial logics, Indigenous peoples are confined to a distant Asian past with no claim to the present. Meanwhile, Asian migrants fail to perform the gendered racialization required for reproducing national identity. These logics foreclosed the possibility of Native Alaskan and Asian migrant relationality—as the former could never be "now" and the latter could never be "here."[22] In Western scientific and colloquial applications, "ancestry" then functions as a means of containment, designating particular communities and individuals as biologically, temporally, and/or culturally incongruent with whiteness and thus US citizenry.

Asian cultures, however, have their own attachments to ancestry, which have been variously politicized by US and European policymakers. Because ancestral veneration is woven deeply into many Asian communities, mis-

18. Day et al., "Settler Colonial Studies, Asian Diasporic Questions," 12.
19. Day et al., 13.
20. Day et al., 15; Woodman, *Picturesque Alaska*; Young, *The Mushing Parson*.
21. Day et al., "Settler Colonial Studies, Asian Diasporic Questions," 16.
22. Pegues in Day et al., 16.

sionaries from the West were conflicted about whether to permit the continuance of ancestral rites when seeking converts. Throughout the Chinese Rites controversy, Roman Catholic authorities deliberated over whether ceremonies honoring one's ancestors were incompatible with Christian belief. Ancestral rites were officially banned with Clement XI's ruling in 1704 and with Benedict XIV's proscription of further debate in 1742. Theologian Sze-Kar Wan describes the term *ancestor worship* as an intentional mistranslation of 祭祖 (*jizu*), which is more accurately understood as commemoration of the dead. The term *worship* (as opposed to *veneration* or *respect*) implied a form of idolatry, which would be anathema in Christian praxis. This word choice helped missionaries pit Chinese tradition against Christian "enlightenment," justifying the eradication of a cultural cornerstone they feared would impede religious conversion.[23] While Benedict XIV's decision was overturned over two hundred years later, the tension between Eastern familial ceremonies and Western scripture extends into present-day Asian and Asian American communities—with the many contradictions characteristic of Asian American racialization.

As "places of return," ancestral relations in Asian culture have been subjected to discordant interpretations that follow the evolution of Western political needs. Centuries after Clement XI's and Benedict XIV's decrees, ancestor veneration was renarrativized as a sign of Asian assimilability to American "family values." In 1966 William Petersen attributed Japanese Americans' "achievement orientation" to the intimate relationship between family and religion—as captured by ancestor veneration. "Whether Buddhist or Christian," Petersen writes, Japanese Americans work toward "the good reputation of the family name, which [is] worshipped through [their] ancestors."[24] Two decades later, Christian philosopher and theologian Rousas John Rushdoony also pointed to Asian family values as a proxy for religious discipline. In *Leeper v. Arlington ISD*, a pivotal legal victory for Christian homeschooling, Rushdoony testified to the importance of religion in providing motivation for learning.[25] When the court challenged Rushdoony with the example of "the orientals" who also seem to have a "strong motivation for education," Rushdoony pointed to "ancestral worship" as an equivalent faith. In his view, the prioritization of the nuclear family, and the "total control" that parents exercised over their children, provided the necessary discipline for younger generations to excel. At the convenience of US racial hegemony, the cultural

23. Wan quoted in Tam, "Culture Clash."
24. Petersen, "Success Story, Japanese-American Style."
25. *Texas Educ. Agency v. Leeper*, 843 S. W.2d 41 (Tex. App. 1991).

traditions denounced by Christian authorities were equated with Christian values.

Far from the dichotomous lens through which Western authorities have tried to interpret Eastern traditions—measuring them by Euro-American values—ancestral relations encompass many different beliefs, worldviews, and practices. Broadly speaking, Buddhist and Confucian-influenced societies practice ancestor veneration through prayer and/or offerings of incense, food, or other symbolic goods. Public commemorations include many variations of ghost festivals and related traditions throughout Malaysia, Indonesia, Singapore, Korea, Taiwan, Vietnam, Cambodia, Laos, Sri Lanka, and China. In the US, many Asian Americans keep shrines or altars in their own homes. Some have even reinterpreted ancestral veneration in concert with Protestant faith, despite its formal prohibition of ancestral rites. While an overview of ancestral practices throughout Asian, Asian American, and Pacific Islander communities is beyond the scope of this book, it would be fair to say that the vast majority of these practices differ from Western conceptions in their emphasis on cross-generational engagement.

Whereas DNA tests are used to investigate long-lost and otherwise unreachable ancestors, ancestor veneration is premised on continued intimacy between the living and the dead. Descendants continue to seek guidance from, pay respect to, and speak with their predecessors, who are in turn affected by these intercessions. Both Polynesian and Asian traditions involve food offerings for their ancestors. It is also common for folks from Taiwan, Hong Kong, Singapore, and China to burn joss paper—or, "ghost money"— so that their loved ones can live comfortably in the afterlife. This emphasis on family continuity was described memorably by Chinese American actress Anna May Wong as "the consciousness that each of us is only a link in a long life chain. The important thing is the family."[26] In patrilineal societies, however, the imperative to prioritize (implicitly heterosexual) family formations suppresses queerness while reinforcing patriarchal structures of wealth and inheritance. As with "love," the topos of ancestry figures frequently in both American and Asian contexts in ways that subject diasporic queers to multiple displacements.

Ancestor veneration, however, is not particular to Asian cultures or even to dominant cultures. Toni Morrison, Audre Lorde, Jacqueline Jones Royster, and Alexis Pauline Gumbs have written extensively about ancestral relations as the grounding through which Black writers can access and reclaim "discred-

---

26. Wong, "I Am Growing More Chinese—Each Passing Year! (1934)," 181.

ited knowledge."[27] Gumbs's Mobile Homecoming precedes the Visibility Project and the QAP in identifying, preserving, and mobilizing QTPOC ancestral knowledge through community-accountable pedagogy.[28] The spirituality of Gloria Anzaldúa's Chicana feminism also kept her in ongoing dialogue with her ancestors,[29] and scholars of Native American rhetorics emphasize the role of ancestral connections in cultivating decolonial knowledge and practices.[30] In composition studies, two important precedents for this chapter come from Aja Martinez's use of counterstory to engage her intellectual genealogies[31] and Eric Darnell Pritchard's exploration of ancestorship as literacy practice among Black LGBTQ writers.[32] As these scholars, artists, teachers, and activists have shown, many minoritized authors and creators have adapted and reinvented ancestral practices to address historical erasures that denied them knowledge of their pasts and their communities.

Through a communal focus, ancestor veneration becomes a means of locating rhetors along a continuum, answerable to predecessors who enabled their lives and responsible for a future where subsequent generations can find connections. Gumbs's Mobile Homecoming not only sustains the legacies of Black feminist leaders but also devotes educational and financial resources to subsequent generations of Black LGBTQ+ folks and to sharing models with allies. In rhetoric and composition, Riley-Mukavetz and Powell teach Indigenous rhetorical practices by telling stories that situate each rhetor within a "web of relations" accountable to their physical geography, their ancestral relationships, and their communities' pasts and futures. The land-based emphasis of Indigenous rhetorics enables students to explore how stories carry places, histories, and belonging, or, put differently: "when textual practices travel, they take their 'home' with them."[33] The Queer Ancestors Project echoes these commitments, querying—in the words of Shō Nakashima—how our survival strategies and "our mere existences are tied directly to the dreams of our ancestors and communities."[34] Throughout the QAP, Nakashima and their peers concretize these ties by storying their places within imagined webs of (gender)queer relations.

27. Morrison, "Rootedness," 342; Lorde, *Zami*; Royster, *Traces of a Stream*; Gumbs, *Dub*.
28. Mobile Homecoming, "About Mobile Homecoming Project."
29. Anzaldúa, *Borderlands* and *Luz en lo Oscuro*.
30. Powell, "Listening to Ghosts"; Riley-Mukavetz, "On Working From or With Anger"; Driskill et al., *Sovereign Erotics*; King, Gubele, and Anderson, *Survivance, Sovereignty, and Story*; Anderson, "Remapping Settler Colonial Territories."
31. Martinez, *Counterstory*, 86–95.
32. Pritchard, *Fashioning Lives*.
33. Riley-Mukavetz and Powell, "Making Native Space for Graduate Students," 146.
34. Nakashima, "Moro's Head," 2019, 43.

From Queer to Kuaer Pedagogies

> The Queer Ancestors Project is devoted to forging sturdy relationships between LGBTQI people and our ancestors. Using history as a linchpin, we build community by providing Queer and Trans artists, age 18 to 26, free interdisciplinary workshops in printmaking, writing, and Queer history.
>
> —*The Queer Ancestors Project*[35]

The Queer Ancestors Project is offered annually, tuition-free, for trans and queer youth. The printmaking workshop, led by Chrysalis studio director Katie Gilmartin, uses linocut printmaking to explore the work of LGBTQ+ artists, activists, and theorists. The writing workshop, helmed by Celeste Chan, moves across written genres to engage, (re)imagine, and/or invent LGBTQ+ ancestors. In 2018 and 2019 Foglifter Press published the first two anthologies of QAP work. Titled *Tender* and *Flower of Ancestry,* the two collections combine full-color prints with poetry and essays. Among the archives I examine in this book, the QAP is the only project not dedicated specifically to Asian American / Pacific Islander histories. Still, it is undeniably a site of QTAPI rhetorics. Chan describes herself as the child of immigrant parents from Malaysia and the Bronx and has been an active contributor to Asian American and QTPOC artistic landscapes. The QAP students represent a wide range of racial and ethnic perspectives, but the majority identify as Asian American / Pacific Islander or Latinx. The ancestors whom instructors and students bring to their workshops include Asian and Asian American deities, artists, and pop culture figures. While racial and ethnic heritage is *one* measure through which QAP participants trace their ancestral relations, however, it is far from the only one. With story as navigational medium, the QAP moves through queer lineages predicated on more expansive conceptions of relation, family, and belonging.

When I sat down with Celeste Chan, she described the suppression of queer and non-Western histories as "our power being kept from us."[36] Her artistic and pedagogical undertakings, including the Queer Ancestors Project, are pursuits of "knowing what's possible—knowing our lineages, knowing that people like us always existed, knowing what past generations did or how they organized, how they networked."[37] These lineages and generations are not bounded by normative categories of race—nor, however, do they ignore the effects of race or the cultural and intellectual contributions of different ethnic

---

35. "Queer Ancestors Project."
36. Chan, personal interview.
37. Chan.

communities. Rather, Chan hopes to "resurface submerged histories—trying to write into the ghost spaces of what's not known."[38] Instead of imposing extant assumptions about race, gender, and sexuality onto historical narratives, the QAP queries history as a process of discovery—an openness to what we do not know about our origins and our connections to others. This process, which I'm calling *kuaer pedagogy*, pursues knowledge by reaching toward the *un*known, embracing instability and the rupture of presumed truths.

Within critical studies, queer theory was instrumental in deconstructing the essentialized, fixed notions of identity exemplified by the booming genetic ancestry market. Even so, many queer theorists—in the words of E. Patrick Johnson—posited a "ground zero" of subjectivity that failed to account for or to address the very real injustices perpetuated by identity-based discourses. In other words, to say that all identity is performed falls short of accounting for the myriad forces that constrain the performances and their reception. Johnson thus offers a "quare studies" that emphasizes race and class as important vectors through which individuals experience gender and sexuality. In his critique, queer theory's willingness to dismantle *all* notions of identity neglected the embodied experiences of queers of color. "On the front lines," he writes, "where the racialized and sexualized body is beaten, starved, fired, cursed-indeed, where the body is the site of trauma,"[39] queer theory requires a more dexterous understanding of identity—a both/and approach that can "*strategically* embrace identity politics while also acknowledging the contingency of identity."[40] From Johnson's womanist approach to queer experience and knowledge-making, Wenshu Lee then developed "kuaer" theory, providing a transcultural epistemology resonant with the origins and practices of the Queer Ancestors Project.

A Mandarin transliteration of Johnson's *quare*, Lee's *kuaer* is inherently transnational, made meaningful in the interstices between continents. Focusing on wordplay and the multiplicity of meanings, Lee posits kuaer theory as a transnational turn to the already race-conscious and intersectional quare intervention. In Mandarin, *kuaer* is not one word but actually several phrasal permutations. Depending on tonal inflection, *kua* could be 跨, meaning *crossing*, or 誇, meaning *proud*. The suffix, 兒 (*er*), means *youth*. Kuaer could then be youth who cross (boundaries, nations, worlds), proud youth, or perhaps youth who take pride in their crossings. Only with its phonetic origins in English, however, does kuaer tie specifically back into queer culture and studies. Kuaer accrues meaning as a transcultural theorization of queer experience,

---

38. Chan.
39. Johnson, "'Quare' Studies," 5.
40. Johnson, 13; emphasis original.

taking pride in the knowledge that emerges from boundary-transgressing accounts of race, class, gender, and sexuality.

In my analysis of the Queer Ancestors Project, I connect Lee's kauer theory with queer pedagogy, which combines critical pedagogy and queer theory. Pushing against what Paolo Freire identified as the "banking model" of education, queer pedagogy is more interested in questions than in fixed answers. In fact, Susanne Luhmann describes queer pedagogy as an approach that poses knowledge as "an interminable question"[41] and that "aims at the infinite proliferation of identifications."[42] She elaborates: "What is at stake in this pedagogy is the deeply social or dialogic situation of subject formation, the processes of how we make ourselves through and against others."[43] The knowledges that students have at their disposal condition the possible avenues through which they conceive of themselves and their communities. Queer pedagogy multiplies those possibilities.

Like the queer theory that E. Patrick Johnson critiqued in 2001, the dominant articulation of queer pedagogy has been mostly silent on how racial and other identities intersect with experiences of gender and sexuality. Kuaer pedagogy, as I conceive it, shares queer pedagogy's understanding of identity as discursive. Like Deborah Britzman—another germinal theorist of queer pedagogy—I understand pedagogy as the practice of questioning/disrupting old certainties, of exploring new relationalities, and of cultivating an inter-relational "practice of the self that can exceed the self."[44] When Britzman proposes that reading practices can catalyze a "proliferation of one's own identificatory possibilities,"[45] however, she offers little to account for how such imaginings clash, connect, or combine with the racialized or disabled body-mind that—in Johnson's words—is starved, beaten, and traumatized for the ways it is inescapably read. Identity, for those whose bodyminds mark them as other, cannot be theorized as a purely imagined construct, as if identifications were simple labels we imagine and claim. Rather, identity must be addressed as both socially/ideologically constructed *and* grounded in lived experiences—in bodyminds that are subjected to physical threat, containment, and displacement/migrations. Like Johnson's quare studies, kuaer pedagogy acknowledges the plasticity of identity while also mobilizing it for "contingent, fragile coalitions [. . . in] struggles against common oppressive

41. Luhmann, "Queering/Querying Pedagogy?," 151.
42. Luhmann, 151.
43. Luhmann, 153–54.
44. Britzman, "Queer Pedagogy," 303.
45. Britzman, 297.

forms."[46] As a border-crossing epistemology, it also builds on recent calls for trans*formational pedagogies that "proliferate possibilities for the doing, thinking, and practicing of trans* genders."[47]

In what follows, I argue that the anthologies produced by the Queer Ancestors Project are kuaerly pedagogical. I explore alliances and frictions among texts, querying how this collection of trans and queer experiences challenges understandings of race, gender, ancestry, and identity—and the ways we pull from these categories to create spaces of (un)belonging. To better identify the promiscuous[48] relations enabled by these rhetorics, I also access the legends, stories, and histories through which QAP students claim their ancestors. Diasporic listening requires that I travel with their narratives, moving across presumed borders. Like the Visibility Project, this archive also disrupts the presumed stability of normative taxonomies. However, in a kuaerly pedagogical turn, they approach identification as an "interminable question." The relations claimed here deconstruct dominant taxonomies while also exposing that normative ancestries are only *one* story of our places and peoples of origin. While the nonce taxonomies of the preceding chapter emerge from rhetors' specific identifications and the labels they reappropriate with conviction, the QAP's ancestries meander into the ephemera, absences, and ambivalences of LGBTQ+ and migrant experience. What does it look like to make knowledge from what can never be known? In my listening, I am both rhetorical critic and QAP student, learning from and alongside the participants of the Queer Ancestors Project.

In the foreword to *Tender,* the 2018 QAP anthology, Celeste Chan queries: "How do we create when we don't know our own histories? How do we locate invisible stories and ancestors?"[49] Over nine months, QAP students explore these questions, "create[ing] original art about queer/trans history, locat[ing] themselves within it."[50] In these classrooms, James Baldwin, Justin Torres, Amir Rabiyah, Kai Cheng Thom, Audre Lorde, and other QTPOC luminaries become mentors and guides. They lead students across geographic and temporal landscapes, providing theoretical lenses and artistic techniques for engaging individual and communal identities. By foregrounding these voices as artistic and spiritual predecessors, the QAP seeks out ancestral connections indifferent to biology. The ancestors they choose outline a trans and queer heritage defined by shared struggle, resistance, and uplift. In this community,

---

46. Johnson, "'Quare' Studies," 10.

47. Nicolazzo, Marine, and Galarte, "Introduction," 368.

48. Gopinath, *Unruly Visions,* introduction.

49. Chan, *Tender,* v.

50. Chan, v.

self and interpersonal love are acts of defiance, rejecting the racist, homo/transphobic, and ableist norms meant to isolate us. More, pedagogy becomes a means of querying possible relations—reaching across timelines and geographies for sturdy, imaginative family formations. In Celeste's words, *Tender* intentionally arranges these students' voices "in conversation [. . . forming] a stirring collective"[51] that queers the heteronormativity of many ancestral traditions and detaches "ancestry" from its contemporary associations with scientific racism. My analysis in this chapter focuses on *Tender* and the 2019 anthology, *Flower of Ancestry*, listening for how students' approaches to homing dream up bolder lineages and constellations of care.

Diasporic Listening and Deconstructing Ancestry

The cover of *Tender* is a linocut print by madhvi trivedi-pathak, titled "Reminder for the Tenderhearted." The image shows two hands splayed open, palms up. A heart-shaped gap opens where the edges of the hands should meet, creating symbolic space for connections beyond the physical. In their artist's statement, trivedi-pathak dedicates the piece "to the tenderqueers in my life, the ones with the hearts that have been so broken so many times by community, lovers (ex) and wh(y), the state, the sadness, the ancestral silence."[52] The print itself is paired with an anonymously crafted poem, which describes the speaker's "palms cup[ped] so / that the deep line / that runs off my left palm / ends / where the line on the right / begins."[53] With this print, trivedi-pathak chooses and speaks to a nameless ancestor, claiming that "ancestral silence" as generative.

A "naan-biryani queer gujarati thali 1 part community organizer 2 parts dillwalla dog lover,"[54] trivedi-pathak opens the collection by naming the cross-cultural forces that often leave diasporic queers without access to community or knowledge of their own histories. Here, gender norms, state institutions, cultural distance, and heteronormative genealogies entangle in economies of abandonment. In a world where biological lineage provides the default tether to community and security, LGBTQ+ migrants are particularly vulnerable to cultural and social isolation. In defiance of those patterns, trivedi-pathak extends a bloodline to this unnamed poet, whose concluding stanza insists: "interdependently. / how we need each other to exist." "reminder for the ten-

---

51. Chan, v.
52. trivedi-pathak, "Reminder for the Tenderhearted," 3.
53. trivedi-pathak, 2.
54. Chan, *Tender,* 64.

derhearted" responds to Celeste's call to action, rendering visible the "ghost spaces of what's not known" and inviting kindred spirits to fill those spaces. These open hands are an invitation. In the subsequent pages, trivedi-pathak's peers answer with essays, poems, and prints that entwine real and imagined histories to—in trivedi-pathak's words—"remake reality." This section constellates QAP entries to consider how these students *unmake* conventional understandings of kinship and ancestry by storying into the silences of their pasts.

Absence, unknowing, and loss pervade these texts, marking the emotional and physical ways that queer and trans children are distanced from their biological lineages. That same emptiness, however, also becomes a blank canvas on which to render new imaginings of individual and shared ancestries. QAP students fill these ghost spaces with desire—with trans and queer yearnings for love, family, and community—and their journeys in pursuit of those desires. Kimiko Goeller, for example, "a queer Japanese American from the bay area,"[55] writes to parents who "tighten the hold of the name you gave me."[56] The speaker of her poem recalls "chiseling myself to fit that arch of your mouth / as you painted praises of your perfect daughter." Spoken praise from her parents reifies an idealized femininity that "carve[s] away" the excess of queer desire. This is the only shape she knows to pursue—the only future she can imagine until she finds queer predecessors who "taught me the difference / between butterflies and caterpillars / reminded me that by shedding its past self / a supernova becomes bright enough to outshine galaxies."

Like Wenshu Lee's 跨兒, "children who cross horizons,"[57] Goeller's speaker moves between wor(l)ds of meaning. The second stanza brings her to the care of gender outlaws who "cradled those scraps / explained that they were seeds not blight."[58] The elements of herself for which she was shamed find light and nourishment through trans wisdom. With this insight, 跨 shifts to 誇—as in 誇贊 (*to praise*) and 自誇 (*to boast*). On this cultural horizon, the poem finds pride in *both* the speaker's origins and their queer crossings. The final stanza returns to address her family of birth. To her parents, the speaker says, "you mourn the loss of your daughter and yet / you are the one that taught me / to shape myself / if the mold no longer fits." With this assertion, the speaker rejoins her family on her own terms. She claims as her familial inheritance the courage to defy expectations. She *is* her parents' daughter in her ability to grow beyond their imaginations.

---

55. Chan, *Flower of Ancestry*, 2:73.
56. Goeller, "Reminders."
57. Lee, "Kuaering Queer Theory," 337.
58. Goeller, "Reminders."

Bahaar Ahsan likewise must leave her parents in order to return more comfortably as herself and documents this tension in her own homeward journeying. Her untitled poem uses translingual movement to explore the disparate, concomitant influences that give her life. The poem opens "when I moved out of my parents house," marking this departure as a new beginning. The stanza continues:

> i began to unlearn how to change into dresses in public bathrooms
> i acquired new kinds of language for this body
> gherti baazi became trans femme,
> avazi became gendernonconforming
> distortions of ancestral images
> rendered hypervisible—rendered invisible
> their bodies bent beyond (re)cognition[59]

Like Goeller, Ahsan begins with the limits of conventional ancestry and maneuvers toward kuaer wisdom. These children had to unlearn the lessons of their parents. Neither poem assigns blame for the trauma of this inherited knowledge. Instead, they expose the normative frameworks that heteronuclear families model for their children, and the restrictive relational vocabularies that these frameworks often impose. In both poems, the speaker also retains a tenderness for their parents, expressed through a desire for (re)connections that enable and embrace trans and queer identities.

Bringing together these contestatory desires of queer diaspora, Ahsan's poem encourages manifold interpretations. When the line breaks at "distortions of ancestral images," it leaves room for contradiction. A reader might infer that *avazi,* Persian for *not right*—or, more overtly, *bitch*[60]—was redefined by queer celebrations of gender nonconformity. In other words, the speaker learned corporeal and linguistic grammars that undermine her inherited understandings of (un)acceptable gender presentation. In this case, the "ancestral images" belong to her family of birth—to her parents and the notions of propriety carried from one generation to the next. A different reading, however, could begin the sentence with "distortions of ancestral images / rendered hypervisible—rendered invisible . . ."[61] refusing to assign agency to the verb. In this iteration, imposed gender norms distort the legacies of the speaker's queer ancestors, whose bodies are simultaneously hypervisible (as threat) and invisible (as people) within binary logics. As the poem goes on to

---

59. Ahsan, "Untitled."
60. Thank you to Fereshteh Abbasi for her invaluable translations.
61. Ahsan, "Untitled."

reveal, the speaker is continually pulled by divergent desires: the needs of her bodymind and her yearning for the people and places she knew as home. By emphasizing the indeterminacy and conflict characteristic of queer diaspora, Ahsan insists on the ability to question and revise one's lineages as integral to queer diasporic survival.

Ahsan's use of ambiguity—rather, her invitation to find multiple, contested meanings—also resists the dichotomous thinking that often discounts experiences of LGBTQ+ migrants. The poem's speaker recalls how she "stayed up all night in the library trying to uncover my past / mistook my mother for archive / only to find the professor regarded my childhood as 'ornamental at best, / possessing some formal value but lacking any thematic complexity.'"[62] This is a familiar reproach for students from marginalized backgrounds, who find that their histories are regarded as objects of analysis but rarely as sites and methods of knowledge production.[63] Instead, they are expected to cut into their home cultures with traditional academic tools. Or, in Ahsan's words: "i disassembled my own body, / tore it apart limb by limb /called this praxis." As the poem reveals, however, some wisdom defies translation. Ahsan's following lines are designed for fellow border-crossers, who can make meaning of the seams between languages and worlds.

In the last stanza, the speaker switches entirely to Persian. The audience shifts as she addresses her mother directly:

maman jaan,
man khodam ra daram assir msiham
hala chi kar konam[64]

Using the term of endearment *maman jaan,* the speaker recognizes the intimacy and affection of this relationship. The following line, like Lee's *kuaer,* uses English transliteration to proliferate possible readings. *Assir* could be عصیر, meaning *extract* (as wine is extracted from grapes), or اسیر, meaning *captive or chained,* or اثیر, meaning *ethereal.* The passage plays on multiple, contrasting images of struggle. The speaker could feel pulled from her places of origin, enchained by this bodymind, or she could feel as if she were evanescing—unseen and unmoored without her family to ground her. She concludes, "hala chi kar konam," meaning *what shall I do now.* The poem comes

---

62. Ahsan.

63. In rhetorical studies, Malea Powell has discussed how scholars who theorize and historicize race are assumed to be working in an area outside or at best peripheral to rhetorical studies writ large. See Agnew et al., "Octalog III."

64. Ahsan, "Untitled."

full circle, beginning with a departure from her mother's house and returning to ask her mother's advice. In the inquisitive vein of queer/kuaer pedagogy, Ahsan ends with a question: what shall I do? How can she reconcile the will of her bodymind with her familial roots and her desire to belong? The question, as a dialogic form, is also an invitation—a reminder that her mother, as implied audience, could respond in ways that ease this struggle.

Ahsan's poem uses translingual movement to demonstrate the epistemological insight of border-crossings. While monolingual readers can glean partial meanings based on context, only a reader who bridges English and Persian can fully grasp the poem's manifold meanings. In her author's biography, Ahsan explicitly identifies as a product of multiple lineages. Ahsan is "a diasporic Iranian trans femme writer, abolitionist organizer, and community member [who . . .] contextualizes her existence and her work within several lineages and legacies including but not limited to the women in her own family of origin and the Black and brown trans femmes who have come before her without whom her own survival would not be possible."[65] By crediting her survival to Black and brown trans femmes, she highlights the limitations of straight genealogies. Especially for those who exceed social bounds, the narrow foundation of familial units too often buckles beneath social pressure. Ahsan acknowledges the expansiveness of her ancestry—the cultural convergences and transgeographical and transtemporal connections that have made her existence possible. Including both her family of birth and her historical inspirations, Ahsan's kuaer ancestry honors those who give us life and those who show us ways to live amid ongoing threat. Conventional ancestry—that is, through genetics, geography, and race science—is just one story "made up" about where we came from.[66] Ahsan and her classmates dare to find other routes home.

Whereas Ahsan's poetry focuses primarily on linguistic border-crossings, other QAP writers transport cultural icons or images across contexts. In "Ngin Ngin," Jai Lei Yee revisits and revises their relationship with their grandmother through the figure of Guan Yin, the bodhisattva associated with compassion. Yee's poem appears alongside a corresponding linocut print, and the pair of texts serve as both prayer and ancestral offering. In the poem's opening line, the speaker tells Ngin Ngin "I make this altar for you"[67]—this statue of Guan Yin, which stares back from the following page. In Yee's print, the bodhisattva sits on a backdrop of deep red—the color of fortune and celebration, and the color of envelopes that children receive from their elders on the Lunar New

65. Chan, Tender, 63.
66. Gumbs, Dub, "a note."
67. Yee, "Ngin Ngin."

Year. Guan Yin looks traditionally feminine, as she does in most contemporary Chinese depictions. She is seated in the lotus position. In one hand, she holds mala beads, and in the other, a portrait of Ngin Ngin. In the foreground is an incense altar, where descendants offer prayers and other devotions to ancestors who have passed.

Yee writes: "This statue of Guan Yin / is my only keepsake of yours."[68] This relic, however, is marked by human imperfection and the fraught relationship from which it emerges. In Yee's description, "Dust gathers in the creases of [Guan Yin's] cloth and hands / Hides her haphazardly glued on middle finger / Broken because I dropped her." An apt vessel for the speaker's late confessions, Guan Yin's scars and blemishes capture the family tension that Yee unravels through verse. Yee writes: "I pray to you through Guan Yin [. . .] I never came out to you / Since you passed away when I was nine / Too young to find the words to tell you." In asking Guan Yin to carry these words to the afterlife, the poem captures and responds to a longing for the super-natural—for a conversation that stitches past with present and seals old wounds.

The reunion staged in this poem, however, is also troubled. As the speaker continues, they burrow deeper into the past, excavating yet more language for the forms of harm embedded in their familial relations. "Ngin Ngin," the speaker says, "You asked me to be a protector like you / To put my five-year-old body between / My dad's fists / and my mom's screams."[69] While the five-year-old provided meager protection, Ngin Ngin posed only further threat. The last stanza augments the tender address of the opening:

Ngin Ngin,
Mom says you beat me often
I don't remember
Can I trust her stories?
My first memories are what my mom tells me

In revealing this violent past, the final stanza sheds new light on its opening scenes. What, for example, was the reason or the consequence for dropping Guan Yin's statue? What other factors prevented the speaker from coming out to their family? Concluding with uncertainty, with the injuries they cannot remember, Yee touches on the gaps in memory that can result from individual and inherited pain. While earlier contributors refer abstractly to intergenerational trauma, Yee anchors that reality in their father's fists, in

68. Yee.
69. Yee.

Guan Yin's fractured hand, and in the phantom recollections of their mother's stories. Here again, questioning appears as a queer/kuaer form of knowledge, inviting readers into the lasting trauma of uncertainty—of having no access to the truth of what happened.

In calling upon Guan Yin, Yee joins other contemporary TGNC folks who have reappropriated the bodhisattva as a genderfluid icon.[70] Though depicted as feminine in contemporary Chinese contexts, Guan Yin took masculine forms prior to the Song dynasty and remains masculine in other cultural traditions. *The Lotus Sutra* describes Guan Yin as able to inhabit any form to teach the dharma. A consummate rhetorician, Guan Yin could appear as "a monk, nun, layman, or laywoman . . . a boy or a girl . . . a human [or] a nonhuman"[71]—whatever shape would make audiences more receptive to their message. Through this corporeal dynamism, Guan Yin was able to spread mercy and compassion and "relieve the suffering of the world."[72] The Western term *transgender* would be an inaccurate label for Guan Yin, though she does have a history of transnational movement and cultural dexterity. In Sanskrit, she is known as अवलोकितिश्वर (Avalokiteśvara) and often assigned a more masculine appearance. In Tibet, his name is སྤྱན་རས་གཟིགས (Chenrezig). In Korea, he is 관음 (Gwan-eum), and in Japan, 観音菩薩 (Kannon Bosatsu). As Cairo Mo does in their print of Mulan, Yee insists on the perdurance of queer existence without having to assign Guan Yin any Western gender category.

Whereas chapter 2's Visibility Project exploited the power of naming, many QAP students find empowerment by refusing to name—by storying affective bonds that do not require explicit identification. In praying to and through Guan Yin, asking the bodhisattva to carry this yearning for familial connection, Yee insists that Guan Yin—commonly known as the "most popular" and widely beloved of Buddhist divinities[73]—also belongs to QTAPI traditions and that queers, too, deserve her compassion. Like queer scholars assembling scavenger methodologies to (re)engage information that has been "deliberately or accidentally excluded from traditional studies,"[74] the QAP's homing narratives explore scavenger lineages to establish new possibilities for family, community, and belonging. As they story through memory and fantasy, they posit kinship as a relation that is tendered—as in gifted from

70. Bailey, "Embracing the Icon"; Gelinas, "Creating a Sustainable Buddhist Feminist *Thealogy*"; Rubin Museum of Art, "Fluid Depictions of Gender and Identity in Himalayan Art."

71. Kumārajīva, *The Lotus Sutra*, 298.

72. Kumārajīva, 301.

73. The Editors of Encyclopaedia Britannica, "Avalokiteshvara."

74. Halberstam, *Female Masculinity*, 12.

one generation of (gender)queers to the next—and tended, as in cared for by subsequent generations who inherit and grow from these legacies.

While some QAP participants use language and printmaking to (re)connect with their families of birth, others reimagine the stories of their chosen ancestors. In "A Thousand Deaths, Not My Own," Lia Dun reinterprets an iconic portrait of Anna May Wong. The first Chinese American actress to gain Hollywood recognition, Wong spent most of her career playing "passive 'butterflies' or deceitful 'dragon ladies.'"[75] Dun's title was inspired by Wong's own words, having "died a thousand times" as her characters inevitably met tragic and/or violent ends. After Wong co-starred in *Shanghai Express* with Marlene Dietrich, the two actresses were rumored to be romantically involved. That unsubstantiated fragment of history has made Wong a prominent figure in QTAPI lore. The original photograph, captured by Carl Van Vechten, features Wong surrounded by artificial flowers. The oversized petals are positioned around her face so that her head seems to be part of the overall bouquet. Dun writes, "I think the original [photo] is super creepy and objectifying, so in this print, I was trying to show how the original photo made me feel and all of the violence it represents."[76] Accordingly, Dun's print has replaced the flowers with detached heads on pikes. Wong's face looks gaunt and lifeless. Dun imagines that Wong has exacted revenge on those responsible for her lifetime of objectification "but didn't emerge from everything unscathed." The macabre imagery deconstructs the fetishizing gaze of the initial photo while reflecting Dun's own feelings through Wong—how Dun conjectures the actress felt about being hypervisible in a white, heterosexual industry. As with Yee's depiction of Guan Yin, Dun reclaims an element of Asian American canon, situating a landmark figure of Asian American popular culture within QTAPI history.

In the same volume, Nidhi Parixit Velani imagines a much gentler past for another queer actress. Disha Ganguly, also rumored to be in a lesbian relationship, took her own life in 2015—nearly a century after Anna May Wong rose to Hollywood acclaim. In her artist's statement, Velani laments that "often times, queer people and their stories are only made visible through instances of violence."[77] Stories like this are how she discovers "evidence of South Asian queer people." Rather than compounding that violence, Velani chooses to represent Ganguly and her lover as content in one another's company. The linocut print, etched in shades of purple, shows Ganguly drinking from a bottle with her arm around Suchandra Banerjee, another South Asian actress

75. Dun, "A Thousand Deaths, Not My Own," 53.

76. Dun, 53.

77. Velani, "Disha & Suchandra," 19.

speculated to be Velani's lover. Both women's eyes are closed and a cigarette hangs from Banerjee's lips. Whereas Dun channeled her disgust and rage into her image, Velani gives life to a desire for peace. Both rhetors, though, channel elements of their own stories and emotions through the re-presentation of these ancestors. Dun revises Wong's portrait into the shape of their own rage, and Velani etches her longing into an image that serves as both salve and critique, providing sharp contrast to the tragedy that overshadows too many LGBTQ+ stories and lives.

Through kuaer movement, these texts carry linguistic, visual, and other cultural artifacts across contexts to highlight elements of QTAPI experience—whether that is alienation from family or limited and objectifying representation in news and popular media. At the same time, their reappropriations of spiritual and cultural figures—Guan Yin, Anna May Wong, Disha Ganguly—pay tribute to forms of gender and sexual diversity that either had no direct English translation or could not be named in any dominant vernacular. These ancestral (re)turns evoke Kai Pyle's "trans*temporal kinship," deployed by transgender and Two Spirit Indigenous people to establish kinships "across time, with both ancestors and descendants."[78] As in Pyle's trans*temporal relationality, the connections forged by QAP students are rooted in cultural specificities—reaching through their sprawling personal lineages to (re)claim forms of gender and sexual variation obscured or fetishized by Western norms. Notably, Yee, Dun, and Velani never make specific claims about the gender or sexual identities of their ancestors. As in Britzman's queer pedagogy, kuaer pedagogy's primary concern is not "getting identities right or even with having them represented as an end in themselves."[79] Nor, however, is identity a free-for-all that can be claimed or reassigned at will. Through homing, they story their own experiences of race/ethnicity, gender, and sexuality in concert with those of these ancestors, paying homage to the legacies of gender-variant kin while building the archive of QTAPI history for relations past and future.

Reappropriating Ancestry and Togetherness-in-Difference

As the only archive in this study that does not focus specifically on Asian American histories, the Queer Ancestors Project places QTAPI experiences in dialogue with other positionalities and perspectives. Each rhetor's culturally grounded terms and references interlace with their classmates' in variegated

78. Pyle, "Naming and Claiming," 576.
79. Britzman, "Queer Pedagogy," 304.

explorations of individual and ancestral histories. Categories like race, gender, and sexuality are regarded not as biologically ingrained truths but as imperfect names for the ways we encounter the world and one another. Through these terminologies, the participants of the QAP situate themselves within legacies of colonialism, imperialism, and resistive moments. Their variegated stories then explore the responsibilities and possibilities that attend different points of entry within distinct and entangled "long life chains."

Bení Alí Ávalos, "a queer chican@ performing artist," exposes the limitations of Euro-American gender categories with their poem "I want to write about." This "road map survival guide to being queer" explains: "I was a man in the ladies' room, a woman in the men's room. / Always being myself, always in between, always disappearing."[80] While others might inhabit these terms with less conflict, for Ávalos they are assigned stigma. Calling someone a man in the women's room or a woman in the men's room is less about identification than about demarcating how the individual fails the standards of either category—about enforcing their unbelonging. Ávalos then turns to gender epistemologies indifferent to binaristic norms. They write:

> People like me are shamans and leaders; our art has always been censored or erased.
> We are the Two-Spirited of Turtle Island, the Xanith in Saudi Arabia, the Hijra in India.
> We are the Queens who fought back at Stonewall, the first ones executed by Spanish Captains.
> We are the Bacha dancers in Afghanistan, our cousins in Russia who did not live to see 2018.[81]

Through kuaer diasporic movement, Ávalos sifts through different cultural reference points for gender variance, locating promiscuous intimacies among disparate pasts. Notably, Ávalos does not fold these identities back into a homogenizing Western category. At no point in the poem do they use the terms *trans, transgender,* or *third gender,* resisting the easy claim that these iterations of gender variance are simply "alternative" iterations of Western gender transgressions. Rather, Ávalos conjures a "we" that calls these different experiences of gender diversity into community while signaling their cultural specificity. They write, "It was so easy to abandon who we were, where we come from. / After they forced us to forget and made us change our names."[82]

80. Ávalos, "I Want to Write About," 46.
81. Ávalos, 46–47.
82. Ávalos, 47.

These gender-diverse terms have appeared with growing frequency in recent transgender scholarship and advocacy—a phenomenon that has prompted criticism by some transgender and Two Spirit writers. Towle and Morgan in particular examine the tendency of Western scholarship to relegate all genders from the Majority World to a "junk drawer" of "non-Western gender miscellany."[83] In these cases, hijra, xanith, and other folks appear as evidence that nonbinary genders should be accepted in Western settings. The "other" is rendered exotic and flattened into a counterpoint rather than acknowledging the full complexity of their worlds and lives. Ávalos does not fully explore those intricacies in this one poem, but the polyvocal nature of the QAP enables my analyses to take shape in the convergences and divergences of different texts. Diasporic listening compels me to hear Ávalos's words in concert with those of their classmates and of the relations they conjure.

jorge mata flores, for example, narrates their linocut print as an attempt to connect with Two Spirit ancestors. The piece is titled "ancestral shifts." On a yellow backdrop, a thick white line meanders. As it narrows near the center of the page, it winds into a dense loop. Two other clusters of lines, scribbled into abstract shapes, are positioned in the top-left and bottom-left quadrants of the image. In the artist's statement, worth reproducing in full, mata flores writes:

> Using the concept of intergenerational trauma as a jumping off point, this untitled piece is an exercise in accessing ancestors. Taking the idea of trauma being passed on a cultural and genetic scale, this piece asks the question whether more than trauma is passed on. If we still hold trauma in our bones surely the resourcefulness, resilience, and ways in which we found to hold onto our sense of self must be in our spirits too.
>
> Historically, for indigenous people, two-spirit or gender variant people have been thought to be bridges. Before western ideas of gender and sexuality were brought to the Americas two-spirit people were held in high esteem often called "joyas" or jewels. They had roles in society as healers, bridges, and in some cases were thought of as having magic.
>
> Through the process of colonization much of the history and visibility of queer and gender variant people has been suppressed, forcing people to hide their magic as a means of safety. Still, we found ways of existing and displaying our magic. Untitled comes through the act of letting my hand move freely as a ritual to let my ancestors speak through me. If lived experiences and spirit are passed on as deep as genetics, and two-spirit people are

---

83. Towle and Morgan, "Romancing the Transgender Native," 484.

thought to be bridges, for this piece I am merely serving as a vessel for the story my ancestors are trying to tell me.[84]

Between the image and the written reflection, mata flores invites readers into their process of ancestral inquiry. Beginning with intergenerational trauma, their artists' statement reverses the exoticizing gaze through which consumers have approached genetic ancestry tests. Whereas GATs promise connections to distant and otherwise invisible pasts, intergenerational trauma imposes past harms on the present. The inheritors of this trauma may not be able to name it, let alone identify its source, but they live its consequences. Race cannot be quantified by genomic data, but social manifestations of race intrude through material and psychic harm that ripples across generations. mata flores chooses to find hope in this fact—that others have carried this burden and forged their own means of survival.

Far from the removed, sanitized process of GAT laboratory analysis, mata flores offers themselves as vessel for this inherited wisdom. They present their flesh and bone as evidence of trauma that gets encoded into subsequent generations. The movement of their hand—this meandering line—captures a defiant faith in their ancestors and the collective resilience of Two Spirit folks across time. Staging their body as a bridge to the spiritual, mata flores disrupts the presumed division between biological connection and "fictive" kin. Equally striking about this image is what is *not* shown. The abstraction of mata flores's drawings spotlights the distance through which many experience intergenerational trauma—how its inheritors are often denied clear answers about its origins or avenues toward healing. The printed lines, which themselves resemble a "road map," track meandering, uncertain routes that often dead-end or double back.

mata flores's usage of the term *Two Spirit* is telling. Another product of cultural crossings, Two Spirit emerged in 1990 as an intertribal designation for gender-variant folks in Native American communities. An intentionally political and decolonial label, it is a challenge not only to the derogatory terms imposed by non-Native researchers but also to the "white-dominated GLBTQ community's labels and taxonomies."[85] Unique to Two Spirit critique is its anchor in Indigenous gender frameworks. The fact that Two Spirit folks "*are* 'normal' within traditional worldviews" positions Two Spirit politics as "an antiassimilation stance against colonial projects" that have sought to eradicate Indigenous sexualities and gender systems."[86] In prioritizing Two Spirit

---

84. mata flores, "ancestral shifts," 15.
85. Driskill, "Doubleweaving Two-Spirit Critiques," 73.
86. Driskill, 83; emphasis original.

people as their ancestors, mata flores claims an identity that predates settler colonial presence in the Americas but that also was named in response
to colonial taxonomies. In the words of Kim Tallbear, "without 'settlers,' we
could not have 'Indians' or Native Americans. Instead, we would have many
thousands of smaller groups or peoples defined within and according to their
own languages, by their own names."[87] Two Spirit is then an assertion of
self-determination and coalition in response to colonial knowledge systems.
Like the language-crossing *kuaer,* it is a term engendered by human movement and friction. These terms acquire their meanings—to paraphrase Gloria
Anzaldúa—where one world grates against the other and bleeds.[88] In claiming Two Spirit identity, mata flores insists that Indigeneity matters—not in the
reductive sense of DNA tests used to claim Native ancestry but in the forms of
knowledge and ways of living made possible by Two Spirit folks then and now.

Far from an example of "alternative gender," then, Two Spirit is a political orientation grounded in decolonial worldviews and forms of community.
As Cherokee Two Spirit and queer scholar Qwo-Li Driskill explains, Two
Spirit critiques align with many elements of queer of color and queer diasporic critiques—particularly in drawing from intersectional experience to
"disrupt white supremacist heteronormative strategies" that marginalize people of color, nonheterosexuals, and others who exceed rigid gender norms.[89]
Driskill finds, however, that frequently these perspectives leave out Native
people and Native resistance. Ze adds: "While I don't think that scholars
need to change the focus of their work, I do expect scholars to integrate
Indigenous and decolonial theories into their critiques."[90] This imperative is
a pressing need within Asian American studies, which has only a few inter-
mittent explorations of what it means to occupy—as perpetual foreigner,
as refugee, as undocumented, and/or as an (im)migrant subject to the economic pressures of global capitalism—land claimed by force. More, what
does it mean to have shared a racial category with Pacific Islanders until the
year 2000? To still be grouped together in "Asian Pacific American Heritage
Month" or the Smithsonian's "Asian Pacific American Center"? How does one
live in the body used for Indigenous erasure?

Though the students of the QAP are not embedded in the same disciplinary conversations as Driskill—at least, not to the same degree—they
demonstrate awareness of hir critiques and the imperative to consider their
relationships to colonial histories of the lands they inhabit. Shō Nakashima's

---

87. Tallbear, "The Emergence, Politics, and Marketplace of Native American DNA," 22.
88. Anzaldúa, *Borderlands,* 25.
89. Driskill, "Doubleweaving Two-Spirit Critiques," 75.
90. Driskill, 78.

print "Kubi Dake Ni Natte Mo (Moro's Head)" is particularly striking for its rumination on what it means to be a "queer nisei who grew up in the white suburbs of Detroit that occupy Anishinaabe lands, and [who] currently resides in the colonial-settler city of San Francisco occupying Ohlone lands."[91] They describe the print specifically as a response to the "many-faced" violences they witness, experience, and are embedded in "as a queer, disabled Asian body in the U.S."[92] "Kubi Dake Ni Natte Mo" is inspired by *Mononoke-hime* (*Princess Mononoke*), one of the most-recognized Japanese animated films in the West. On a gold backdrop, Nakashima has etched a wolf's head. Its lips pull back to reveal sharp teeth clamped around a severed arm. Its eyes are open beneath furrowed brows. In the artist's statement, Nakashima identifies this as the decapitated head of Moro, the wolf god from *Princess Mononoke*. In the film, Moro's detached head surges back to life to attack Eboshi, an industrial developer whose ambitions have bled the land of life and resources. Nakashima describes this image as an attempt to "capture and re-interpret this scene," which they see "reflected in the U.S. and globally, especially for queer and trans communities of color."[93] Though Nakashima provides a brief gloss in their artist's statement, the piece bears greater impact for those familiar with the film and popular interpretations.

Described as filmmaker Hayao Miyazaki's "most mature work,"[94] *Princess Mononoke* stages a clash between capitalism and the natural world. With Miyazaki's signature ambiguity, the film avoids easy distinctions between heroes and villains, inviting more nuanced explorations of morality in our long-broken worlds. Eboshi, in bringing iron manufacturing to the area, also provides employment and shelter for lepers and prostitutes who had been abandoned by samurai culture. The people of Iron Town respect and admire Eboshi. They credit her with rescuing them from exploitation and/or neglect and providing them the conditions to lead their lives with dignity. Eboshi also arrives after the shogunate had already exiled the Emishi, the Indigenous peoples of the land, to the north. Ashitaka, the Emishi prince at the center of the film, spends most of the movie trying to broker compromise between conflicting parties. His failure to reach a neat resolution is often seen as commentary about the inevitability of capitalist destruction. This is where Nakashima departs from popular reception.

The film opens with Ashitaka killing a boar god who had been driven mad by an iron bullet, which appears to eliminate any possibility of preindustrial

91. Chan, *Tender*, 64.
92. Nakashima, "Moro's Head," 2019, 4.
93. Nakashima, 4.
94. Abbey, "'See with Eyes Unclouded,'" 114.

ways of life. As the conflicts escalate, all the humans survive, but almost none of the animal gods do. Kristen Abbey, a professor of comparative literature, summarizes the themes of *Princess Mononoke* as such:

> Industrialization destroyed the forest, and the Japanese relationship to it as a sacred space, inevitably, was part of the growth away from feudal injustice and toward modernity. While modernity has more potential for social justice, everywhere it has destroyed the land and displaced Indigenous peoples. Modernity is neither desirable nor escapable, but it is also not evil. Like any tragic hero, it means well. Mononoke-hime offers no solutions that will make everyone safe and happy.[95]

While viewers might empathize with the strong yet cold Eboshi, with the wolf-raised Princess Mononoke, or with the mediator Ashitaka, Moro and her fellow animal gods are almost always regarded as inevitable casualties of human progress. There may be no victors in *Princess Mononoke,* but the inevitable destruction of human progress is its certainty.

Nakashima's choice of Moro—or, more specifically, Moro's reanimated head—as ancestor pivots away from most interpretations of *Princess Mononoke.* The death of the gods as well as Ashitaka's departure from the Emishi community are typically taken to mean that there is no return to a world before the ravages of capitalism and economic competition. Nakashima, though, writes toward the possibility that other futures can be made by knowing the preindustrial past. Even if ways of life prior to "imperialism, queer and trans erasure, and colonization and genocide more broadly"[96] cannot be "returned to" in a pure sense, Nakashima insists on the power of reviving and connecting with those forms of knowledge. The "capitalism, industrialism, and democracy"[97] captured by Iron Town and the shogunate are not inevitable so much as accepted forms of futurity. The brief revival of Moro's head, in Nakashima's words, "illustrates how we are sometimes brutally 'decapitated'—destroyed and deprived of life and joy in this economy—and yet, we are still able to resist and be a nuisance to those in power beyond our physical lives."[98] That is, even when cut off from resources or from our own histories, we can find disruptive potential in what remains. The world that we build after that

---

95. Abbey, 118.
96. Nakashima, "Moro's Head," 4.
97. Nakashima, 4.
98. Nakashima, 4.

rupture will not be the "same," but it also does not need to align with the "extractive, violent, non-communal economies"[99] normalized by modernity.

In reaching toward a presumedly foreclosed past, Nakashima explores how connecting with discounted or fantastical ancestries might open up novel worldviews and worldmaking. Ancestry, in this view, is not just about anchoring one to a distant past but about how the story of that past spills into the present and carries us into particular futures. What solutions would we pursue if we did *not* regard the ravages of human expansion as inevitable? How could we distinguish between the irreversible damage of past harms and the ongoing violence of passivity? How would that revise our relationships to the injustices we inherit? What potential alliances and communities would those relationships reveal? For the many of us who are born into and benefit from exploitative social arrangements, this means that inaction is still violence; it accepts the injustices of our present as if they were predetermined and unchangeable. Nakashima's homing practice models ancestral dialogue as a means of accessing "what power we have, amidst both violence and death,"[100] to unsettle these legacies and to choose otherwise.

Becoming Ancestors

Like the other archives of this study, the QAP engages in an ecology of API, trans, and queer rhetorics. As such, it creates opportunities for future rhetors to engage, and for present participants to carry their work beyond the bounds of this nine-month course. For example, some QAP artists find agency by reflecting on their responsibilities to subsequent generations. Inspired by Alexis Pauline Gumbs's *In Your Hands* project, participants wrote from an imagined future—when they, as ancestors, speak to descendants about a queer past. In "Return Address," Keira writes to a nameless "starchild" from the view of an elder wishing she could reach through time.[101] As ancestor, Keira mourns that "there are no words, no pictures, no old ledgers . . . to hint at the lives we lived." She enjoins the unnamed child to imagine their ancestors' stories and their love—ancestors who would embrace them "however you may be, however you may wish to be." Keira-as-ancestor says, "Hi-story is still stories, after all, with endless truths between. (re)create what has been stolen."[102] Keira's essay functions as both critique and curative, exposing how the erasure of

---

99. Nakashima, 4.
100. Nakashima, 4.
101. Keira, "Return Address," 24.
102. Keira, 25.

LGBTQ+ history denies subsequent generations models for navigating suppressive realities. In leaving this letter, though, Keira writes back against that erasure.

In a related gesture, Queen Sen Sen etches an image of themself as queer and trans guardian. Their self-portrait takes up half the linocut print, their head stretched to an empty sky as they cast light toward an open door. On the other side of the page, many hands reach for the light. Describing their three-day stint in jail following a protest, Sen writes: "I remembered yearning for sunlight to touch my body and also felt disempowered while my body ached from bruises and wounds. In this piece, I wanted to re-imagine myself as a divine protector for all Queer and Trans prisoners."[103] This print draws from the artist's own experience of deprivation to envision protection and guidance for their community. Though more metaphorical than Keira's letter, this piece also simultaneously captures the critique and response, spotlighting the rampant imprisonment of LGBTQ+ folks while positioning Queen Sen Sen as a developing voice in LGBTQ+ communities.

In their bio, Sen explains that they wanted to participate in the Queer Ancestors Project to facilitate their work as an artist and teacher who explores relief printing as a means of "cop[ing] with CPTSD and depression."[104] Influences from the QAP appear throughout Sen's emerging career. Following the QAP, both of their linocut pieces from the 2019 anthology are offered as digital prints sold through their online store. As of 2020 they teach visual arts to youth in Oakland, still focusing on "visual storytelling through images of historical ancestors" and "dismantl[ing] systematic oppression among Indigenous, Black, Fat and Transgender bodies."[105] One of Sen's prints for the QAP, a tribute to Marsha P. Johnson titled "Liberation for All of Us," appears at the top of an interview they did with arts and literary journal *The Ana*. In the interview, Sen describes how their art emerges from and gives back to their communities—how they were taught and amplified by other queer and gender-nonconforming artists, and how their art has connected them with other fat folks who "express how [Sen's work] has helped them through their own self-love."[106] Sen's journey traces the interconnectedness of ancestral practice—how communing with ancestors can provide LGBTQ+ folks environments and strategies for healing and prepare them to become guides and mentors for others.

---

103. Queen Sen Sen, "Sun," 31.
104. Chan, *Flower of Ancestry*, 2:73.
105. Queen Sen Sen, "About."
106. Sen quoted in Pinkney, "Fat Femmes Rise Up!" 50.

Also like the DFP and the VP, the texts of the QAP are rhetorically significant in both their creation and their distribution. Curricula centered on the creativity, compassion, and power of queer community and survival both insist on and *make* these stories meaningful, giving them new life in the memories and artistic productions of QAP students. These productions are then circulated through events and publications. The printmaking workshop, for example, culminates in an art installation. Students' prints are framed and exhibited at Strut Health Center, home to the San Francisco AIDS Foundation. At opening night, there are prints available for purchase as well as free food and drinks and free sexual health testing via Strut's mobile health unit. The exhibit remains on the wall throughout the five months of the writing workshop, and at the closing reception, students share their poetry, essays, and stories in front of their artwork. Afterwards, all these texts—the prints, the artists' descriptions, and their creative writing—are collected in an anthology published by Foglifter Press.

While not all students need to or even want to pursue further publication, some do and carry these conversations about trans-and-queer-of-color histories into new settings. In addition to Queen Sen Sen, who continues to sell their prints in a broader artistic collection celebrating queer, trans, and fat bodies, Lia Dun revised and published an essay that first appeared in *Tender* as "Kurama." In the critically acclaimed *Catapult* magazine, Dun's essay is retitled "Redrawing the Lines: How Anime Helped Shape My Nonbinary Identity." Examining the texts side by side, readers can witness Dun's view of their past, their family, and themself all sharpen through more precise language. Their familial resentment takes a reflective turn, focusing instead on "how lucky I was to have a parent who was so feminist or who loved me so unconditionally."[107] Whereas the initial draft tracked the author's self-doubt ("Maybe I'm just a silly American girl who likes to pretend she doesn't have a home here."[108]), the *Catapult* essay considers how such thoughts are encouraged by cultural pressures. Kurama, a character from the anime *Yu Yu Hakusho,* comes to stand in for Dun's genderqueer desires. The character, who moves between worlds, "was never wrong for being who he is. It was the world that needed to change."[109] Folding this reflection back onto their own life, Dun insists: "I try to remember that this is not my fault"—that their struggle to find a place between the poles of masculine and feminine was an indication not of Dun's shortcomings but of the exclusions of binary gender.

---

107. Dun, "Redrawing the Lines."
108. Dun, "Kurama," 21.
109. Dun, "Redrawing the Lines."

In approaching identification as an "interminable question," the QAP students disrupt taxonomies that have organized dominant views of lineage, loyalty, and belonging. What if who we think "we" are is just one story among myriad possibilities? What events, past and present, would we see ourselves as connected to and responsible for? The rhetorical impact of the QAP collections is found less in specific claims than in the questions they explore and their willingness to unmoor themselves from old certainties. Moving differentially among far-reaching cultural touchpoints, languages, and bodily experiences, these rhetors explore a kuaer pedagogy that is open to novel identifications while grounded in material inequities and corporeal difference. As opposed to fixing themselves to one "long life chain," these writers and artists find home in the moments their stories touch others'.

Storying toward the homes they need, QAP participants summon the myriad possibilities of kuaer ancestry. A community blossoms between madhvi trivedi-pathak's open hands. Bahaar Ahsan finds sites of belonging in the supposed divide between Persian and English, and Lia Dun fuses their rage with (what they imagine as) Anna May Wong's to haunt those who exoticize and exploit Asian women. Jai Lei Yee situates trans Asian Americans as inheritors of Guan Yin's compassion. Bení Alí Ávalos and jorge mata flores position TGNC folks as allied in envisioning worlds outside of Euro-American epistemologies, and Shō Nakashima imagines futures accountable to and emergent from precolonial wisdom. These artists and writers demonstrate how the worlds we make are shaped by the communities for whom we make them.

The meanings I constellate from these texts derive from my own angle of approach, which is particular to my cultural influences. Readers in other geographical and temporal settings will arrive at different commonplaces and insights. For me, the most exciting lesson from journeying alongside the QAP students is the possibility of *unknowing*. If the story we tell of our lineages is only one (restrictive) means of accessing kinship, how else could we draw our networks of care and our homeward journeys? How would doing so hold us accountable for settler exploitation, racial injustice, trans and queer phobia, ableism, and a wounded planet? What languages would we invent to access and nurture those connections? I ask these questions by writing with and to the artists of the Queer Ancestors Project—stepping into Celeste Chan's ghost spaces, as one of trivedi-pathak's tenderhearted, and believing in Nakashima's promise of a world beyond extractive, violent economies. For subsequent generations of LGBTQ+ Asian Americans: we hope you find shelter in these conversations, and that you'll carry them forward. These stars are yours now, for you to chart your own path among them.

// That's how it is with Asian American identity—nothing brings it out like other people's expectations and a sense of danger.[110]
    —*Eric Liu,* The Accidental Asian

In his memoir, writer and political commentator Eric Liu recalls a childhood of searching for "Chineseness." Like many Chinese Americans, he had balked at the homogenizing assumption that there were any essential qualities binding people of Chinese descent together—let alone all of Asian America. At a turning point in the narrative, though, Liu recalls stepping into the role of Public Asian. As a member of the Clinton administration, he appeared on a news show to discuss a magazine cover that depicted the president, vice president, and first lady in yellowface—a commentary about the 1996 campaign finance scandal. When another guest—an Asian American staff writer from the magazine—remarked that "normal people" were not offended by the caricatures, Liu responded with outrage. Surprised by his own defensiveness, Liu reflects: "I'd become the righteous, vocal Asian American. All it had taken was a stage and a villain."[111]

I empathized with Liu's resistance to Asian American identification—with the way he balked at the conflation of his skin tone and hair color with an entire distant continent. I heard echoes of my own experiences as he recalled letting slip his ancestral tongue, failing to see himself in "the" Asian American story, and mining his father's memories for some tenuous connection to a distant land. Unlike Liu, though, even the threat of Asian American stereotyping did not stir me into a protective defensiveness of Chinese cultures, which I had experienced as threat just as often as Western xenophobia. Had I been better acquainted with my histories, I might have known that rigid and binaristic views of sex and gender arrived in China with the influence of Western biomedicine.[112] I might have known that Taiwan's present-day leadership in LGBTQ+ rights in Asia draws from the island's amalgamated histories—from the diverse gender roles and identities of Indigenous Taiwanese; from the gender outlaws who persisted before, during, and after the Republic of China's militaristic regime; and from strategic appropriations of US queer cultures following its Cold War interventionism.[113]

I never really feel Asian American or queer—or, more importantly, both—until I arrive in Celeste Chan's classrooms. I meet the 2017–18 cohort of the QAP in a dressing room at SOMArts, where we gather around a single long table. Celeste has again brought snacks. An offering of granola bars and candy greets us at the entrance. I think of Cherríe Moraga's definition of Third World feminism, which "is

---

110. Liu, *The Accidental Asian*, 62.
111. Liu, 62.
112. Chiang, *After Eunuchs.*
113. Chiang and Wang, *Perverse Taiwan.*

about feeding people in all their hungers."[114] I think of Kitchen Table Press, named for the spaces where work, care, and survival entwine. I think of teaching as an act of curation—as the selective organization of information, people, and texts; as an act of care.

We begin with Audre Lorde's "Litany for Survival," reading it aloud, passing the lines between us like an incantation. Though I already know this poem, it takes new life in the mouths of these students—all queer nonbinary Asian Americans in their early twenties. When we first walked in, we followed members of a theater troupe who were rehearsing or building or perhaps even performing just beyond the adjoining wall. I don't know because I must not have noted any of the noise they made as the evening progressed. In my memory, this room is a fortress. For three hours, nothing rattles the walls that hold these students and the sound of them trying on voices that can assert their truths. As the sun drifts lower in the sky, Lorde's verses fill the space between us. I have read this poem countless times, but today each line is its own revelation—a prayer for "those of us . . . who love in doorways coming and going / in the hours between dawns."[115]

Fantasy, history, and memory converged as each text opened broader discussions about the challenges and joys of trans, queer, disabled, and Asian American life. The students' stories are not mine to repeat. I did, however, share one of my own. Celeste had asked that I bring something to share with the class and I selected a work in progress. Though I had been experimenting with story as method, theory, and criticism for years, this was the first essay I would publish that narrativized my own experience as rhetorical inquiry, using my queer trans embodiment to press the boundaries of Asian American rhetorical studies. This essay was the first time I wrote publicly as trans and nonbinary. It was in part an argument about my own existence—about the existence of all of us in this room together and about our claim to Asian American history and rhetorical innovation.

I was so worried that I would bore the students—that I would lose them in the segments that dip into disciplinary history and minutiae. They stayed with me every step of the way, however, as I recounted the troubled hope, anger, and (un) (be)longing that shaped my academic journey. I continue to hold their generous responses close, as a reminder that giving and receiving stories is the lifeblood of connection. I am so grateful for their willingness to dream with me; to suspend reality; to believe in a world of our making. A few weeks after this class, the essay found a home in a journal issue on Asian American rhetorics. Having a voice in that conversation is meaningful to me, but not without this moment before it—not without the affirmation of LGBTQ+ Asian Americans seeing elements of their own

---

114. Moraga, *Loving in the War Years*, 132.
115. Lorde, "A Litany for Survival."

struggles and aspirations. I did not want to write another essay that contorted their experiences—our experiences—beyond recognition.

I cannot help but imagine that I might have been one of these students. Had I lived in the Bay Area and been born five or six years later, I could have been among this cohort, searching for our lineages. To my surprise, one of the students reflects that rumination back to me—seeing themself in Celeste's journey and in mine. This writer, whose thoughtful reflections and artful prose haunt me long after this evening, looks from Celeste to me and says, "I used to think that as a queer nonbinary Asian American, I could never make it in academic settings. But the fact that you are here—you are proof that it's possible. That we can make it." We make it, I'm learning, through moments like this, when someone calls us into community. This is the moment that I become a vocal Asian American—not with Eric Liu's righteous anger but with communion, and with the desire to create a world that will shelter and nourish and lift up these students.

When we depart for the evening, I find myself dwelling with the final verse of Lorde's poem. I had heard it as imperative—as an ancestor's charge to her inheritors: "So it is better to speak / Remembering / we were never meant to survive."[116] I hope, too, though, that it is a promise—that these open-hearted young folks will continue to write and draw and dream in whatever genres will give form to the worlds they need—we need—to thrive. //

---

116. Lorde.

CHAPTER 4

To Make a Home

Bodymind as Archive

Stories, like the DNA used to trace our histories to distant lands, are never completely ours. I cannot extricate my life story from the aspirations my parents carried with them halfway around the world and into the American Southwest. I would not exist without the Hart–Celler Act, which allowed my father—an engineering student—to study at Texas Tech. My mother joined him within a few years, and I was born in the university hospital, our family's first and only US citizen and a beneficiary of family reunification.

After graduating, my father took his first job in Arizona, where I was raised on desert soil and unrelenting sun. My story would not exist without the peoples who nurtured this arid ground, nor without land theft and its denial so that I could grow up unawares on earth that belongs to the O'odham, Yavapai, Hohokam, and Akimel O'odham—a peoples from whom my middle school took its name: Akimel A-al, meaning children of the river. The school sits on Akimel O'odham land—on a segment of the Gila River Indian Reservation that was incorporated into the Kyrene School District in 1956. As a twelve-year-old, I had no idea.

At no point in school did I learn how the "children of the river" were cut off from their lifeblood when non-Native farmers carved up the Gila River with dams and diversion structures. I did not learn about the shipments of canned and processed foods that the federal government provided as "relief" from the famine they precipitated, or that the Akimel O'odham now experience the highest rate of type 2 diabetes in the world. As of 2021, drawing upon centuries-old intertribal collaboration, the Akimel O'odham and the Piipaash are building the Pima-Maricopa Irrigation Project, an irrigation system that will deliver water to 146,300 acres of reservation land.[1] At twelve years old, I also did not know that the names of our counties—Pima, our southern neighbor, and Maricopa, where I lived—were the names the Spanish had given to the Akimel O'odham and the Piipaash, words they have since adopted as their English names.

I have been writing about, through, and around this story my entire life—this story that is not entirely mine. I have been trying to tell a story that fits me into trajectories of globalization, human movement, and cultural conflict, extraction, and exchange. As an MFA student of creative writing, I learned that ethnic stories were rewarded for their pain. How authentic, the striving of this immigrant other. How beautifully fraught, the cultural distance cleaved between generations. I wanted to write a story that was about being Asian American and queer and sick but that wouldn't be *only* about those things. To do that, I needed the help of the Dragon Fruit Project, the Visibility Project, and the Queer Ancestors Project. I needed the richness and depth of QTAPI experience to give me context—not a shining exemplar, but a point in a constellation.

As an antidote to the damage-centered narratives expected of structurally marginalized people, Eve Tuck proposes desire. Controverting Deleuze, who describes desire as "perfectly meaningless," Tuck *desires more*. She insists on a desire that is purposeful, intentional, and agentic.[2] Desire, in Tuck's view, is a living archive of ancestral knowledge—a constellation of scattered influences. Let me rephrase without Deleuze: people historically objectified by settler colonial researchers are often written about as if they have no desires of their own. They are hopelessly tragic, without self-determination, and/or so completely colonized that their hopes and dreams have been reshaped by dominating scripts. Inspired by Tuck, I want to make space in this chapter for the complexity of Asian American, trans, queer, and disabled desires—inevitably affected by global and national scripts, by the values of those who raised us and those whom we love, but also replete with our own creativity, stubbornness, and experiential insights.

This book, for example, attempts to amplify the desires expressed by QTAPI folks for more conscientious, nuanced representations of QTAPI experiences. Written in the first few years of my tenure-track job, it is also shaped by the expectations of academic reviewers, publishers, and other authorities

1. Gila River Indian Community, "History" and "Pima-Maricopa Irrigation Project."
2. Tuck, "Breaking Up With Deleuze," 645.

who will adjudicate the future of my livelihood. The version that you're reading is unavoidably shaped by the expectations of my profession and by the predilections of my editors. It is also, however, driven primarily by my desire to find and foster a stronger sense of LGBTQ+ Asian American community. I ask: What does trans and queer Asian American rhetoric look like, and what can it do? How do LGBTQ+ Asian Americans and Pacific Islanders imagine and enact community across so many national, ethnic, sexual, and gender identities?

Homing, as writing praxis—as a method of locating buried intimacies, as a theory of how our worlds come together, and as survival—is the process through which diasporic subjects continually reinterpret events that have shaped their places of origin and connect with (real and imagined) sites of belonging. In chapters 1 through 3, I explored how QTAPI rhetors inquire into the events that inform our lives, taking the raw material of experience and building powerful reflections on social and political histories—insights that in turn open imaginative avenues for change. This chapter documents the particular changes that this book has effected for me—reshaping not only my understandings of and orientations toward my personal, familial, and ancestral histories but also my intimate circles. Composing this book has connected me with stories and people who have changed my perspective and my life. It has brought me to communities that provided linguistic and emotional resources for self and communal advocacy—for desiring and demanding more of the spaces I work and live in.

Throughout the following sections, the voices of Asian American, trans, queer, and/or disabled authors provide navigational guides for my own explorations of love, resilience, and ancestry. Inspired by queer-of-color collectives such as the Third World Women's Alliance, I call upon their voices as a reminder that I am not speaking alone. Generations of QTPOC before me have beaconed out their prayers, their calls to arms, and their survival strategies without which I would not be here today. These narratives also remind me that my speech and silence affect more than just me—that narrative scarcity means that any story of QTAPI experience is laden with disproportionate representational burden. I hope that by filling this book—my small plot of textual terrain—with an abundance of QTAPI experiences, I have edged us closer to narrative plentitude. I also hope these stories provide context for my own—that, amid a chorus of other trans and queer Asian American voices, I might have the range to be broken, petty, or mediocre without diminishing the vibrant diversity of Asian American lives.

Home, which haunts all the preceding chapters, surfaces here as commonplace. Through my journeys into, encounters with, and departures from archives of QTAPI rhetorics, I consider how the stories at my disposal have shaped my possibilities and pursuits of belonging. Constellating these experiences with those of other trans, queer, and/or disabled people of color, I consider how QTAPI insights might facilitate Chela Sandoval's democratics. That is, I consider what QTAPI stories reveal about how narratives exclude, marginalize, and abandon, and what our stories can contribute toward more liberatory futures. In the spirit of homing, this chapter is more journey than direct argument, but also journey *as* knowledge. As I listened to the preceding archives, I ask readers for a similar openness to moving with—and perhaps being moved by—the stories that follow. Using homing to re-place individual experience within surrounding narratives, this chapter revisits some of the preceding ghost passages and anecdotes to provide broader context and to explore how seemingly personal accounts deconstruct and/or reappropriate cultural patterns. All narratives are selective renderings, but I have tried my best to provide fair and thoroughly researched accounts. I have also, however, reserved my right to refusal, using constellatory connections to re-center the systemic rather than to scrutinize the decisions and motives of the people in my life.

Bodies of Memory

A week before I left for San Francisco, before the first time I shared physical space with Celeste Chan, with the Queer Ancestors' Project, APIENC, or the Visibility Project, my house caught fire—rather, the half-house I was renting from some listing on Craigslist caught fire. I had spent the year living in a duplex adjacent to three guys in their early twenties. These neighbors slept through the day and hosted parties that began at approximately 10:00 p.m. Nearly every night, their guests crowded our shared driveway, and as I got ready for bed, their stereo rattled our shared wall. If the dog woke me to go out in the middle of the night, we dodged orange bulbs of cigarette stubs lobbed over our fence.

// How do you make a home when no one wants you there?
    —Celeste Chan[3] //

I spent most of the year tolerating their disregard, knocking on their door only when their guests—still inebriated from the night's festivities—had

---

3. Chan, personal interview.

blocked my car into the driveway. Twice, they opened the door to see that it was me and disappeared back inside without a word and without moving the car. When I called a rideshare to take me to work, the driver was incensed on my behalf.

"This is about race," he insisted, meeting my eyes through the rearview mirror. "And it's about gender."

"I know." It's about the fact that I look like someone who won't fight back—who isn't supposed to cause trouble, but who by nature of gender illegibility, already *is* troubling.

Then one Saturday morning, after another night of party noises, my dog would not stop whimpering. As I tried to write at the kitchen counter, she paced a small circle around my legs, whining insistently. Through the wall, I heard the smoke detector sound from next door, blaring intermittently every few minutes. I called our landlord to let him know. My own smoke detector had been malfunctioning the previous week, so I did not think enough of it. How easily repetition can inure us to the sound of alarm. It wasn't until I smelled smoke that I stood to investigate. Then I heard the crack of wood splitting on the other side of the wall. I threw a harness on the dog and opened the door to an onrush of smoke and sirens.

For an entire snowy morning, I sat in the parking lot of the gas station across the street, watching firefighters hack their way into the garage, extinguishing someone's car that had melted in the inferno. I watched them hose down a kitchen charred beyond repair and move systematically through the house to assess the damage. At the end of the driveway, my neighbors comforted the young woman who had left her car in their garage. At some point, I called a friend who lived a block away. At some point, I left my dog with her and spoke to my landlord and the fire marshal who determined when it was safe for me to re-enter my half of the house. I must have sifted through the debris and stuffed the cleanest clothes I could find into an overnight bag. I don't really remember any of that, though. I remember watching the smoke drift down the street, recalling the discomfort I had felt on the day I moved in. A guilty ache settled in my stomach, as if my body had tried to warn me—as if I had heard its warning and accepted this day as fate.

I have spent so much time residing in unsettling spaces that I have difficulty expecting or seeking comfort in the places where I live. I have moved every one to two years since age eighteen. In college, it was just in and out of the dorms each year and to wherever I had a summer job or internship. After graduation, I briefly shared a Brooklyn sublet with bedbugs and occasional rodents. In graduate school, the one time I lived alone was in a basement studio, where I trapped mice in the kitchen by chasing them down with oversized bags and releasing them in the woods behind the house. I moved from that studio to a condo with two undergraduate students. At twenty-nine years old, I came home to a fraternity party in full swing, a bathroom covered in vomit, and my own towels having been used to sop up regurgitated beer. The duplex in Arkansas seemed like a natural progression from these spaces—right down to the Confederate flag that appeared in a neighbor's window the week I moved in. I had learned to accept "home" as a space of unease. I had also learned discomfort as my natural habitat.

Having explored in previous chapters archives as sites of meaning-making, I propose here that the body, too, is an archive—that we carry with us our experiences and the stories we are given. We exceed them, too, but these are the materials from which we build our worldviews. For months after the morning that Tali (the dog) and I fled our duplex, I found myself sitting near the exit of every room. Four years later, the smell of smoke still sends my pulse into a sprint. Even Tali, who never minded sirens before, now whimpers when fire trucks charge by our house. I propose that these memories are cataloged in the responses of our bodies—in the dog's tremble; in the tightness of my shoulders; in the panic storming my chest when I leap from bed in the middle of the night. Four years after the fire, I still wake to the phantom smell of smoke. Each time, I search the house for evidence—as if the fire were an intruder crouched in the shadows. The house is still, though. The air is clear. I return to the bedroom, where the only sound is my partner's steady, untroubled breathing.

The fire is an easy example—a direct line from disruptive experience to sleepless nights. Following that thread, I can feel its connections to my other experiences of home—to my habituation to unease, learning not only to accept but to *expect* discomfort in my places of residence. The fact that I had never known "home" as a place that was mine—that I never felt authorized to paint the walls, claim peace or silence, or take up space—had inured me to the disregard of my neighbors. How far and wide can we follow those threads, though? How much of my complacency was trained through the teachings of Asian femininity—how we are taught to hold ourselves and behave long before we are capable of critical distance or analysis? How much of my complacency is survival—how we learn to subtract comfort from safety; to reserve our crip energies when trying to work at the pace of a capitalist consumption; to find the limits of what we can live with in order to keep living?

How far back can we trace these threads—to my parents' own trainings in Confucian ethics? To their parents' experiences of nation as an unstable, precarious thing that is lost and won by force? How much is enabled by colonial narratives that caution migrants, people of color, queers, and disabled folks that our lives are always contingent and precarious? How many of our decisions are shaped by the knowledge that violations of our behavioral imperatives are punishable by deportation, imprisonment, or murder? How do these connections entangle us—indebt us—to people who have risked more and lost more than we have to combat these mechanisms of violence? The connections we find through our mappings will be incomplete and muddled with our own complicities, biases, and predilections, but the telescopic view—the constellation offered by our piecemeal sketches—stretches closer to a more comprehensive understanding of our mutual entanglements.

On Love

// My mom's acceptance of me is not about her going to a meeting, it's not about her going to march in a parade, it's not about her having to tell other people that she has a queer daughter. It's that she put [my] books up [beside] my dad and grandmother and it's about our family heritage. It's about letting my ancestors know . . . that you should know this about your daughter [. . .] Having the altar, which she totally believes in—that's going to mean something to her, that is where I can understand that she loves me, that she has unconditional love for me even if she doesn't believe in gay marriage. You know what? Okay, I can live with that contradiction.
    —Alice Y. Hom, Dragon Fruit Project[4] //

Unlike Alice Hom, I am not the first member of my family to earn a PhD. I came in second behind my father. I never know where to begin with stories of my parents, so perhaps I'll start here: in the dingy apartment behind Arizona State University, where my parents built a home from a graduate student's stipend. In this sunless kitchen, my mother made epicurean meals from ramen and bok choy. Here, she once baked egg tarts from scratch for my entire kindergarten class. She called them "egg towers," which is a literal translation of their Chinese name.

Unlike me, my father did not become an academic. He was discouraged from doing so because of his accent; they presumed American students would never understand him. I do not remember my parents' accents as particularly thick, but I do remember having to translate for them in restaurants and doctors' offices. I remember thinking even then that this had less to do with how they spoke than with how people listened. Instead of teaching, my dad found

---

4. Hom, [166].

a stable job as an engineer. He kept that position for his entire career, earning a steady salary while my mother went back to school, while I decided I would not become a doctor, or a lawyer, while I called home from college to tell them that I wanted to tell stories for a living.

I want to tell you about the three of us discovering the American Southwest—going hiking in Sedona and horseback riding in Payson. I want to tell you about the seven-hour drives we took just to visit L.A.'s Chinatown, and about the nostalgia that filled my parents' voices when they told me about Taiwanese bakeries and night markets and their brothers and sisters and parents, who all still live on the island. I want to tell you about my mother's culinary genius and the Asian American fusion of her chorizo fried rice and adzuki bean turnovers. I want you to see me running out to meet my dad in the evenings, when he biked home from his classes at ASU. I want you to see us—me riding on his handlebars, both of us spinning circles in a parking lot, watching the desert sky burn to dusk.

Any story I tell will be only a partial truth, so I want to start with these shards of memory: See my father building the first piece of furniture for my bedroom—a sturdy wooden shelf that will first hold knockoff Lincoln Logs and stuffed animals and eventually fantasy novels and SAT workbooks. See my mother emptying her purse for quarters so that she can win me a stubby, stuffed alligator that I sleep beside for years. See us move to the suburbs, grill steaks in the backyard, and then stir-fry leftover sirloin with broccoli and eggplant. See us laugh and cry and hurt and learn to till this arid soil. See, this is where I begin: with love and its many imperfections.

// I grew up in a very old world, old school immigrant family, where telling their children "I love you" is just not done.
—Alice Y. Hom[5] //

As I recall it, the aching heart of every conflict I had with my parents was family—the unsteady earth on which we found little common ground. At first, we fought about typical things (or what I imagine as typical)—the tone I took; the tidiness of my room. Over time, these arguments became freighted with everything we could not say. The fights about the dress I would not wear were also about the gender comportment we could not name. Their relentless enforcement of girlish norms was about the world that would punish me for gender illegibility. My outrage was about my body being taken from me—the way I forgot how to stand, how to hold my limbs when vested for a role I

---

5. Hom.

could not play. We were fighting about how my parents had dreamt for me a life easier than theirs, and about the dreams I could feel but not yet name.

Without words for our longings or fears, my parents and I lashed out in the coarse vocabularies we had. I don't know if there is a way to write these scenes without the specters of migrant and queer clichés: intergenerational conflict; cultural dissonance; the clumsiness of words that could not fill the shape of our wounds. If you're going to see me in a pattern, try to see the whole of it. See that only half of trans folks have all their immediate family members in their lives—that of those who come out to their families, nearly half experience a form of rejection including refusal of their gender identity, attempted conversion therapy, and/or expulsion from their family home. See that 40 percent of homeless youth identify as LGBTQ+. See the crushing disproportionality of homelessness and poverty among people of color and disabled folks. See their structured neglect and abuse in educational, employment, and health care settings.[6] See this richest country in the world—where my parents staked their dreams—abandoning those who do not play by its rules.

"No one in Taiwan was . . . like that," my mom said, years after I came out to her—after we started talking *around* queerness, though not about it. I assumed that she was mistaken; queers are everywhere. I wanted to tell her that neither she nor my father had friends or family who felt safe enough to come out to them. Another version of that story, though, is that *I* was the first person in their lives with enough security and comfort to try on and discard sexual and gender identities. My parents were born into and raised entirely in a country governed by martial law. Under this regime, which taught Confucian "family values" as the foundation of moral education, homosexuals and gender-transgressors could be and were arrested for "violating the natural order" or "good mores."[7] Public discourse made very little mention of homosexuality, and many Taiwanese physicians, compressing ableism and homophobia, viewed same-sex attraction as mental illness produced by troubled adolescence. This was the definition my mother gave me when I was a child—the only explanation I had for the first stirrings of a desire I could not name.

I should emphasize that, too—that in the US, even decades and oceans removed from my parents' upbringing, I also did not know any openly LGBTQ+ people until age sixteen. A friend asked me over the phone before confessing that he, too, was gay. As far as we knew, we were the first queer

6. Grant et al., *Injustice at Every Turn.*
7. Damm, "Same Sex Desire and Society in Taiwan, 1970–1987," 69, 75.

people one another had met in person. We were both only children of Asian migrants, trying to reconcile what we knew about ourselves with the security our parents had wanted for us. We spent a night whispering our truths over the phone, trying on new words like new wardrobes, practicing names for who we were and could become.

Before that night, the only story of a real-life queer person I'd known was that of Matthew Shepard. News anchors recounted his slow, merciless death as the camera panned over the fence rails where he had spent his last conscious hours. The dizzy dread that churned inside me was perhaps one of the first confirmations of what I was. This wasn't just a story about a distant tragedy but a referendum on what I was: something punishable by unthinkable violence. I wonder whether stories like this were also my mother's first introductions to queerness. I wonder what I would do to shield my child from that possibility. How do I explain anti-assimilation to someone who gave her homeland for the promise of my belonging? We aren't absolved of our choices, but can we view the choices in context? Can we acknowledge that the choices, too, are bound by constellations of precarity and privilege?

// *Difference is that raw and powerful connection from which our personal power is forged.*
　—Audre Lorde[8] //

There is a night I think of as a point of rupture in our familial unit and the strained peace we had held for eighteen years. I was preparing to leave for college—1,800 miles away, which was as far as I could get on scholarship money. My parents wanted to spend the summer in Taiwan. They knew better than I did that college and early adulthood would rob me of the time and resources to return. I knew, though, that these were the last months I had to spend with the close-knit group of misfits I had come to know as kin. My parents and I were fighting about the different communities in whom we had invested our time and care. We were also fighting about, but not talking about, the past year I had spent sneaking out and staying out with the girlfriend I could not name. In the end, I refused to go to Taiwan. I refused to see my parents' own aging parents. Because they stayed in the US with me, I also denied them that time with their loved ones—our homes split across seven thousand miles.

That was the problem, of course—that I saw our Taiwanese family as my *parents'* siblings and nieces and nephews. To me, they were people I had met only a handful of times, who often spoke to my parents about me as if I were

---

8. Lorde, "The Master's Tools Will Never Dismantle the Master's House," 95.

not in the room. Mandarin was my first language—my only language until my mother dropped me off at preschool—but my relatives had always referred to me as "the American." Naming is power, and that designation became prophecy as I distanced myself from my mother's tongue, as I gradually let slip the language I used to speak and write and dream in. By the time I was eighteen, I felt I had little to do with the distant world of my parents' birth. By association, it seemed, my parents felt I had little to do with them.

We argued as if this one decision were at issue—this one trip to Taiwan. Behind the words, though, was the heft of everything we had not said. While I now have the privilege to think of "queer" as one of my many identificatory traits, the weight of its secret at the time made it feel defining. It was who I was at the expense of everything else. My parents had spent my lifetime pressing me, with increasing desperation, to adopt any of the traditional accessories of femininity—not because dresses or makeup were especially important to them, but because they had only stereotypes from which to draw their knowledge of queer existence and were looking for any sign that I could be "normal." We never said it. I did not even know the words for *queer* in Chinese, but the specter behind all our conflicts was the friction of our desires in a world that persecutes deviance.

After my mother and I said too many things we could never take back, my father separated us into different rooms. It is the only time I remember him playing peacemaker. Through the wall, my father said something that I cannot recall. My mother's response, though, I can still hear, torn from her throat like the words of a woman drowning: "If the daughter I have is not who I thought she was, I'd rather not have a daughter at all." With the wisdom of retrospection, I can hear a mother's hope that her child is not as alien and unreachable as they seem. In the moment, though, I could only think that I was definitely *not* the daughter she thought I was—that we were already unintelligible to one another.

There is a version of my story that is about how my traditionalist parents needed to shed their "old world" values to love their queer child. This story presumes Western progressivism will liberate backward Eastern countries. It is a story I believed as I packed eighteen years of unreflective anger into my college suitcase, fleeing 1,800 miles across appropriately scorched earth. As I wandered the expanse of this country, however, I found myself reaching for grounding in old familiarities. In Houston, my roommates and I drove weekly to Chinatown, where we stockpiled childhood snacks that we had once abandoned for pantry goods at Target. In New York City at Lunar New Year, I walked with my partner from Canal Street to East Broadway, winding through sidewalks lined with red lanterns and paper cuttings, trying to recall our early lessons in Mandarin. I did not realize until later how fortunate I was to have grown up in environments bustling with diversity. These spaces are far from perfect, of course, but I had lived in some of the most populous and racially variegated cities in the country. My high school and college (though also not perfect) were both minority-majority. I'd always had access to Chinatowns and Chinese schools. My childhood friends came from households that spoke Vietnamese, Thai, Cambodian, Japanese, Korean, French, German, Spanish, and variations of world Englishes. Until I no longer had access to such vibrant heterogeneity, I didn't understand what a privilege it was to have spent my life surrounded by difference—what a gift to have always known it as a strength.

// I was finding my place in US history and the American narrative through Asian American studies. Through the curriculum that reflected my and my family's experience, my friends' experiences, my community's experiences.
—Alice Y. Hom[9] //

In both of her interviews with the Dragon Fruit Project, Alice Hom acknowledges *This Bridge Called My Back* as a landmark text that brought her to women of color and, eventually, to Asian American feminism. For me, this book was also an awakening—and a humbling encounter with my betrayals. The essays in *This Bridge,* written seven years before my birth, mapped a history to which I already belonged and had abandoned. These essays spoke "a language I knew—in the deepest parts of me—existed."[10] Late in my graduate studies—already drafting my dissertation—I was stricken by Cherríe Moraga's confession that "I had disowned the language I knew best—ignored the words and rhythms that were the closest to me."[11] Like many before me, I had once resisted the unwieldy vocabularies of my seminars—the stiff rhythms of journal articles, and the detached scrutiny with which researchers talked about people who looked and lived like me. Like many before me, too, I studied and lived in those rhythms until they became the backbeat to my own thoughts. Gloria Anzaldúa says it better: "*I have not yet unlearned the esoteric bullshit and pseudo-intellectualizing that school brainwashed into my writing.*"[12] With the guidance of her comadres, I am trying to hear my own heartbeat again—to trust that it also derives from melodies with much deeper histories than mine. I am finding places and people who will move with me at cadences attuned to my body.

---

9. Hom, [169].
10. Moraga, "La Güera," 26.
11. Moraga, 26.
12. Anzaldúa, "Speaking in Tongues," 163.

The authors of *This Bridge* reminded me that I had been drawn to writing for its intractability—its wild imagination. While the essays of *This Bridge* are often discussed as if they *document* a momentous transformation in academic practice, they were also a means of that change. Editors Gloria Anzaldúa and Cherríe Moraga called for a "theory in the flesh" that makes knowledge of our experiences, forging a "politic born out of necessity"[13] from the physical realities of marginalized peoples. This writing exposed knowledges that academic conventions were made to conceal—the exploitation of Black and brown peoples; the denigration of nonwhite cultural forms; and the abuse and isolation of "unfit" scholars and students in these institutional spaces. Writing in *un*disciplined (or, as Anzaldúa says, untamed) tongues, contributors to *This Bridge* refused "easy explanation[s for] the conditions we live in."[14] Instead, they roved through experience's excess to capture the elisions of traditional "research." Their position on the frontera provided particular insight into the friction and feracity of borderlands, where "the lifeblood of two worlds merg[e]."[15] While the border itself is a dividing line—a cut between the sanctioned and the profane—a border*land* is the world made in spaces in between. In this "vague and undetermined place,"[16] the authors of *This Bridge* claimed their power. This collection was, then, more than a reminder of my dormant faith in the inventive potential of writing; it was proof that such worldmaking was possible.

In the final stretch of my formal schooling, my work pivoted toward the possibilities imagined by writers of color who refused to bury their difference. ("*They'd like to think I have melted in the pot. But I haven't, we haven't.*"[17]). In fact, their insistence on their unique standpoints exposed the limited vocabularies at use for identity and belonging. To be bridges across difference, these Third World feminists became aware of and responsive to the ways they move among different vectors of power. Exploring intragroup differences, they also highlighted the heterogeneity of categories like *queer* or *women of color*—not as facile models of diversity but as strategic coalitions that require ongoing dialogue, reflection, and mutual respect.

With guilty revelation, I read Cherríe Moraga's confrontations with privilege, "both when it worked against me, and when I worked [with] it, ignorantly, at the expense of others."[18] Like Moraga, I was given a sturdier

---

13. Moraga and Anzaldúa, *This Bridge Called My Back,* 19.
14. Moraga and Anzaldúa, 19.
15. Anzaldúa, *Borderlands,* 25.
16. Moraga and Anzaldúa, *This Bridge Called My Back,* 25.
17. Anzaldúa, *Borderlands,* 108.
18. Moraga, "La Güera," 29.

foundation than generations before me and wore my education with "a keen sense of pride and satisfaction."[19] Educational institutions, though, were made not to dismantle structured discrimination but to absorb the Other into existing arrangements. I could not see the limitations of formal schooling so long as I kept my head down and did as I was told. From within this established territory—this conquered land—I could not see that whiteness, heteronormativity, ableism, and gender binaries were not the actual norm but standards contrived to naturalize white dominance. Moraga's words spotlighted my silence (and my lack of curiosity!) as complicity. How had I not known or even hoped that other worlds were possible?

I am far from the first writer of color to make this discovery. Had I the wisdom to seek out *This Bridge* sooner, I would have read Mitsuye Yamada's resonant experience when she stopped playing "the submissive, subservient, ready-to-please, easy-to-get-along-with Asian woman."[20] This is the bind of Asian belonging in white spaces, a story much older than the term *Asian American*: we are tolerated, even necessary, as passive accessories to anti-Indigeneity and anti-Blackness. Stepping out of this role, however, is also to abandon its tenuous shelter. Like Yamada, I found the limits of my protections when I broke from racialized gender norms. While it was fine for me to be, theoretically, (gender)queer and Asian American and disabled, it was not okay for my histories, my body, and my needs to affect our professional spaces. The model minority is inseparable from yellow peril; when we refuse to endorse hegemonic norms, we threaten them.

// I write to record what others erase when I speak, to rewrite the stories others have miswritten about me, about you. [. . .] To convince myself that I am worthy and that what I have to say is not a pile of shit.
—Gloria Anzaldúa[21] //

The stories from *This Bridge* put words to the unease I had felt but never been able to name. They charted the vast network of (largely unspoken) bodily and behavioral expectations that govern safety in public spaces—insight that could not have come from the analytical methods that created those spaces. Among the important legacies of *This Bridge* is this insistence—and proof—that our knowledge matters. The strategies that trans and queer people of color cultivate for our own and one another's survival—the ways we learn to map institutional power; to redraw our trajectories of love, resilience, and

---

19. Moraga, 23.
20. Yamada, "Invisibility Is an Unnatural Disaster," 32.
21. Anzaldúa, "Speaking in Tongues," 167.

ancestry; and to tell our truths despite repression and gaslighting—are worthy of attention. These perspectives have value not just for fellow *kuaers,* who cross the bounds of white respectability, but also in the broader project of envisioning more compassionate, more equitable ways of co-existing. Building shared knowledge from the specificity of their experiences, the authors of *This Bridge* insist that social architectures *must* be evaluated and revised by those they were made to exclude—those with vantage points from which to see the system's barriers and fractures.

These were critiques my parents had always made, without a background in critical theory or decolonial studies. When I was a kid, they pointed to Eurocentric and Orientalist threads throughout the media I enjoyed, but I dismissed their opinions as vestiges of their traditionalism. Having been born into and steeped in these narratives, I lacked their perspective—the global and historical positioning that gave them a better view of Western mythmaking. Taiwan's history is a series of outside incursions—dubbed by historian Arif Dirlik as "the land colonialisms made."[22] Originally home to numerous Austronesian tribes—sixteen of which are now recognized by the Taiwanese government—the island was subjected to Dutch and Spanish occupation, then the House of Koxinga, followed by Manchu (Qing dynasty) control. The Qing ceded Taiwan to fifty years of Japanese colonization, which was replaced by the Chinese Nationalist Party (KMT), which imposed martial law from 1947 to 1987. Because it has been traded as the spoils of war, Taiwan experienced these regime changes with no input from the actual inhabitants of the island—primarily Austronesians and the overwhelming influx of Hoklo and Hakka people of Han descent. These communities were more likely to identify with their ethnic or tribal affiliations than with Taiwan itself. Like "Asian American," Taiwanese is an aggregative identity that collapses intragroup conflict, vast experiential disparities, and still a tentative (or sometimes reluctant) optimism about the power of collectivity.

Before all these invasions, Taiwan was quite likely the originary site of Austronesian migration.[23] The island remains home to the greatest diversity of Austronesian languages, seventeen of which survive today and nine of which are exclusive to Taiwan. In recent decades, grassroots Indigenous movements have gathered momentum and attracted public attention, precipitating significant developments such as the establishment of the Council of Indigenous Affairs and the passage of the Basic Laws of Indigenous Peoples.[24] Still, reso-

---

22. Dirlik, "Taiwan."

23. Diamond, "Taiwan's Gift to the World"; Bellwood, *First Farmers.*

24. Huang and Liu, "Discrimination and Incorporation of Taiwanese Indigenous Austronesian Peoples."

nant with the colonial legacies of the US, the first peoples of Taiwan continue to experience disparate health outcomes—undoubtedly tied to structures that limit access to education, health care, and employment.[25] Debate continues among Indigenous leaders about whether to pursue a route of parallel governance—that is, gradual disassociation from Han institutions by establishing separate educational, judiciary, legislative, and representative bodies—or to mobilize toward greater autonomy and influence within dominant (and dominating) structures.

As recent movements toward "Taiwanization" strengthen support for Taiwan independence, these questions complicate the development of a cohesive national identity. The island's rapidly growing democracy has garnered frequent praise in English-language press, but this democracy is still quite young, having yet to surpass the thirty-eight years of martial law that preceded it. It has yet to contend with the meaning of *Taiwanese* after the rapid succession of colonial regimes that both exacerbated and muddied interethnic divisions. The "Four Great Ethnic Groups" of Taiwan—the Austronesians, Hoklo, Hakka, and Mainlanders who arrived with and after the KMT—carry among them centuries of conquest, betrayal, and distrust. As the island remains neglected in global politics, though, often regarded as a bargaining chip between the US and China, its inhabitants have also grappled with the urgent need to assert a vision for the land with which they live.

Growing up half a world away, I did not know any of this. My family members are, in their own words, private people, who do not often share personal stories. However, the fact that I did not learn even their general histories until adulthood is also damning evidence of where my interests lay. I distanced myself from most things Taiwanese, associating them with "old world" values I was desperate to leave behind. The more my education widened the rift between who I was and where I came from, the more I relegated my family of birth to the backward worldviews that Western researchers have traditionally assigned to Other cultures.

Because White people were my guide into queerness, I mistook gender diversity as a Western invention. I wonder whether my parents did as well (*"No one was 'like that.'"*). Before graduate school, my first encounters with queer worlds had been through whitestream media. Lesbian identity was defined by Ellen DeGeneres and the cast of *The L Word*. Queer angst was soothed by Melissa Etheridge's raspy vocals and the Indigo Girls' crisp harmonies. Even when I discovered queerness as a field of study, it was an intellectual terrain mapped by Judith Butler and Michel Foucault. I learned definitions of femi-

---

25. Huang and Liu.

nism and queerness that would never accommodate my experiences of gender or sexuality, and when I could not fit their words to the contours of my story, I assumed it was my fault.

// [Find] the voice that lies buried under you, dig it up. Do not fake it, try to sell it for a handclap or your name in print.
  —Gloria Anzaldúa[26] //

Let me try this story again. Let me place it in constellation. My mother's parents grew up in the Taiwanese underclass governed by Japanese empire. My mom's father, the youngest son of a poor family, missed out on early education when he was drafted to work in a child labor camp in Japan. While her mother was born into better economic fortune, she was also denied an education by her traditionalist family, who believed women should tend to the home. This, my mother has often said, was one of my grandmother's great regrets. In Mandarin, they are considered 本省人 (literally, *this province people*), whose family lineage is rooted in Taiwan for as long as anyone can recall. This term masks complex histories of enmity, alliances, betrayal, and miscegenation that shaped centuries of Han Chinese movement onto Austronesian land.

Over the centuries, Han settlers included merchants, soldiers, tradesmen, and farmers; laborers recruited by the Dutch East India Company; administrators of Qing prefectures and their opposition; and still others. Solidarities and identifications were at times drawn along ethnic lines but often also along familial or interpersonal intimacies, class solidarities, or places of origin.[27] Each new political regime reshuffled the relationships among Hoklo, Hakka, and Austronesians (including many subgroups split between "plains" or "mountain" aborigines). With high rates of intermarriage and colonial taxonomies that did not account for mixed households, families might have identified as "Han" or "Aborigine" depending on which label was available to them and whether it carried more freedoms at the time.[28] To expedite Indigenous assimilation and erasure, Japanese and KMT policies also sometimes eliminated the classification of Aborigine altogether. My family's particular place in these events, along with much of Taiwanese history, is difficult to discern within formal accounts actively rewritten by a succession of colonial

---

26. Anzaldúa, "Speaking in Tongues," 171.
27. Brown, *Is Taiwan Chinese?*
28. Lin, "I Choose to Stand With Taiwan's Indigenous Peoples."

regimes.[29] Taiwan's diplomatic isolation amid the neocolonial tactics of US–China power relations, too, has left it ignored by many English-language historians and cultural critics—the only language in which I am equipped to study these histories.[30]

In contrast to my mother's side, my father's pathway to Taiwan is much easier to pin down. My dad is the youngest son of an army officer for the KMT. He and his brothers were their family's first generation born in Taiwan, after the Nationalist Party retreated to the island and seized political power—simultaneously refugees, exiles, and colonizers. In Taiwan these people are called 外省人 (*outside province people*) to distinguish those who arrived with the KMT after 1949 and the uneven privileges they were afforded under martial law. "Our families did not support us being together" was all my mom said of it. I filled in the blanks by listening for deeper histories, mapping the chronology of our bloodline onto narratives I read in translation. After my parents met, though, several of my mom's sisters also married across political lines, and most of my father's family have by now withdrawn their support of the party despite its overwhelming influence on their childhoods. My parents and aunts and uncles join Taiwan's long and convoluted history of intermixing—of seemingly irreconcilable peoples who grew up on the same land and saw their futures aligned.

The simultaneous mundanity and rapidity of this shift awes me: a few generations of children grew up alongside one another, learning one another's languages, and falling in and out of love with one another. They established affective ties that would necessitate new social and political configurations. Lee Teng-hui, the first KMT president born in Taiwan, who himself grew up under Japanese colonialism, led efforts to eliminate the laws that his own party used to suspend democratic functions. His campaigns enabled the first democratic election on the island, after which he was re-elected to become the first president chosen by popular vote. His successor was then the first president from the Democratic Progressive Party, effectively ending the KMT's fifty-five years of continuous control and ushering in Taiwan's first peaceful transition of power. These events are shot through with bitter contestations, lingering controversies, and partisan divisions, but I cannot help also seeing the force of intimacy in the island's rapid transformation. If love is a plot we give to desire, Taiwan's recent political transformations are stories made by new attachments and the worlds they need to flourish.

---

29. Chun, "From Nationalism to Nationalizing"; Jacobs, "The History of Taiwan"; Wang, "Affective Rearticulations."

30. Chun, "Democracy as Hegemony"; Wang, "Affective Rearticulations"; Storm, *Connecting Taiwan.*

In the past few decades, Taiwan has experienced a surge in youth-led activism, sparking long-overdue conversations about what Taiwanese identity should be, and how its people can reconcile the many layers of oppression and resistance they inherit. These young people, who have only ever known this island as home, have been integral to pivoting Taiwan politics away from the KMT's One-China Principle. Lee's political reforms were expedited by the Wild Lily student movement, which staged a six-day demonstration for democratic reform. Their actions foretold the Sunflower Movement of 2014—a mass mobilization against a KMT-backed trade agreement that would have made Taiwan more vulnerable to Beijing's control. Their occupation of the legislature, amid the West's growing concern about Chinese influence, managed to draw global attention to Taiwan.

This moment, often acknowledged as a generation's political awakening, also exemplifies the potential and pitfalls of interethnic alliances. Indigenous students were on the front lines of the Sunflower Movement, among the first to break into and occupy the legislature. Street events throughout the occupation included Indigenous concerns.[31] Still, they received less media coverage, and little mainstream discussion has explored how Indigenous causes differ from those of their Han allies. While many Han Taiwanese were moved to protest by the government's betrayal—or more broadly by the history of suppression under the KMT—Austronesians have a much longer history of maltreatment and active persecution on their own land. After the KMT was pushed from office, some Sunflower participants formed third parties that have thrown their weight behind recent elected officials. While their ability to shift Taiwanese politics may seem like a win for the Han majority, these developments do little for Austronesians working toward autonomous conservation of their histories and cultures. In other words, intimacy is inseparable from history—our connections will only hold when they are accountable to the unequal lineages that carried us here.

Grappling with these responsibilities, Taiwan's nascent conversations are incomplete and imperfect, with both significant promise and quite likely future betrayals. Prominent pro-independence leaders have, along with leaders of Indigenous rights movements, continued to highlight resonances among their causes. They aspire to an independent Taiwan that can, in the words of Sunflower Movement leader Lin Fei-fan, "understand, confront, and revise the relationship between the state and all the people of this land—especially the original people of this land."[32] In Lin's priorities are the recognition

---

31. Ho, *Challenging Beijing's Mandate of Heaven,* 160.
32. Lin, "I Choose to Stand With Taiwan's Indigenous Peoples."

that a world beyond empire requires Indigenous knowledge and leadership—which by nature models ways of living and thriving outside of colonial and imperial domination. The search for a Taiwanese togetherness-in-difference postulates homing as an interminable, relational process—constellating our shards of memory with the peoples affected by those histories, and the futures we can cobble from these fragments of sky. Taiwan's experiments in democracy-building are filled with missteps, and the island is far from the democratic "miracle"[33] that the West would believe, but these emerging movements have also taught a new generation the power of organizing and civic contestation—have proved that listening and building across difference can tip the scales of power.

No matter how much I research, whatever I write about Taiwanese history and politics will be from a remove. I have to read the reports in translation, or very slowly with my clumsy second-grade literacy. I have to compare news accounts, critical analyses, and social media posts with the stories my family gives me—undoubtedly shaded by their own political affiliations and personal histories. My father's father fought and waged war for the regime that conquered my mother's homeland, which was already conquered, already colonized, and already didn't belong to her or our people, though her ancestors have been on the island for too long and with too much external violence and erasure to know where else they belong. My bloodlines have moved too far too quickly for me to tell you where I am "really from." I do not have an argument to make or a conclusion to draw from this. I am telling these stories to map some other means of belonging, to forge a place in the world that is not just a passive recipient of violent histories. I am trying to find connection, if not healing, in harm that cannot be undone.

// Throw away abstraction and the academic learning, the rules, the map and compass. Feel your way without blinders.
—Gloria Anzaldúa[34] //

For most of my life, the obvious chasms between my parents' perspectives and my own convinced me that their histories were irrelevant to my life and worldview. The further I venture into these narratives, though, the more my own journey seems inextricably bound to theirs. I come from three generations who have experienced language as the medium through which knowledge is accessed, controlled, and challenged. My mother's parents attended

---

33. Chun, "Democracy as Hegemony."
34. Anzaldúa, "Speaking in Tongues," 171.

segregated schools designed for a segregated workforce, where Taiwanese children were taught Japanese language and morals—the 修身 or "shushin" that William Petersen celebrates in his account of Japanese Americans' "success story."[35] My mother attended schools under KMT oversight, which changed the national language overnight from Japanese to Mandarin. Both languages are mutually unintelligible to the Hokkien that my mother's family spoke at home. Like the Japanese officials, the KMT filled the curricula with a curated version of history and with its own moral education, this time based in Confucian principles and staunchly heteropatriarchal ethics.

The trajectory that carried me away from their house was undeniably influenced by their early lessons on language and education as power. I saw writing and deep study as a means of exploring cultural conflict, marginalization, and myriad forms of everyday harm that go unacknowledged. Despite my better efforts, I have internalized the "immigrant work ethic" that my parents championed—a disposition that helped me not because "working hard" is a panacea but because my parents migrated to the US when the model minority myth became politically expedient. As a child, I had the benefit of an educational system that encouraged my success and rewarded my ability to play the diligent student. The privileges and complicities I inherited enabled my life trajectory, through which I learned to diminish the insights of my ancestries.

It was also writing that brought me back to my parents' house—to see this place, too, as a site of family. Scholar-activists such as Gloria Anzaldúa and Alice Hom provided models for sitting with the incongruencies of queer diaspora. They taught me to deconstruct the "frames and metaframes"[36] that earned me a place as an "academic writer" but cut me from my bloodlines—biological and forged. It would be too simple (and condescending) to say that my parents were simply products of their cultures—to say that they had learned queerness as precarity and were only trying to save me from that fate. It would be reductive, too, to say that queer pop culture and intellectualism convinced me of Western progress. The truth is that my parents worried for me *and* believed and perpetuated homophobia. The truth is that I subscribed to narratives of Asian inferiority long before I found solace in lesbian sitcoms and melodrama. My parents and I have hurt one another in ways deliberate and passive. We are moved by larger cultural currents, but we also are not helpless within them. We have learned to listen better to and to grow with one another, even as we continue to disappoint and fail one another. My mother has, it turns out, kept me in her life without having a daughter at all.

35. Petersen, "Success Story, Japanese-American Style."
36. Anzaldúa, "Speaking in Tongues," 165.

I have come to *"live with that contradiction,"* as best I can—through and in dialogue with the stories of Alice Hom, Gloria Anzaldúa, and the many narrators whose voices precede and accompany theirs.

On Resilience

// every survivor is splendor
every spoon is sacred.
every cough is an altar on the bend of ribcage.
every cane is a drum calling into the earth.
[...]
when your bodies are carnal waves collapsing.
Remember: together we can find the shore.
  —Kay Ulanday Barrett[37] //

I have this poem saved in the photo album of my phone. I have carried it with me to the emergency room—held it in my palm like a prayer. My family was never devoutly religious, but we spent time in Buddhist temples when I was younger. I learned to meditate—to chant "amituofo" as I passed mala beads through my fingers. I never kept with the practice, but it finds me in moments of desperation. I can almost feel the sandalwood when I hold Kay's words on my tongue, each word a bead, each line a borrowed breath, each verse a glimpse of the distant shore.

When I became sick—when I learned sick as something I *am* rather than as a passing condition—I lost a third of my body mass in three months. It was so quick that it felt like an ambush—like my body being burgled in the night. I remember less a gradual change than waking one day to discover that I inhabited a cage of bones that could not move or sit or stand without aching. I remember a lot of tiredness and cold. I remember loss—of energy, of stability, of so many relationships that could not span the distance of my pain. I remember that it was the first time anyone told me that I looked like my mother. I remember seeing the gaunt face of a stranger in the mirror and finding in it my mother's cheekbones, her slender neck. I remember wondering if this was the price of femininity.

Since then, I have spent twelve years cycling through doctors, medications, and (mis)diagnoses. With luck and privilege, I completed a PhD; started a tenure-track job; adopted two dogs; met and moved in with my beautiful, gen-

---

37. Barrett, "To Be Underwater & Holy."

erous partner; found joy, community, and conflict in weightlifting and combat sports and other sites of physical culture; and continue to migrate unpredictably across the spectrum of (un)wellness. I survived, not by individual fortitude but by having access to people, goals, and stories that I wanted to move toward—and having the means to get there.

Disabled writers, trans and queer writers, and writers of color taught me to envision futures worth the pain of tomorrow. Eli Clare exposed diagnoses as ideologically laden rhetorics;[38] José Esteban Muñoz provided utopic futures;[39] Dean Spade identified the "administrative violence" of medical, educational, and other institutions;[40] Alison Kafer modeled ways of "yearning for an elsewhere" or an "elsewhen" in which disability is understood as political, valuable, and integral;[41] and of course Audre Lorde provided a litany for we who "were never meant to survive."[42] For me, the writings of these scholar-activists are more than citations. They are traveling companions—in the words of Sara Ahmed, they are texts "whose company enabled you to proceed on a path less trodden."[43] These companions gave me permission to step off the paths I was given—to believe in the possibility of new roads and more promising destinations.

Creating such possibilities is ultimately the work of storytelling—of inventing new plots for unsanctioned desires. Shahd Alshammari recalls the need to "recreate a new life narrative" when "what works for the majority" pushed her to believe she was failing.[44] Disability studies and gender studies helped her compose a new definition of the good life, as these fields do for so many for whom oppression is not merely theoretical. Alshammari insists on such scholarship and education as "a necessary constituent of making sense of living in a different body."[45] Like Alshammari, I found in these disciplines analytical vocabularies that broadened the scope of my senses. I came to see, hear, and feel the ways that social and professional worlds are disabling—how my experience of my bodymind could not be separated from the environments in which it must move.

It's impossible to discuss—or experience—disability in academia without also noticing the profession's aversion to embodiment. Academics are envi-

---

38. Clare, *Brilliant Imperfection.*
39. Muñoz, *Cruising Utopia.*
40. Spade, *Normal Life.*
41. Kafer, *Feminist, Queer, Crip,* 3.
42. Lorde, "A Litany for Survival."
43. Ahmed, *Living a Feminist Life,* 16.
44. Alshammari, "On Survival and Education."
45. Alshammari.

sioned as floating brains, above the crude considerations of flesh and experience. To live in a body that cannot conform to the rhythms and spaces of public life, however, is also to understand bodies and their misalignments as co-constitutive with the conditions of public safety and comfort. The relentless schedules of full course loads, conference programs, and/or research institutes and university orientations presume mechanistic bodily efficiency—bodies that do not require rest, fresh air, movement, or other forms of stimulation; bodies that do not need to eat or shit or sleep; bodies without dependents; bodies made for production. In such spaces, those with less institutional power are also less likely to feel comfortable discussing their disability status. What if my advisor thinks I can't handle the work? What if my colleagues think they can't count on me? How will my supervisor frame this in my annual evaluation?

When even medical experts emphasize health as a matter of individual resilience, illness feels like a personal failing. When my body began to suffer, my brain assumed that it would get better; it knew only the stories it had been told—that sickness is temporary and healing is individual responsibility. I thought, surely, the next doctor or the next drug would help. When they didn't—when the next doctor and their next drugs made me sicker—I assumed it was my fault. I wasn't diligent enough with my own care. Perhaps it was all the late nights mainlining coffee, the student diet of frozen dinners and protein bars, or the stress I put myself through. Doctors lectured me on relaxing. Well-meaning friends recommended yoga or diet trends. As I tottered through tree pose and paleo, gluten-free, and ketogenic regimens, my body careened toward sickness.

As a queer trans nonbinary Asian American, I have also consciously and unconsciously imbibed narratives of immigrant toughness and masculine embodiment that continue to condition my responses to pain. This is the distance between having a *theory* of the oppression and having a *method* of excising it from my own behaviors and self-talk. My attachment to reductive notions of physical fortitude and intellectual productivity kept me silent through many years of sickness. I cannot help but remember the ways my own parents worked through illness and injury. I recall how they saved sick days so that they could care for family in Taiwan, could pay for my piano lessons, could tender our bloodline's past and future. I remember the Taiwanese dentist we visited in Phoenix—the way he extracted a loose molar from my mouth without anesthetic because "Asians are tougher than Americans." Like many who experience chronic pain, I wonder how strong I really am—how others would answer the unrelenting scream of their body—as if my capacity for suffering were a measure of my worth.

// The idea is that if we work hard enough, individually, we too can be successful.
What happens when you cannot be a brown laborer in physical productivity?
—Kay Ulanday Barrett[46] //

When I first became sick, I was twenty-one years old and I still believed in the cruel optimism of "cure." That was, after all, the logics of my world until this point. Like many kids with able-bodied privilege, I had gotten colds and stomach bugs and bad flus, but they always resolved. Even the severe asthma that plagued my early years had receded to an emergency inhaler that I now sometimes forget to refill. When the fatigue became pain became nausea became wildly erratic nervous and digestive systems, I believed I could work myself back to wellness. I tried every fad diet and took up a rigorous, likely counterproductive fitness routine. I was trying to discipline myself into yet another role I could not play.

At the time, I was working in New York, interning for a literary agency that paid in lunch and a Metro card. We were there for my then partner, an architecture student who had landed an internship with a prestigious firm. While she went to her better-compensated nine-to-five in the Financial District, I spent my day reading submissions from a slush pile. In the evenings, I biked from our Bed-Stuy apartment to Park Slope, where I waited tables at a hip new ramen joint owned by Australians. I was living on Tylenol and coffee. There was an espresso machine at the agency and I went through at least four cups a day—on top of the ones I drank before and during my restaurant shifts. I couldn't sleep anyway, so I also got up every morning to perform dumbbell circuits in our living room. At some point—a transition too gradual to notice and too sudden to prevent—I forgot what it felt like to feel rested, to feel warm, or to exist without pain. My world narrowed to the self-control it took to get from one minute to the next, from one job to the other, from bed to work and back again. That was all I had the energy for.

There's not enough space in this chapter to tell you about the relationship we demolished in the remaining months I spent in New York, though this story is incomplete without it. It was the sort of consuming romance made possible by teenage fearlessness (and foolishness). We were both only children of Asian migrant families, both drawn to big emotions and ambitious stories with unlikely heroes. Our corporeal and emotional vocabularies felt as effortless as the Chinglish we phased into when recounting childhood memories. She felt like the first person in the world with whom I wasn't speaking in translation. This was a relationship for which we both defied our parents—a

---

46. Leibowitz, "Dapper Crip."

gesture that held particular gravity for only children who anchored our parents to this continent. Our love was the line drawn in the sand; it was the vision of family we were willing to risk everything for. I had never been so certain of anything.

I had no precedent for understanding how pain cleaves away at you until you are fragments of inchoate, unbearable *feeling*. I was embarrassed by my suddenly volatile, fragile body. I was furious at its inadequacy. I was devastated every new morning when I was not magically on the mend. As if the problem would somehow evanesce through denial, I refused to discuss it with my partner or with my friends. I understood the betrayals of our bodies as private, impolite topics. I thought that to admit to them would be weakness and that weakness made me less deserving of anyone's love. As far as I remember, I consulted only one doctor in those months. None of the clinics in New York accepted my health insurance, so I took the train to New Jersey, fevered and half-delirious, to see a doctor who told me that I had caught a bad bug and needed rest. I missed my transfer on the way back and rode the R train down to Bay Ridge before turning around amid the shuffle of evening commuters. A month later, after I left the city altogether, the Architect called and told me she rode the subway end-to-end because she didn't want to return to the space we had built together.

By then, I was back in my parents' house, where I stayed for the few months between New York and the start of my graduate program. I should have been grateful for the time in my old bedroom, for the meals my mother tried to cook for me and that I failed to keep down, for the alarm in her eyes when I arrived in Phoenix a shadow of the child who had left for college. I might have appreciated this time to rebuild, but all I could hear when we talked was the relief in her voice when I told her I had left my best friend and the life we had dreamt together. Even the words tasted like bile as I recalled the many years my mother had spent insisting to me that I could walk away from the person I loved. I knew that my grief sounded to her like hope, like the possibility that I could now live a life of complacent heterosexuality. What I didn't know was how many other narratives orbited our own and the things we believed or could imagine.

My resentment came quickly to the surface, and the few months I spent at home were filled with mistrust and mutual damage. Pain is an accelerant. It cuts me down to the quick—the rawest version of myself. Especially in those early years, I was an open blade, all edges and folded steel. I know this is not everyone's reaction to pain—that others withdraw into themselves rather than brandishing their wounds. I hate that this is *me*, amplified, rather than illness. I can hear in my impatience my father's short temper—his sharp reactivity that terrified me as a child. Before I learned to curb my worst impulses, my anger burned through some of the strongest relationships that I had.

// I propose an analytic that builds from pain—my "critical" and "severe" pain—foregrounding an experience often considered the most unincorporable disability experience.
—Alyson Patsavas[47] //

My primary symptoms were all things whose severity or very existence are subjective: immobilizing fatigue, pain, full-body aches, nausea, and vertigo. Without physical symptoms apparent to outside observers, I was continually dismissed by doctors. I was in my early twenties, with an unremarkable medical history of asthma and occasionally low blood pressure. When I kept losing weight, I received lectures about energy balance and consuming enough calories. Exhaustion was expected of young adulthood. "You seem like the Type A sort," a doctor said in the first minute of our appointment. "You should try reducing your stress." I was told so often that I was fine that I wondered whether it was all "in my head." If your body screams and no one is listening, is it even real? Are you even here? I wanted a gaping wound. I wanted to gush viscera all over a hospital floor. I wanted to look like the emergency I could feel detonating beneath my ribs.

Without the response of medical providers and with all my most intimate relationships in disrepair, I obsessed over finding my own answer. I began reading medical journals between my actual studies. I joined a Cross-Fit gym, where the culture of hardline machismo fulfilled a fantasy I could not yet name. The version of me writing now is flabbergasted that I paid $100 a month for a Marine Corps veteran to yell at me while I threw myself at pull-up bars and barbells in a filthy gym. At that moment, though, it assuaged an unexamined need to feel strong in the most superficial senses of the word. It also fulfilled an expectation that I should be punished—that, for my inability to control my body, for the ways I (believed I had) disappointed or burdened my loved ones, for the ways I had squandered the opportunities given to me, I deserved the pain. I can see why personal resilience is such a seductive concept: even as the person in unexplained agony, I found it more comforting to believe there was a reason—that I was somehow responsible and could thus *take responsibility* for its resolution.

Unexplained, but not inexplicable agony. It wasn't cure that saved me, but crip epistemologies. It was Kay Ulanday Barrett's poetry, Robert McRuer's crip

---

47. Patsavas, "Recovering a Cripistemology of Pain."

theory, the Disability Justice Collective's visionary worldmaking,[48] and Alyson Patsavas's cripistemology of pain that gave me a future free from the imperative of wellness. These theorists, artists, and activists helped me understand that even this—even my narrow channel of pain—is relational. I learned from crip writers ways to map my experiences within structures of privilege and precarity. Alyson Patsavas's cripistemology locates her pain within ableist narratives while simultaneously acknowledging her own positionality to mark the limits of her knowledge claims.[49] The simultaneity of these things is important. I have class and racial privilege that enables me to even seek care that others could not access. While moving through these spaces, though, I inhabit a body almost always overlooked in their design.[50] Embedded in my experiences is knowledge of how medical and other cultural institutions inflict, *inflect,* and amplify pain on deviant bodies.

// Disability is experienced in and through relationships; it does not occur in isolation.
  —Alison Kafer[51] //

Long before I was sick, I was a small human with something to prove about my toughness. When I was caught fighting on the playground, I was terrified to tell my parents. The principal sent me home with a disciplinary letter for a parent to sign. When I showed it to my father, he scribbled his signature with a laugh. He told me about how, after school, he and his classmates used to rearrange the desks in an empty classroom so they could brawl. I liked that this felt like a transgression we shared—that, in this one thing, he shielded me from the principal's condescension. I liked that this made me feel strong like him—my father, whom to this day I have only seen cry once. Neither of us had the perspective to note that Black and Indigenous children in this country have been suspended, expelled, and/or arrested for much less—that the same racial architecture that presumes our docility also curtails Black and brown lives through assigned criminality. It was many years before I could read my life in relation with others'—before I could see or could *feel* that the isolationism of US life is an illusion. We are far more intimately bound than white supremacy would have us believe.

---

48. Berne, "Disability Justice"; Piepzna-Samarasinha, *Care Work.*

49. Patsavas, "Recovering a Cripistemology of Pain," 205.

50. For more on how physical and social spaces anticipate particular (cisgender, white, nondisabled male) bodies, see Hamraie, *Building Access*; Kern, *Feminist City*; Criado-Perez, *Invisible Women.*

51. Kafer, *Feminist, Queer, Crip,* 11.

For much of my life I believed the bootstrapping mythology of my parents' lives—that they had come here alone and made it alone, speaking a fraction of the language and even less of the cultural mores. I had not accounted for how much the timing of their migration mattered, arriving with the influx of students following the 1965 Immigration and Nationality Act, with the stratospheric rise in Asian migrants who could build Chinatowns and Chinese schools and newspapers and forged families. I had not considered, too, the stabilizing influence of their own families, who could provide, even from half a world away, emotional grounding and the knowledge that they would have a place to go home to if all else should fail. This is not to say that my parents didn't work hard, suffer racism and xenophobia, and overcome adversity, but to say that they were able to do so through a range of social factors inseparable from their individual experiences. For a long time, though, I considered them models of individual striving.

My sense of isolation was heightened by my move to central Pennsylvania, by far the smallest and most racially homogenous place I had ever lived. The town of forty thousand—83 percent white—was a far cry from Phoenix, Houston, and New York City. The impersonal protocol of medical practices affirmed my feeling that I was in this alone. At the university health center, I never saw the same doctor twice. Each time I renarrativized my symptoms, the story got shorter and more details disappeared. When I think back on those initial doctor visits, I can see how unfamiliar I was with self-advocacy in medical contexts. It was and still is reflex for me to defer to authority in public spaces. This is neither natural nor comfortable; it is a defensive posture produced by a lifetime of punishment for transgressing the demands of Asian femininity. The stakes of this behavioral calculus feel more dire in doctors' offices, where I can be and have been denied care—through explicit refusal and through the passive dismissal of my concerns and experiences.

For the first seven years through which I went undiagnosed and untreated, I earned a graduate student's salary—well below a living wage, though it was considered above average for humanities PhDs. I supplemented my pay with freelance writing, CrossFit coaching, communications gigs, and whatever else I could find in the margins of my schedule. In addition to the time and energy that additional jobs required, I lived in constant fear that a sudden flare would put me behind on my writing or teaching. When my encounters with medical professionals were unpleasant, discouraging, and already demanded more time, money, and energy than I had, it seemed easier just not to go. I cannot overstate this: there are many without my luck who are forced to drop out of school, who take far more dangerous jobs to pay for medical bills, and who get sicker and die. I am surviving systems that murder people with experiences adjacent to mine. I had the random fortune to be born into privileges that no one should need to fulfill basic human needs.

As if my body had accepted the desperate bargain I made with it throughout graduate school, it carried me through my dissertation defense before my symptoms accelerated with frightening rapidity. Within the next year, I had three diagnoses that required three different specialists and a weekly pill dispenser to manage my continually changing treatment plans. These diagnoses, like the "gender dysphoria" for which I began testosterone in late 2020, are just approximate names for my experiences so that I can access the bloodwork, MRIs, and treatment I need. In my years of medication roulette, some approaches helped, some made me worse, and some required protracted exchanges with the voicemail inbox of my physicians' office until I could receive an answer about the side effects I was experiencing. My body is regarded as an endocrine system, a gastrointestinal tract, and a nervous system—all with separate appointments and medications. Medical knowledge, like much of academic research, is compartmentalized into coarse categories with limited applicability to lived experience.[52] While medical education, funding, and research are channeled through specialized arenas, bodies are experienced holistically. Research trials focus on participants with only one condition to limit confounding factors, but many patients will in fact confound the results with their comorbidities.

Comorbidity: the co-existence of two or more diseases, disorders, or pathological processes in one individual.[53] Linguist Michiel de Vaan also connects the root word, *morbus,* with *mori*—"to die."[54] He traces both to the proto-Indo-European root *mer-*, responsible for other death-bound words such as mortal, mortuary, and murder. To be sick is to be closer to death, or to be associated with death, or, in too many cases, to be resigned to it by an ableist world. In her essay, Patsavas observes how mainstream portrayals of chronic pain suggests that the experience of pain is "a fate worse than death."[55] Films such as the Oscar-winning *Million Dollar Baby* valorize the hero who would rather die than face a disabled and painful existence. The message, writes Patsavas, is clear: "death is the only way to end my suffering."[56]

By placing people with chronic pain or chronic illness on a singular trajectory toward death, these narratives constrain public imagination—that is,

---

52. Emery, "Our Unsustainable Culture of Medical Specialization"; Anderlini, "The United States Health Care System Is Sick."

53. *Oxford English Dictionary Online*, s.v. "comorbidity, n."

54. Harper, "Morbid (adj.)."

55. Patsavas, "Recovering a Cripistemology of Pain," 203.

56. Patsavas, 208.

they limit the disabled futures that people can picture or pursue. This "cultural logic of euthanasia"[57] presumes that disabled lives are by nature not worth living, and it deters attention from the social factors that render disabled lives particularly difficult. Understandings of illness and pain as individualized, self-contained experiences omit the many historical and systemic factors that make particular people more vulnerable to certain conditions while depriving them of care. The moralization of health as individual responsibility further compounds the experience by making sickness and pain feel even more isolating. Finally, individualist narratives of personal overcoming occlude the sociality of health, success, and thriving. Sickness, pain, and suffering are inherently relational; we do not experience anything in a vacuum.

// I speak to leave evidence for the people like me who are searching for reflection and recognition and a "yes, we exist."
—Mia Mingus[58] //

I have only begun speaking and writing publicly about my experiences of illness in the past few years. For the most part, I was inhibited by narratives of precarity that are both true *and* mechanisms that silence scholars and students on the margins of their institutions. We are the few who made it. Do we know how easily they could expel us if we spoke up, declined their asks, missed the deadline, or otherwise made our presence known? What, though, is the point of being here if we can't *be* here? Creating enough space for ourselves and our communities without losing our place altogether requires delicate calculations. My own arithmetic changes depending on where I am, what allies and resources I have in this space, and what alternatives I have available—in Kay Ulanday Barrett's words, "*how much in community I am, how comfortable I am, how joyful I am.*"[59] Experiences are made in relation.

Learning to fold illness into race and gender and sexuality has also been active practice—a search for vocabularies that can write closer to and from the places where I live. The lack of intersectional vocabularies for co-constitutive oppressions limits resistance efforts to single-axis approaches, which will inevitably complement extant structures of power rather than reimagine them. Put another way: if we talk about gender at the exclusion of race, queerness, disability, and class, we have a feminist movement powered by white, wealthy, cisgender and heterosexual women. Learning to discuss how my illness is compounded by mythologies of masculinity and immigrant resilience—how

---

57. Garland-Thomson, "The Cultural Logic of Euthanasia."
58. Mingus, "Moving Toward the Ugly."
59. Barrett, "Kay Ulanday Barrett—New York."

it is shaped by the ways that health care providers encounter my racial and gender identities is part of an ongoing effort to open up critical discussions to more comprehensive analyses. It is also an acknowledgment of how I have unintentionally reified ableist narratives in all the years I spent concealing how terrible I felt—how I made myself feel more terrible in order to meet deadlines, attend classes and social gatherings, and prioritize the comfort of those who would otherwise not have to think about our physical fragility. In demanding those things of my body, I was also asking that other disabled people do the same—that we subordinate our lives to the comfort of our able-bodied and neurotypical colleagues. I was valuing individual resilience over collective—over the strength of a world where we all can participate.

Fortunately, pain cuts me down to the quick. It bleeds me of my patience for politeness and its imperatives. When I began pressuring the policies and expectations that exclude disabled folks from participation, others began to share their resonant experiences and needs. As disabled scholars have long demonstrated, ableism presumes idealized bodies and lives that rarely apply to anyone in practice. What is merely "inconvenient" or occasionally frustrating for some folks, however, is inaccessible or actively harmful to others. Communities created and led by those harmed, then, necessarily imagine wholly different ways of working and being together.

// I want to be with you. If you can't go, then I don't want to go.
—Mia Mingus[60] *//*

Mia Mingus, Leah Lakshmi Piepzna-Samarasinha, and Stacey Milbern— three disabled queer Asian femmes—dreamt up Creating Collective Access in 2010, when they decided they were sick of remaining an afterthought in conference planning. They did not want another gathering where they would have to accommodate ableist policies, so instead they sent a call to other disabled folks for a community-led access effort. Attendees formed pods that then relayed to event organizers their access needs and their resources; some could make food runs, some were great at coordinating, others had vehicles or access to other transportation. Piepzna-Samarasinha recalls that one attendant took another's spare manual wheelchair to the nearest restaurant and filled it with shawarma orders to take back to everyone who could not walk that far.[61] It was a space with care as its guiding principle. Everyone here knew what it was like to be left out, and they refused to do that to anyone else.

---

60. Mingus, "Wherever You Are Is Where I Want to Be: Crip Solidarity."
61. Piepzna-Samarasinha, *Care Work*, 50.

I have not shared in anything as revolutionary as the now-legendary CCA, but I recognize in Mingus's description of crip solidarity the rare gift of being surrounded by other folks committed to accessibility as a practice of care. Our access needs are almost never the same, nor are we always aware of one another's access needs upon meeting, but there's a fluency around access that breathes air back into the room. Your needs are the foundation of this space—not an imposition on it. I delight in the imagination of crip innovation—of jury-rigging our environments to fit all of us with our chairs, our tics, our migraines and stiff joints. I cherish the conversations that flow through text and signing and screen readers. I am moved each time by the significance of this gesture: it is most important to us that you can be here, fully, as yourself; everything else can change. I have never felt as fully present as I am able to be in these spaces, where the needs of our bodies are as integral to the shape and rhythm of our conversations as the contributions of our minds and hearts. We know these things are inseparable—that we are not floating organs and ideas but whole humans with intricate histories and lives. The process is never perfect—accessibility is a process, not a destination—but it also feels like a collective problem we are solving together. I am energized by learning from and with people with whom I want to build places and practices of refuge; this is work that gives me life.

I know that I am supposed to end on that note—the feeling of crip solidarity in a room of people dreaming together about disability justice. I am wary, though, of disability narratives with neat resolutions. Some of us live whole (emotive, fulfilling, difficult) lives in the muddy terrain between "well" and "dead," and I want to make room for those stories. ("*Yes, we exist.*") The truth is that CCA disbanded after a year—that it encountered the pervasive conflicts shot through other DJ collectives: What happened when members had competing access needs? What was "fair" when some got too sick or tired and others braced themselves and gritted through? What about when those who were safer in nondisabled spaces were thus more visible and received more credit for the work of the collective? Under the familiar pressure of these tensions, the initially fervent community of the CCA dissolved.

This dissolution, though, is not failure. Piepzna-Samarasinha describes it as "another worthy, imperfect model in my body's archive,"[62] providing knowledge and tools for the care she continues to build in her communities. There is a moment in her book, *Care Work,* when she describes CCA's initial gathering that lingers with me: instead of able-bodied people walking briskly ahead and abandoning those who move at a slower pace—instead of pedestri-

---

62. Piepzna-Samarasinha, 60.

ans pressuring those with mobility devices off the sidewalk or trampling their path—the CCA moved as one slow tide. She writes, "People got out of the way."[63] When they agreed that they would move at the pace of their slowest member, when they committed to leaving no one behind, they reshaped the ableist environment around them.[64] They made people notice and adapt. They were more powerful—rather, undeniable—together. (*"Remember: together we can find the shore."*)

On Ancestry

// How do we create when we don't know our own histories?
  —Celeste Chan[65] //

At twenty-four years old, I returned to Taiwan—six years after my mother and I railed over my decision not to travel back. I flew from Pennsylvania, where I'd just completed my degree in creative writing, to San Francisco, where my mother was already waiting after her flight from Phoenix. We ate a quiet lunch of overpriced airport fare—something fast food and bland—before boarding the thirteen-hour flight to Taipei. In Taiwan, my relatives remarked on how long it had been since they'd seen me. In prior trips, the comments were routine, but this one came with the guilty knowledge that I had actively avoided this trip for years. They were as shocked as my mother was the first time she saw me after I got sick—forty pounds stripped from a 5'2" frame, almost unrecognizable. While the weight-loss remarks had been rampant in the US, I was still stunned by how my emaciation was celebrated in Taiwan. I could not help but hear in the compliments an affirmation of frailty as feminine beauty. I was most appealing when I was disappearing.

As we do every trip, we traveled from the city to the northern coastline, where there's a cemetery built into a mountainside, overlooking the East China Sea. It is the final resting place for my mom's mom and my dad's parents. Though my dad stayed in the States this time, we rode with his brothers and their families. It was pouring rain, which is usual for the mountains. The trunk of the car was filled with food that we laid out for ancestors. In prior trips, we brought joss paper to burn in a giant outdoor kiln, but the Taiwanese government was beginning to cut down on burnt offerings to mitigate pol-

---

63. Piepzna-Samarasinha, 51.

64. Reminiscent of Adrienne Marie Brown's moving "at the speed of trust" (drawn from Mervyn Marcano and Stephen Covey). Brown, *Emergent Strategy.*

65. Chan, *Tender,* v.

lution. I have always been comforted by that ritual, though—the notion that destruction in this world can bring abundance in the next.

I really only have one memory of my maternal grandmother. During an early visit to Taiwan, my mom left me with her mother for a couple hours. I remember that we spoke very little—that I sat beside her as we watched television, and that she gave me a can of cold congee to eat. In college, my roommates and I drove to Chinatown to stock up on those aluminum containers. We would eat them at our prefab desks in the lost hours between dusk and dawn, dipping plastic spoons into syrupy porridge. These are the scraps I have of the people my parents know as family: a cramped Taipei apartment; television commercials in Mandarin; the taste of sticky rice soaked in sugar.

I have even less of my father's parents. His mother passed before I was born, and his father had Alzheimer's for most of my life. By the time I was old enough to remember 爺爺, he had already forgotten me. My memory of him rests on the side of this mountain, where gravestones line the hills. The view steals my breath every time—the impossibly green canopy of the island meeting sea foam and boundless ocean. It looked even more surreal in the rain as my uncles drove my mother and me up the steep mountain roads. Storm clouds darkened the horizon, dumping sheets of water so that it was impossible to know where the air ended and the sea began. After we parked the car, my mother and I followed my dad's brothers and sisters-in-law, each of us carrying wide black umbrellas.

The graves here are as daunting as the view, identical slabs of polished dark marble, marked by pillars of engraved stones. I was still staring out at the sea when my uncle, my father's oldest brother, chastised me to turn around. He pointed at the names of his parents, and—to my surprise—made a joke: "You can't read these, can you?" Defensive, I pointed to the first character and read it aloud: "許." Hsu. In Chinese, the family name comes first.

"What about the rest?" my uncle asked. I only shrugged, and he laughed and nodded toward his brother as if I had confirmed something for them. "You don't even know 爺爺's name," he added, the laughter still in his voice. I wondered whether to him this was just a fact—some trivia about his brother's kid, whom he sees once or twice a decade. To me, it was a reminder that I was playing house, making theater of an intimate, reverent practice.

More than one relative has teased me about the distance of my language. At other times, in this same place, other uncles and aunts have reminded me that my grandparents do not understand English. In Mandarin the phrase for "does not understand" is 聽不懂. Translated literally, it means *hear, not comprehend*. I have wanted to believe that the language of prayer doesn't matter— that my ancestors and I might hear each other better across spiritual borders than across national ones. My relatives' teasing, however—what I'd guess they regard as mild ribbing—reminded me that I'm never fully certain that anyone is listening. As a queer kid raised on soil where I am always alien, I am always a little afraid that I will never have any grounds from which to speak.

// Our histories are a collage of scattered ashes, burned memories, and stolen art. —Bení Alí Ávalos[66] //

My parents' families are both fairly close. At least, they look that way to me. Taiwan is less than fourteen thousand square miles, which is 5 percent of the landmass of Texas. Most of my relatives live in Taipei, but even those who don't are only a short train ride away. As the only member of either side raised outside of Taiwan, I grew up without them, but I didn't grow up without family. In Arizona, we formed a tight-knit group of Taiwanese American families, at the core of which were five other households we saw weekly, though there were more who drifted in and out of our circles. I called the adults 阿姨 and 叔叔, as I did my actual aunts and uncles. Our weekends were boisterous, loving affairs. We spent Saturday mornings at a local park, where the adults played tennis and talked and the kids roamed the bike trails. In the evenings, we reconvened for sumptuous potlucks with full spreads of home-cooked Taiwanese comfort foods: braised pork over rice, stir-fried noodles, and fried mantou buns. For dessert sometimes, one of the aunties broke out her hand-cranked shaved-ice machine. We took turns filling our bowls with flurried snow, which we topped with condensed milk and fresh boba. We also vacationed together—a caravan of cars on the desert interstate stopping at a Travelodge where we filled a block of rooms with connecting doors. Whenever one household traveled to Taiwan, we delivered items for others' relatives and friends and returned with suitcases full of gifts to share.

These were the people who raised me, and whom I helped raise. We spent our summers at the house or workplace of whoever could hold us, and after each of the children turned twelve, we became de-facto babysitters for the others. When my father was hospitalized with a severe infection, Aunt L[67] picked me up from school. I remained at her house until he was discharged, so that my mom was free to move between work and the hospital. The first night that Aunt L set me up in her daughter's room, she lingered by the door, checking that I had enough blankets and pillows, that I had remembered my toothbrush, and that I knew what time to get up in the morning for school.

66. Ávalos, "What Was Born," 4.
67. Pseudonyms are used in this chapter to protect people's privacy.

I remember the concern in her voice, but I do not remember feeling scared or worried. I was too young to grasp that my parents were not immortal. I could not reconcile the news of my dad's sickness with his sturdy, sometimes intimidating presence. I was confident in his recovery and the safety of this house, which felt like all the clamorous warmth of long dinners, spirited conversations, and holidays.

In this migrant enclave, I learned "family" as a bulwark of care indifferent to biology. Perhaps this was actually my first encounter with queerness. We supported one another in ways that stood in for and exceeded traditional kinship structures; this has always been migrant culture. In the early years of Chinese migration to the US, forged families resulted in a "queer domesticity"[68] pathologized and stigmatized by white officials. The diversity of Chinese American household formations violated the only legible standards for "family"—that is, "a male patriarch, a sole wife, and their children"[69]—such that US census enumerators could only conclude that these homes were sites of prostitution and sexual deviance. These officials could not grasp the imaginative intimacy that sustained those who were excluded from the nation's social safety nets, decrying how women and children were "herded together with apparent indiscriminate parental relations, and no family classifications."[70] Around the same time, beginning with the Dawes Act, the US government seized nearly 150 million acres of Indigenous lands and parceled them back to those who would renounce tribal belonging in favor of white familial structures. This is, of course, the same country that has always directed policy toward sundering families of color—through slavery, Native American boarding schools, Japanese internment, and now immigration enforcement, the criminal justice system, and a child welfare system designed to cleave generations apart.

// diaspora haunted, we
hunt for pregnant pauses . . .
. . . ghost children drawing maps in the margins/
of a place called No Homeland
   —Kai Cheng Thom[71] *//*

When I was thirteen, my Chinese school teacher assigned each student a passage from the Confucian *Analects* on which to write an essay. "In ministering to his parents," my passage began, the son "may (on occasion) offer

68. Shah, *Contagious Divides*, 13–14.
69. Shah, 84.
70. Farwell, *The Chinese at Home and Abroad*, 9.
71. Thom, *A Place Called No Homeland*, 8.

gentle remonstrances; when he sees that their will is not to heed such, he should nevertheless continue to show them reverent respect, never obstinacy; and if he has to suffer, let him do so without murmuring."[72] I composed a long response on how these values were outdated for contemporary forms of family and relationality. I have no explanation for why I showed my parents except that I did not yet understand the extent to which our worldviews diverged. Perhaps I also thought that they, of anyone, might resist the latter part of that passage, which advised that "whilst the parents are still living, [the son] should not wander far." They yelled until I agreed to rewrite it. I do not remember the specifics of the final product—just that it praised Confucian wisdom and guidance, and that my teacher was so taken with it that she had me read it aloud to my classmates the following week. It was not the last time I wrote to placate authority, but it was the only time I have argued against my convictions. I quit Chinese school within the year, accelerating the atrophy of my first language and my alienation from my family of birth.

The teacher, whom I suspect was also raised in Taiwan during martial law, had experienced these aphorisms as an integral component of her own education. Confucian teachings have been used as moral training since the Warring States period—long before China was China but was rather an imbroglio of bitter rivalries. Confucianism emerged as one of the competing philosophies for self, familial, and state governance, drawing a direct line between disciplined individuals, heteropatriarchy, and national fortitude. Viewed through the lens of narrative, Confucianism is one particular story about ancestry—both what it means and how it is practiced. We descend from the people who give us birth, and the abiding tether of blood will map our networks of intimacy.

Both Western and Eastern theorists have speculated about whether these "traditional" principles are conducive toward democratic societies.[73] It takes little imagination, however, to see resonant principles ingrained in the social and legal entrenchment of the "American family." In addition to the representative prevalence of the nuclear family (e.g., portraits of the president with *his* wife and children), marriage and heteronormative reproduction are codified into law through property rights, employment, medical, and consumer benefits, and other protections. All these legal and social measures follow the same narrow tract of imagination that elevates the heterosexual dyad above all other relations.

<hr />

72. Confucius, *The Wisdom of Confucius*, 24.
73. Vogel, *The Four Little Dragons*; Chun, "From Nationalism to Nationalizing"; Chia, "The Elusive Goal of Nation Building."

What if, however, we began with queer diaspora as a means of knowing? As in, what can we learn from distance and deviance—from how queers are denied access to structures of privilege and inheritance while also cut off from histories and ways of knowing conducive toward their own survival? What can we learn by deconstructing the heteronuclear family structures that have been used to assimilate and/or isolate Black, Indigenous, Asian, Latinx, migrant, poor, and disabled communities? What would we learn about the elisions of social forms that we consider self-evident? What innovations and reappropriations of kinship could have brought me to the altar of *This Bridge* sooner? What words can honor such poetry, scholarship, and stories as prayers for those who precede and follow us? How do we pay tribute to the narrative threads that have been cast to us as a lifeline, and how do we further their reach? Here, too, the answer comes to me in Anzaldúa's voice: *"Write with your eyes like painters, with your ears like musicians, with your feet like dancers. You are the truthsayer with quill and torch. Write with your tongues of fire . . . Put your shit on the paper."*[74]

On the Way Home

In summer 2019 I am back in California, where I get coffee with Un Jung Lim, witness Celeste Chan in a Performing Resilience showcase, and meet Jasmin Hoo, who succeeded M. Lin as APIENC's Community Organizer. I still reach out to M. Lin, though. We have no more formal business for my research or for APIENC, but I take the train from Oakland to Hayward to meet them for dinner. It is the highlight of my trip. Halfway between my Airbnb and their new workplace, away from the frenetic rhythm of San Francisco's Chinatown, they pick me up from the BART station. We drive to a Laotian and Thai restaurant, where we talk about their new job, the stress and exhaustion of organizing, and the ways we both try to reconnect with and relearn Mandarin. M. Lin considers me over plates of braised pork and Lao sausage, and says, "We've known each other for a while now . . . and I feel like each time I see you, you've grown a little more into yourself. Do you feel like that's true?"

This is the sort of dialogic space I have come to associate with M. Lin—where they invite self-reflection through the guise of an observation or personal opinion. As I scoop more rice onto my plate, I respond, "I think that's true." I think it's due in no small part to people like and including M. Lin, who have modeled forms of confidence, community, and care to which I could

---

74. Anzaldúa, "Speaking in Tongues," 171; emphasis original.

aspire. I think it is due to the constellated memories of the Dragon Fruit Project, the powerful storytelling of the Visibility Project, and the thoughtful, deeply caring pedagogies of the Queer Ancestors Project. It is due to finding enough belonging in these spaces to have histories that I want to sustain, futures I want to pursue, and family with whom to do those things.

Meeting M. Lin and the members of APIENC was the first time anyone asked me my pronouns—the first time anyone invited me to identify differently from how I had been assigned all my life. In these few years, M. Lin has watched me come out as trans nonbinary and explore what that looks like and feels like on this body. They have watched me navigate professional and community spaces, in scavenger style, pilfering survival tactics as I go. My sense of self will probably always be in process, but M. Lin is right in that I have become more comfortable with this provisional state that I am in, and with whatever future adaptations will come.

If, as I proposed at the beginning of this chapter, our bodyminds archive the experiences we encounter, then homing not only assigns meaning to those archives, but channels that meaning into new ways of encountering ourselves and one another. Homing is the narrative cord that Gloria Anzaldúa extends to "mujeres de color, companions in writing."[75] It is the pattern she interweaves with the stories of her writing companions—a story-based tapestry that serves as safety net and security blanket. It is the constellated stories of the Dragon Fruit Project, the Visibility Project, and the Queer Ancestors Project, which explore novel configurations of community, care, and social criticism. For diasporic subjects rendered chronically adrift, homing offers a means of reshaping our social spaces—in pursuit of belonging for ourselves and for those whom we call into community.

---

75. Anzaldúa, "Speaking in Tongues," 163.

Moving Home /
Homing Movements

This book began with the question of community: How do trans and queer Asian Americans forge shared histories and politics from their consonant and contradictory experiences? How do they assemble alliances and actions from social categories that carry no guarantee of commonality? What I found was not a singular thread—no definitive history or clear boundaries—but a network of relations, survival strategies, and distinct but interwoven memories, fantasies, and desires. I found stories as widespread as our national origins, and self-definitions as colorful and diverse as our genders and sexualities—a narrative patchwork whose collective resilience reflects that of the bodyminds that compose it. These stories trace powerful intimacies not just among those who identify as QTAPI but across experiences of racial, sexual, and gender minorities and disabled folks throughout global history. They offer new perspectives on my own histories, personal and communal, and they brought me to people who claimed me as theirs.

The stories collected here demonstrate how identities come to matter through accrued history and collective action but are not fixed or preordained scripts. LGBTQ+ Asian Americans are pulled together by related but not equivalent experiences in distant countries, on North American soil, in their households, and/or out in public when they are aggregated into reductive social and administrative categories. For those seeking to forge and mobilize a communal consciousness, our commonplaces serve as discursive and affective sites of convergence. Our experiences, failures, and revelations of love, our struggles and strategies for resilience, and the kinships we seize provide grounds for connection and negotiation. Some alliances are passing affiliations, and others, enduring bonds. Our relations are always constellating, and our homes are built and lived in motion.

This is a book about LGBTQ+ Asian American and Pacific Islander experiences, but also about queerness, racialization, and the scripting of normative bodyminds to justify conquest and (un)belonging. It is an argument about the relevancy of QTAPI histories and insights to broader global conversations about US colonialism and imperialism. It is a celebration of the resistive strategies that marginalized communities have used to find and hold one another and to build mobile sites of support and healing. I hope that the entanglements of trans and queer Asian American and Pacific Islander histories with other narrative arcs will invite further explorations of these intimacies—of the potential collusions and inevitable frictions that come with proximity.

// I am writing to tell you, I have been spending a lot of time thinking, Who are my people? What determines whose death will storm my chest, will flood my eyes, will make me wanna burn down a city and pray with every ounce of my winded grace that more than the smoke will rise?
—Andrea Gibson[1] //

The journey from Arkansas to Texas is eight hours of freeway—almost a straight shot of black pavement on roads emptied by stay-at-home orders. It is summer 2020 and the COVID-19 pandemic is spreading rapidly across the US with no sign of slowing. My partner and I depart Arkansas with our vehicles packed to the brim—every inch of our two little hatchbacks filled with Clorox wipes, dog toys, small kitchen appliances, and other miscellany that could not go on the moving truck. Moving while most of the country is under social distancing measures is a surreal experience; we could not see any of our friends to say goodbye, and we have no one to meet when we arrive. Sometimes it feels like we are the last two people at the end of the world.

Partway into the drive, Mck speeds ahead without me. A white woman who grew up in small southern towns, she is anxious to beat the city traffic. I, having learned to drive on Phoenix interstates and Houston's twelve-lane beltways, am far more afraid of giving police a reason to chase me down. I never drive more than five miles above the speed limit—not after having been pulled over for five- and nine-mph infractions; not after having been reported to and detained by police for public displays of queer affection; and especially not

---

1. Gibson, "A Letter to White Queers, A Letter to Myself," 36.

now, while a nation under duress ignites with public protests against police violence and racial injustice. I do not carry the same risk that George Floyd, Breonna Taylor, Atatiana Jefferson, and so many other Black and Indigenous people of color do while living in this country—not by a long shot—but even my run-ins with the US legal system have left me with hands fixed to the 10:00 and 2:00 of my steering wheel, constantly checking for the blue-and-red bar of a patrol car in my rearview mirror.

I stop once for gas along the way. After I refill at the pump, I step into the convenience store, where I am intercepted on my way into the women's room. I break out my softest, high-pitched nonthreatening voice, and this time, the embarrassed stranger lets me go. This time I make it back to the car without seeing or speaking to another person. This time I watch through my mirrors to make sure no one has followed me back out as I launch my phone's navigation app and mount it to the dashboard. My body, however, is stuck in the last time. My heartbeat and sweat glands are remembering large fingers biting into my shoulder and my back pressed to tile. *"Trauma time is cyclical,"* and I am thirty-two years old, twenty-nine, twenty-two, and eighteen, just trying to get home safe.

When I cross the Texas border, I think about James Byrd Jr.—a Black man from Jasper, Texas, who was killed the same year as Matthew Shepard, the same year that Shepard's story aired in my parents' living room, that I sat transfixed by this proof of queerness. In 1998 Byrd accepted a ride home from the wrong three white men, who instead drove him to the edge of town, tied him to the back of their truck, and dragged him—fully conscious—over three miles of asphalt. Before that, though, before tragedy was all most people knew of James Byrd Jr., he was the son of a deacon and a Sunday school teacher. He sang and played piano for his father's church. He graduated from the last segregated class of Jasper Rowe High School, and worked for a period as a vacuum salesman. Not that we should have to tell tender, humanizing stories about people before we are willing to condemn their murder.

If Byrd's story aired in Phoenix, in the neighborhood bordering the Gila River Indian Community where I was glued to the television, I did not notice. I did not know his name for at least another decade—not until 2009, when President Obama signed the Matthew Shepard and James Byrd Jr. Hate Crimes Prevention Act. If I had known his story, though, I would not have known to map my own family histories onto the racial architectures that perpetuated Byrd's victimization. I would not have known how anti-Blackness undergirds Asian migration and trans and queer phobia. I would not yet have placed myself in the history that encouraged and condoned his lynching—or asked what I could do about it.

*// I sometimes wonder if I would have been less sick if I had had a home.
—Porochista Khakpour[2] //*

Earlier that year, as we started planning our move, COVID-19 overtook the US, exposing rampant inequalities in health care, housing, and employment. Initially regarded as a distant disaster mismanaged by the Chinese government, the novel coronavirus eventually arrived on Western shores with crushing force. Even as it spread through Europe and into US coastal cities, the majority of the country maintained an insistent denial that such crises couldn't happen here—not in our peaceful hometowns. Ashish Jha, then director of the Harvard Global Health Institute, summarized it as such: "When this outbreak began in China, everyone said, *Thank God it's not here.* It moved to Western Europe and people said, *They have government-run health care; that won't happen here.* Then it hit New York and Seattle, and people said, *It's the coasts.* At every moment, it's more tempting to define the other who is suffering."[3]

As I have written elsewhere, US governing officials and media relied heavily on "epidemic logic," which deploys metaphors of containment to simultaneously generate and assuage public fears.[4] They must make the public afraid enough of the contagion to justify measures that will supposedly contain its spread. This is the paradox of epidemic logic: even as viral proliferation exposes our vulnerability to the bodies and decisions of others, prevailing responses treat bodies and communities as self-containing and isolatable.

While the pandemic is frequently assessed as a failure of the US health care system—or sometimes more expansively as a health-based phenomenon that exploited racial, gender, and class-based divisions—I also see this period as a rupture in the US's increasingly narrow definitions of home. I mean *home* in all its iterations—home as in the fiction of a bounded or justifiable "homeland"; home as in 家, as in the fantasy of a self-sustaining nuclear family; home as in "the place where a person or animal dwells,"[5] as in property, as in the plots we carve from Earth. The virus's rapid spread revealed the porosity of so many presumed borders—social truths that do not hold when they fail to account for material, lived realities. If *homing* enables us to link personal injuries to their contextual causes, then perhaps it might also trace the anguish of

2. Khakpour, *Sick*, 181.

3. Quoted in Yong, "America's Patchwork Pandemic Is Fraying Even Further"; emphasis original.

4. Hsu, "Containment and Interdependence."

5. *Oxford English Dictionary Online*, s.v. "home."

a wounded planet to our individual and collective misdeeds. Perhaps it might also build from our collective desires a more stable foundation for living.

Joining a recent escalation of zoonotic outbreaks, COVID-19 has been examined as another consequence of humans' unchecked consumption. These infections, transmitted from animals to people, are made prevalent by unsustainable land use, extractive industries, and environmental disruptions such as habitat fragmentation and extreme weather events precipitated by climate change.[6] This planet, in other words, is home not just to humankind but to entire ecosystems that sustain plant and animal life in delicate balance, which we continue to disrupt. As human encroachment into animal habitats escalates, these viruses have more opportunities to leap across species, moving through and amplifying many forms of (dis)connection.

With modern transportation and the interdependencies of global economies and cultures, the virus spread quickly around the world, indifferent to geographical and political boundaries. Responses to COVID-19 varied widely and had disparate results, but the US proved particularly ill prepared for the crisis. While countries with fewer resources and less time to prepare still implemented effective quarantine and contact-tracing measures, the US's COVID-19 response was almost universally acknowledged as a catastrophic failure. The virus seeped into and exacerbated existing social divisions. Every attempt to stem the escalation of illness and death became a highly charged, partisan matter. Across the country, retail workers and security personnel were shot for asking patrons to don masks. Protestors in Michigan, decked out with long guns and other military-inspired paraphernalia, stormed the capitol to demand a reversal of the governor's stay-at-home orders. Meanwhile, people of color, poor folks, and transgender, queer, and disabled people bore (and continue to endure) the worst of the economic and physical consequences.

Michigan's armed protestors exemplified a particularly ill-adapted response to adversity, but they were reacting at least in part to the very real strain the virus placed on a system with few provisions for economic, emotional, and physical hardship. People of all political leanings were hard-hit with stay-at-home measures. When "non-essential" businesses closed, unemployment skyrocketed to its highest rate since the Great Depression. Governing officials counterposed social distancing policies with the nation's economic health in a reductive dichotomy—as if the government itself were not capable of issuing economic relief and emergency housing, and as if widespread illness and death would not also devastate the economy. Rather than providing clear leadership, federal and state authorities defaulted to the neoliberal vocabulary

---

6. Randolph et al., *Preventing the Next Pandemic*.

of personal "choice," charging individuals with the responsibility of protecting themselves and one another. Without substantial government aid, however, and without supportive social networks, many people were left without any good choices at all.

The "American home," it turned out, was a grossly inadequate foundation for daily life. This reality—a truth already known to so many trans, queer, poor, disabled, and/or racially marginalized folks in the US—finally drew the attention of the white middle class. Far from natural or neutral, the idealization of the nuclear family helped ensure that normative citizens would become "successful" capitalists while racialized, migrant, and other unfit citizens would struggle.[7] Let me put it differently: the smallness and isolation of the heteronuclear family ensured that in most circumstances, both parents would have to work—would have to have the educational, cultural, and class backgrounds to secure well-paid jobs; would commit long hours to ableist schedules and workspaces; would pay others for child and elder care; would be so bound by the financial necessity of that child and elder care and atomized home living that they could not protest or augment their working conditions. By the time COVID-19 arrived, much of the country lacked the vocabulary and structures for collective organizing that would have provided worker protections and economic and social support.

Beyond exposing the nuclear family as a failed economic project, COVID-19 also exceeded the capacity of the family as a social and emotional network. Those who were able to keep their jobs struggled to balance work responsibilities with full-time caregiving for children, elders, or other household members. The 35.7 million Americans who lived alone were faced with an indefinite future without intimate physical contact. The "loneliness epidemic" that Surgeon General Vivek Murthy observed in 2017 reached new heights,[8] while the US's already "vastly underfunded, fragmented, and difficult to access" mental health system careened toward crisis.[9] Rates of intimate partner homicide surged around the world—as did reports of domestic violence, despite inevitable underreporting when people are trapped at home with their abusers. Amid the crumbling foundations of home, family, and nation, US leaders relied on familiar tropes to scapegoat the East Asian Other for long-simmering domestic instabilities.[10]

---

7. Reddy, "Asian Diasporas, Neoliberalism, and Family"; Hong, "Existentially Surplus"; Wingard, *Branded Bodies, Rhetoric, and the Neoliberal Nation-State.*

8. Murthy, "Work and the Loneliness Epidemic"; Ducharme, "COVID-19 Is Making America's Loneliness Epidemic Even Worse."

9. Wan, "The Coronavirus Pandemic Is Pushing America into a Mental Health Crisis."

10. Hsu, "Containment and Interdependence."

As many have pointed out, however, COVID-19 only exacerbated precarities already pervasive throughout US life. Pain is an accelerant. The virus moved through extant currents of power, taking advantage of those rendered vulnerable by structures of labor and care. Latinx workers, overrepresented in agricultural and service industries, experienced a disproportionate rate of infection.[11] Black Americans, long neglected and often actively harmed by medical professions, were subjected to the highest rate of COVID-19 fatalities.[12] Native American reservations, whose funding and protective equipment were withheld or delayed by US bureaucratic measures, had insufficient resources to stem viral outbreaks.[13] Conditions suspected to exacerbate COVID-19 symptoms—for example, diabetes and cardiovascular disease—are all more prevalent among Black, Indigenous, and Latinx populations because of structured disenfranchisement.[14] Meanwhile, an uneasy public directed its fear toward those deemed perpetual threats to the nation, and rates of anti-Asian violence continue to soar.[15] All this devastation follows familiar patterns in US history. The harms attributed to COVID-19 are not new but an escalation of the nation's pre-existing conditions.

Accordingly, some activists, politicians, and other community leaders call for a reckoning with the institutions that enabled the ravages of COVID-19. In a widely circulated article, the novelist Arundhati Roy sees opportunity in disruption. "Historically," she writes, "pandemics have forced humans to break with the past and imagine their world anew."[16] The US, in particular, has found the limits of its commonplaces. The ideologies behind the US's stratospheric rise in global capitalism also established an ethos of glorified individualism and social fragmentation that made it especially vulnerable to a virus indifferent to national and social boundaries. As COVID-19 ruptured the presumptive truth of our mythological borders, it also demonstrates that these particular orientations to nation, home, and family are actually inhospitable to *any* form of life. These definitions were driven by logics of consump-

---

11. Martinez et al., "SARS-CoV-2 Positivity Rate for Latinos in the Baltimore–Washington, DC Region."

12. Yancy, "COVID-19 and African Americans."

13. Givens, "The Coronavirus Is Exacerbating Vulnerabilities Native Communities Already Face." Also important is that in 2021 Indigenous nations distributed their vaccine doses with such efficacy that they then extended vaccines to settlers in the US and Canada long before state and federal governments were able to do so.

14. Wallis, "Why Racism, Not Race, Is a Risk Factor for Dying of COVID-19"; Beyer and Joint Economic Committee Democrats, "The Impact of Coronavirus on the Working Poor and People of Color"; US Department of Health and Human Services, *National Diabetes Statistics Report, 2020.*

15. Gover, Harper, and Langton, "Anti-Asian Hate Crime during the COVID-19 Pandemic."

16. Roy, "The Pandemic Is a Portal."

tion, bleeding earth, sea, and sky of resources so that experts have long been warning of zoonotic outbreaks. The same extractive greed renders humans similarly expendable, prompting the eugenicist logics undergirding US federal responses to COVID-19.

This is a continuation of the story that begins with Indigenous dispossession and continues with the importation of enslaved Africans and Asian indentured laborers. This is a story that rhetors throughout this book have traced through the denial of Hawaiian sovereignty, the betrayal of Marshall Islanders, the instantiation of white gender performances among communities of color, and myriad other narratives and structures that render trans, disabled, queer, and other "deviant" lives as disposable. History has shown that the US nation-state actually depends on these abuses—at times adapted under new guises and names, but inevitable in a political economy that prioritizes profit over any form of life.

With the escalation of so-called natural catastrophes in the past few decades, a wide range of constituencies have issued urgent calls for coordinated and sweeping change. Leading ecologists, biologists, and other public health experts warn of irreversible disaster or even extinction.[17] The Climate Justice Alliance connects consumerism, colonialism, and militarism to position white supremacy as the driving force of climate crisis.[18] The Indigenous Environmental Alliance similarly highlights the damages of the "financialization of nature" and centers Indigenous rights and sovereignty in planetary healing.[19] There is overwhelming evidence that human behavior needs to change. The struggle to lead and shape that change will be a battle waged, in large part, through storytelling. When the ways of living now normalized as everyday life—that so many of us have come to accept as home—are driving us to ruin, we need new narratives. We need plots that dream us into new relations with one another and with the earth that sustains us.

// I think we can heal by realizing that "home" is not a place, but a tapestry of relationships. Home is the place we carry in our hearts, that we call into being in the space between.
—Kai Cheng Thom[20] //

17. Díaz et al., "Pervasive Human-Driven Decline of Life on Earth Points to the Need for Transformative Change"; Algona, "Coronavirus Pandemic."

18. Climate Justice Alliance, "Just Transition."

19. Indigenous Environmental Network, "Indigenous Principles of Just Transition."

20. Thom, "I Want to Find the Place Underneath Rage."

Our house in Austin sits at the city limits. It is a little small for two people and two overactive dogs, a little far for the commute on congested freeways, and definitely too far from my favorite ice cream shop, but it is also the first place where I hang paintings and shelves on the walls. It is the first residence where I want to leave proof that we lived here—with our too-many books and dog toys and my growing collection of fitness equipment. While my partner and I erect a home gym in the garage, while we paint sealant onto the fence and repair the interminably leaky irrigation system, the borders of this country are overrun by disaster. Hurricanes swarm the Gulf Coast and fires consume the western states. In California, journalist Ezra Klein describes the skies as "choking"—how the day fills with burnt haze and his dogs pace and bark.[21] My news feed becomes a collage of charred earth, and my chest tightens with the memory of smoke. I recall with guilt how I ignored Tali's insistent whimpering that morning—how I assumed the alarm next door was a normal part of our everyday; how the continual menace of our everyday inured me to the signs of imminent danger. We are lucky to be living inland, where most of these events seem like a distant phenomenon, but we should and do know better. For those unmoved by the photos of orange skies and of evacuees packed into rescue helicopters—for those unmoved by the suffering of others *right now*—these snapshots of the West Coast should be a glimpse into their/ our future, and a reckoning with their/our past.

In 1850 the Act for the Government and Protection of Indians outlawed intentional burning, criminalizing over thirteen thousand years of Indigenous praxis where the Yurok, Karuk, Hupa, Miwok, Chumash, and other tribes deployed small burns to reduce the risk of larger wildfires.[22] The practice of controlled burns reflects how humans evolved in relation with the land, using strategic fires to clear habitats for elk and deer, and to promote spring flow and drought tolerance, among many other environmental benefits. Burns were executed seasonally and with the rhythms of animal migration; humans worked as a part of the planet rather than against it. This established and proven wisdom was sidelined by colonial prejudice against what they saw as "primitive" practices,[23] resulting in a century of fire suppression that stifled biodiversity. Late to this revelation, Western science has since concluded that fire suppression and the resulting homogeneity leads to poorer crop yields and overproliferation of pests and disease.[24] Diversity, it turns out, is integral to healthy ecologies.

---

21. Klein, "There Are No Good Choices."
22. Cagle, "'Fire Is Medicine.'"
23. Cagle.
24. Kimmerer and Lake, "The Role of Indigenous Burning in Land Management."

After centuries of destruction, there is no seamless return to precolonial conditions. Recent West Coast fires are intensified by autumn winds made stronger and drier by climate change.[25] In California's Tubbs Fire, flames tore through homes at an acre a second, and houses erupted spontaneously from the heat.[26] There are, however, knowledges and ways of life that existed long before colonialism and neocolonialism. Whatever solutions emerge now will need to bridge the ravages of capitalism with the forms of relationality and reciprocity that sustained the earth prior to settler economies and greed—and will need to disinvest from the former in ways that US agencies and residents still seem unprepared to do.

In 2019 the *Guardian* reported that California officials had sought tribal guidance on fire policy, connecting Yurok and Karuk fire practitioners with firefighters. Even then, Bill Tripp, director of environmental policy for the Karuk Tribe Department of Natural Resources, worried about the co-optation and misuse of tribal practices. "We don't have a problem teaching about our principles behind our practice and where, when, why, and how," he said, "but we're not interested in doing that if five years down the line they say OK, we'll do it for you now, and you can just stay in poverty."[27] Predictably, a year later, Tripp decried the continued neglect of US officials, who had allowed fires to spread into Karuk territories while prohibiting intentional burns through bureaucratic measures—"because of liability or because there aren't enough personnel available."[28] As with COVID-19, wildfires and other signals of a distressed planet continue to proliferate, indifferent to human denial. In recent decades, the number of annual wildfires in California has increased fivefold and continues to grow.[29] Meanwhile, rising temperatures and disappearing coastlines threaten an impending wave of climate migration. Sociologist Mathew Hauer estimates that by 2100, cities such as Austin, Orlando, Atlanta, and Houston could receive more than 250,000 new residents due to rising sea levels alone.[30] Already in 2020, Austin's transportation infrastructure is far behind its rapid population growth. The city's long-awaited proposal for a new rapid transit system also risks further displacement of Black, Latinx, and working-class communities who are more likely to need and use that transit

---

25. Goss et al., "Climate Change Is Increasing the Likelihood of Extreme Autumn Wildfire Conditions across California."

26. Lustgarten, "How Climate Migration Will Reshape America."

27. Cagle, "Fire Is Medicine."

28. Tripp, "Our Land Was Taken."

29. Williams et al., "Observed Impacts of Anthropogenic Climate Change on Wildfire in California."

30. Hauer, "Migration Induced by Sea-Level Rise Could Reshape the US Population Landscape."

system, and who are more likely to be uprooted by climate change. The challenges of the coming years look like a house of cards—one disaster collapsing into another. They feel impossible to map—or grasp, even—in their immensity and interdependencies. Those same linkages, however, are potential nodes of connection. Our fates are bound, awaiting the story that will bring us together.

// To understand where we're going, we need to understand the successes and challenges of our elders and ancestors. We want to make new mistakes.
—API Equality—Northern California[31] //

Whatever the future brings, it will not come with neat resolutions or easy answers, so I offer one more story-in-process—another transient home. Sequestered by the pandemic, members of the Dragon Fruit Network (DFN) convene on Zoom. An outgrowth of the Dragon Fruit Project, the DFN uses the archive as a launch point for community conversation and action. Most participants are quarantined at home in California, where in addition to the threat of infection, in addition to choking skies, Asian Americans have reported over eight hundred incidents of targeted discrimination related to COVID-19. Xenophobic attacks continue escalating under a presidential administration that popularized the term *China virus* (or worse, *kung flu*). Though I am halfway across the country, Zoom takes me into Steve Lew's living room, where he takes us all back another thirty years.

As a gay man in the 1980s, Lew was already regarded as a vector of disease—was already persecuted for it. "We sometimes hope that our institutions will lead in a health crisis like this," he says, "but we can't count on that. And we have to think about how we could be changing the narratives in our minds, with each other, with our communities, and with the government to really create a rational response." The year that I was born, Lew co-founded the Gay Asian Pacific Alliance (GAPA), now a long-standing vanguard of LGBTQ+ API community health, culture, and activism. Three decades later, he draws from that history in communion with thirty-seven trans and queer Asian Americans and Pacific Islanders, as we look to the past and the future for strategies of connection and survival.

After Lew offers a list of upcoming town halls and mutual aid efforts, another attendee reports on APIENC's newly formed Ecological Justice League (EJL). The EJL is named as a tribute to and in alliance with Movement Generation, whose pursuit of climate justice is grounded in an appreciation of ecology as "home." *Eco,* from the Greek *oikos,* means "home, dwelling

---

31. API Equality—Northern California, "Building."

place, habitation."[32] *Logy,* the English suffix that signals a "study of," is drawn from the Greek *logos,* or "discourse." Ecology: the study of or a discourse of home. Begun in community listening sessions such as this one, the EJC uses community education to mobilize toward harmonious "local regenerative economies."[33] Grounded in the interpersonal and the local, the EJL envisions planetary change through the power of intimate and immediate connections.

With the added displacement of the pandemic, I am not the only DFN member calling in from outside the Bay Area. Others have stayed up late on the East Coast, or even arisen early in Asia. Some are quarantined indefinitely in college dorm rooms, unable to see classmates or friends. We span at least three generations and a hodgepodge of national origins and ethnic, gender, and sexual identities, but we are bound by these histories we have claimed and the ways we hope to grow from them. Conversations like this do not get a lot of press in chronicles of history, but they are the bedrock of collective power, without which the marches, the policy changes, and the cultural shifts would not be possible.

Place this snapshot, then, this blip in time, back in its narrative momentum. Constellate it with the wide-reaching but interrelated undertakings of other LGBTQ+ API. See the EJL, months later, launch storytelling campaigns where QTAPI share experiences of climate crisis past, present, and future. One floor above the APIENC office, watch Mia Nakano join Chinese for Affirmative Action and "Stop AAPI Hate," which collects and tracks data about anti-API harassment and violence after COVID-19. Down the road, witness Tita Aida and her co-workers at the San Francisco Community Health Center providing food and first aid for unhoused folks during the city's shelter-in-place. Across the Bay, see Celeste Chan shepherd another QAP cohort through a global pandemic while she completes her MFA degree. See Willy Wilkinson co-facilitate APIENC's online workshops on interdependence, on asking for help, and on establishing networks of care. See a world of LGBTQ+ Asian Americans and Pacific Islanders reaching for and finding one another, traversing continents, languages, and generations to build homes that can move and grow with their people.

---

32. Harper, "Ecology (n.)."
33. API Equality—Northern California, "Ecological Justice."

BIBLIOGRAPHY

100+ Asian American and LGBTQ Organizations. "100+ Asian and LGBTQ Organizations' Statement in Opposition to Law Enforcement-Based Hate Crime Legislation." *Reappropriate* (blog), May 12, 2021. http://reappropriate.co/2021/05/75-asian-and-lgbtq-organizations-statement-in-opposition-to-law-enforcement-based-hate-crime-legislation/.

23andMe. "DNA Genetic Testing & Analysis." Accessed September 25, 2019. https://www.23andme.com/?vip=true.

Abbey, Kristen L. "'See with Eyes Unclouded': Mononoke-Hime as the Tragedy of Modernity." *Resilience: A Journal of the Environmental Humanities* 2, no. 3 (2015): 113–19.

Agnew, Lois, Laurie Gries, Zosha Stuckey, Vicki Tolar Burton, Jay Dolmage, Jessica Enoch, Ronald L. Jackson, et al. "Octalog III: The Politics of Historiography in 2010." *Rhetoric Review* 30, no. 2 (March 21, 2011): 109–34. https://doi.org/10.1080/07350198.2011.551497.

Ahmed, Sara. *The Cultural Politics of Emotion.* New York: Routledge, 2004.

———. *Living a Feminist Life.* Durham: Duke University Press, 2017.

———. *On Being Included: Racism and Diversity in Institutional Life.* Durham; London: Duke University Press, 2012.

Ahsan, Bahaar. "Untitled." In Chan, *Tender,* 13.

Ahuja, Bex. "Bex (Rough Cut)." Interview by Mia Nakano, January 23, 2011. The Visibility Project. https://vimeo.com/19086550. Video no longer available.

Aida, Tita. Interview by Vida Kuang, May 4, 2014. Dragon Fruit Project. API Equality Northern California, San Francisco, California.

Alexander, Jonathan, and Jacqueline Rhodes. "Queer Rhetoric and the Pleasures of the Archive." *Enculturation,* January 16, 2012. http://enculturation.net/queer-rhetoric-and-the-pleasures-of-the-archive.

Alexander, M. Jacqui. *Pedagogies of Crossing: Meditations on Feminism, Sexual Politics, Memory, and the Sacred.* Perverse Modernities. Durham: Duke University Press, 2005. Kindle.

Algona, Peter. "Coronavirus Pandemic: A Symptom of Our Mass Extinction." *The Santa Barbara Independent,* April 15, 2020. https://www.independent.com/2020/04/15/coronavirus-pandemic-a-symptom-of-our-mass-extinction/.

Alshammari, Shahd. "On Survival and Education: An Academic's Perspective on Disability." *Canadian Journal of Disability Studies* 8, no. 4 (June 2019). https://doi.org/10.15353/cjds.v8i4.532.

Alvaran, Israel "Izzy." Interview by Le and Ken Quello, July 18, 2015. Dragon Fruit Project. API Equality Northern California, San Francisco, California.

"AncestryDNA." Accessed September 30, 2019. https://www.ancestry.com/.

Anderlini, Deanna. "The United States Health Care System Is Sick: From Adam Smith to Over-specialization." *Cureus,* May 31, 2018. https://doi.org/10.7759/cureus.2720.

Anderson, Joyce Rain. "Remapping Settler Colonial Territories: Bringing Local Native Knowledge into the Classroom." In *Survivance, Sovereignty, and Story: Teaching American Indian Rhetorics,* edited by Lisa King, Rose Gubele, and Joyce Rain Anderson, 160–69. Logan: Utah State University Press, 2015.

Anzaldúa, Gloria. *Borderlands / La Frontera: The New Mestiza.* 4th ed. San Francisco: Aunt Lute Books, 2012.

———. *Light in the Dark / Luz en lo Oscuro: Rewriting Identity, Spirituality, Reality.* Edited by AnaLouise Keating. Durham: Duke University Press, 2015.

———. "Speaking in Tongues: A Letter to Third World Women Writers." In Moraga and Anzaldúa, *This Bridge Called My Back,* 163–72.

API Equality—LA. "Mission." Accessed March 3, 2019. https://www.apiequalityla.org/mission-1.

API Equality—Northern California. "About." Dragon Fruit Project. 2015. Accessed February 22, 2018. http://www.dragonfruitproject.org/.

———. "APIENC: Building Transgender, Non-Binary, and Queer API Power." APIENC. Accessed July 10, 2019. https://apienc.org/.

———. *The Dragon Fruit Project.* Dragon Fruit Project. API Equality—Northern California, 2015. https://www.youtube.com/watch?v=TQ8iwXKM6zo.

———. "Dragon Fruit Project Toolkit," 2017.

———. "Ecological Justice." *APIENC* (blog), 2020. https://apienc.org/what-we-do/ecological-justice/.

———. "Quality Control Checklist," July 20, 2017.

Ásta. *Categories We Live By: The Construction of Sex, Gender, Race, and Other Social Categories.* New York: Oxford University Press, 2018.

Au, Nancy. "About." Peas & Carrots. Accessed July 5, 2019. https://www.peascarrots.com/about.

Ávalos, Bení Alí. "I Want to Write About." In Chan, *Tender,* 46–47.

———. "What Was Born." In Chan, *Tender,* 4.

Baik, Crystal, Joyce Gabiola, Alice Y. Hom, MLin, and Eric Wat. "Beyond Survival, Toward Resistance & Alliance Building: The Making of Queer and Trans of Color Activist Archives." Association for Asian American Studies Conference, 2018.

Bailey, Cathryn. "Embracing the Icon: The Feminist Potential of the Trans Bodhisattva, Kuan Yin." *Hypatia* 24, no. 3 (2009): 178–96.

Barrett, Kay Ulanday. "Kay Ulanday Barrett—New York." Interview by Mia Nakano. Video, 2012. The Visibility Project. http://www.visibilityproject.org/kay-ulanday-barrett-new-york/. Video no longer available.

———. "To Be Underwater & Holy." In *When the Chant Comes.* Topside Heliotrope, n.d.

Beauchamp, Toby. *Going Stealth: Transgender Politics and U.S. Surveillance Practices.* Durham: Duke University Press, 2019.

Beck, Alma. Interview by Mioi Hanaoka, December 8, 2013. Dragon Fruit Project. API Equality Northern California, San Francisco, California.

Beker, Carson, Nancy Au, and Haldane C. King. "The Escapery." The Escapery: Your Art Unschool. Accessed July 5, 2019. https://www.theescapery.org/.

Bell, Chris. "Introducing White Disability Studies: A Modest Proposal." In *The Disability Studies Reader,* edited by Lennard J. Davis, 2nd ed., 275–82. New York: Routledge, 2006.

Bellwood, Peter S. *First Farmers: The Origins of Agricultural Societies.* Malden, MA: Wiley-Blackwell, 2005.

Benjamin, Ruha. *Race after Technology: Abolitionist Tools for the New Jim Code.* Medford, MA: Polity, 2019.

Berlant, Lauren Gail. *Cruel Optimism.* Durham: Duke University Press, 2011.

———. *Desire/Love.* Brooklyn, NY: Dead Letter Office, Punctum Books, BABEL Working Group, 2012. Open access e-book.

Berne, Patty. "Disability Justice—a Working Draft by Patty Berne." *Sins Invalid* (blog), June 9, 2015. https://www.sinsinvalid.org/blog/disability-justice-a-working-draft-by-patty-berne.

Besnier, Niko, and Kalissa Alexeyeff, eds. *Gender on the Edge: Transgender, Gay, and Other Pacific Islanders.* Honolulu: University of Hawaiʻi Press, 2014.

Bessette, Jean. *Retroactivism in the Lesbian Archives: Composing Pasts and Futures.* Carbondale: Southern Illinois University Press, 2018.

Beyer, Don, and Joint Economic Committee Democrats. "The Impact of Coronavirus on the Working Poor and People of Color." US Congress, April 24, 2020. https://www.jec.senate.gov/public/index.cfm/democrats/2020/4/new-report-explains-why-black-latino-low-income-communities-are-disproportionately-impacted-by-the-coronavirus.

Blackpast. "(1966) Stokely Carmichael, 'Black Power,'" July 13, 2010. https://www.blackpast.org/african-american-history/1966-stokely-carmichael-black-power/.

Bonilla-Silva, Eduardo. *Racism without Racists: Color-Blind Racism and the Persistence of Racial Inequality in America.* 5th ed. Lanham, MD: Rowman & Littlefield, 2017.

Borges, Sandibel. "Home and Homing as Resistance: Survival of LGBTQ Latinx Migrants." *WSQ: Women's Studies Quarterly* 46, no. 3–4 (2018): 69–84. https://doi.org/10.1353/wsq.2018.0032.

Brah, Avtar. *Cartographies of Diaspora: Contesting Identities.* New York: Routledge, 1996.

Bratta, Phil, and Malea Powell. "Introduction to the Special Issue: Entering the Cultural Rhetorics Conversations." *Enculturation* 21 (April 20, 2016). http://enculturation.net/entering-the-cultural-rhetorics-conversations.

Brewer, Elizabeth, Cynthia Selfe, and M. Remi Yergeau. "Creating a Culture of Access in Composition Studies." *Composition Studies* 42, no. 2 (2014): 151–54.

Britzman, Deborah P. "Queer Pedagogy and Its Strange Techniques." *Counterpoints* 367 (2012): 292–308.

Brown, Adrienne M. *Emergent Strategy.* Chico, CA: AK Press, 2017.

Brown, Melissa J. *Is Taiwan Chinese? The Impact of Culture, Power, and Migration on Changing Identities.* Berkeley: University of California Press, 2004.

Butler, Judith. *Excitable Speech: A Politics of the Performative.* New York: Routledge, 1997.

Byrd, Jodi A. *The Transit of Empire: Indigenous Critiques of Colonialism.* Minneapolis: University of Minnesota Press, 2011.

Cadena, Keiva Lei Kealohimaka. "A Day Just for Us: A Conversation with Keiva Lei Cadena." Interview by Sarah Hashmall. Accessed August 14, 2020. https://www.thebody.com/article/a-day-just-for-us-a-conversation-with-keiva-lei-ca.

———. *Positively Trans: Meet Keiva Lei Cadena.* Transgender Law Center. Accessed April 15, 2020. https://www.youtube.com/watch?v=BDXBPKchxdE.

Cagle, Susie. "'Fire Is Medicine': The Tribes Burning California Forests to Save Them." *The Guardian,* November 21, 2019, sec. US news. https://www.theguardian.com/us-news/2019/nov/21/wildfire-prescribed-burns-california-native-americans.

Campt, Tina. *Listening to Images.* Durham: Duke University Press, 2017. Kindle.

Caswell, Michelle, Ricardo Punzalan, and T-Kay Sangwand. "Critical Archival Studies: An Introduction." *Journal of Critical Library and Information Studies* 1, no. 2 (June 27, 2017). https://doi.org/10.24242/jclis.v1i2.50.

Chan, Celeste. "Bio." celestechan.com. Accessed July 5, 2019. http://www.celestechan.com/bio.html.

———, ed. *Flower of Ancestry: The Queer Ancestors Project.* Vol. 2. Oakland, CA: Foglifter Press, 2019.

———. Personal interview with Jo Hsu, April 15, 2018.

———, ed. *Tender: The Queer Ancestors Project.* Oakland, CA: Foglifter Press, 2018.

Chang, Clio. "The Familiar Defiance of Wesley Yang." Jezebel. Accessed May 10, 2019. https://jezebel.com/the-familiar-defiance-of-wesley-yang-1832874054.

Chávez, Karma R. *The Borders of AIDS: Race, Quarantine, and Resistance.* Decolonizing Feminisms. Seattle: University of Washington Press, 2021.

———. *Queer Migration Politics: Activist Rhetoric and Coalitional Possibilities.* Feminist Media Studies. Urbana: University of Illinois Press, 2013.

Chen, Jian Neo. *Trans Exploits: Trans of Color Cultures and Technologies in Movement.* Anima: Critical Race Studies Otherwise. Durham: Duke University Press, 2019. E-book.

Chia, Yeow Tong. "The Elusive Goal of Nation Building: Asian/Confucian Values and Citizenship Education in Singapore during the 1980s." *British Journal of Educational Studies* 59, no. 4 (December 2011): 383–402. https://doi.org/10.1080/00071005.2011.591288.

Chiang, Howard. *After Eunuchs: Science, Medicine, and the Transformation of Sex in Modern China.* New York: Columbia University Press, 2018.

Chiang, Howard, and Yin Wang, eds. *Perverse Taiwan.* New York: Routledge, 2017.

Chin, Frank. "Come All Ye Asian American Writers of the Real and the Fake." In Chin et al., *The Big Aiiieeeee!,* 1–93.

Chin, Frank, Jeffrey Paul Chan, Lawson Fusao Inada, and Shawn Wong, eds. *The Big Aiiieeeee! An Anthology of Chinese American and Japanese American Literature.* New York: Meridan, 1991.

Ching, Leo T. S. *Becoming "Japanese": Colonial Taiwan and the Politics of Identity Formation.* Berkeley: University of California Press, 2001.

Chomsky, Aviva. "DNA Tests Make Native Americans Strangers in Their Own Land." *The Nation,* November 29, 2018. https://www.thenation.com/article/dna-tests-elizabeth-warren-native-american-race-science/.

Chou, Wah-shan. *Tongzhi: Politics of Same-Sex Eroticism in Chinese Societies.* New York: Haworth Press, 2000.

Chow, Kat. "'Model Minority' Myth Again Used as a Racial Wedge between Asians and Blacks." *NPR,* April 19, 2017. https://www.npr.org/sections/codeswitch/2017/04/19/524571669/model-minority-myth-again-used-as-a-racial-wedge-between-asians-and-blacks.

Chun, Allen. "Democracy as Hegemony, Globalization as Indigenization, or the 'Culture' in Taiwanese National Politics." *Journal of Asian and African Studies* 35, no. 1 (January 2000): 7–27.

———. "From Nationalism to Nationalizing: Cultural Imagination and State Formation in Postwar Taiwan." *The Australian Journal of Chinese Affairs* 31 (January 1994): 49–69. https://doi.org/10.2307/2949900.

Cintrón, Ralph. "Democracy and Its Limitations." In *The Public Work of Rhetoric: Citizen-Scholars and Civic Engagement,* edited by John M. Ackerman and David J. Coogan, 98–116. Columbia: University of South Carolina Press, 2013.

Clare, Eli. *Brilliant Imperfection: Grappling with Cure.* Durham: Duke University Press, 2017.

Climate Justice Alliance. "Just Transition." Accessed August 24, 2020. https://climatejusticealliance.org/just-transition/.

Coe, Vanessa. Interview by Tawal Panyacosit, January 6, 2011. Dragon Fruit Project. API Equality Northern California, San Francisco, California.

Combahee River Collective. *The Combahee River Collective Statement: Black Feminist Organizing in the Seventies and Eighties.* Albany, NY: Kitchen Table: Women of Color Press, 1986. http://books.google.com/books?id=sEqaAAAAIAAJ.

Confucius. *The Wisdom of Confucius.* Carol Publishing Group ed. Secaucus, NJ: Carol, 1996.

Craddock, Susan. "Embodying Place: Pathologizing Chinese and Chinatown in Nineteenth-Century San Francisco." *Antipode* 31, no. 4 (October 1999): 351–71. https://doi.org/10.1111/1467-8330.00109.

The Creativity Movement. "Declaration of the Women's Frontier." Accessed August 26, 2019. https://creativitymovement.net/declaration-of-the-womens-frontier/. [https://web.archive.org/web/20210924150801/https://rationalwiki.org/wiki/Creativity_Movement#Declaration_of_the_Women.27s_Frontier].

———. "The Sixteen Commandments." Accessed August 26, 2019. https://web.archive.org/web/20210711030453/https://creativitymovement.net/creativity/the-sixteen-commandments/.

Criado-Perez, Caroline. *Invisible Women: Data Bias in a World Designed for Men.* New York: Abrams Press, 2020.

Cvetkovich, Ann. *An Archive of Feelings: Trauma, Sexuality, and Lesbian Public Cultures.* Series Q. Durham: Duke University Press, 2003.

Damm, Jens. "Same Sex Desire and Society in Taiwan, 1970–1987." *The China Quarterly,* no. 181 (March 2005): 67–81.

Dang, Kim. Interview by Yvonne Tran, 2012. Dragon Fruit Project. API Equality Northern California, San Francisco, California.

Dao, Lotus. Interview by Avery Nguyen, November 21, 2015. Dragon Fruit Project. API Equality Northern California, San Francisco, California.

Day, Iyko. *Alien Capital: Asian Racialization and the Logic of Settler Colonial Capitalism.* Durham: Duke University Press, 2016.

Day, Iyko, Juliana Hu Pegues, Melissa Phung, Dean Itsuji Saranillio, and Danika Medak-Saltzman. "Settler Colonial Studies, Asian Diasporic Questions." *Verge: Studies in Global Asias* 5, no. 1 (2019): 1–45. https://doi.org/10.5749/vergstudglobasia.5.1.0001.

Del Hierro, Victor, Daisy Levy, and Margaret Price. "We Are Here: Negotiating Difference and Alliance in Spaces of Cultural Rhetorics." *Enculturation,* no. 21 (April 20, 2016). http://enculturation.net/we-are-here.

Delgado, Richard. "Storytelling for Oppositionists and Others: A Plea for Narrative." *Michigan Law Review* 87, no. 8 (1989): 2411–41. https://doi.org/10.2307/1289308.

D'Emilio, John. "Capitalism and Gay Identity." In *Powers of Desire: The Politics of Sexuality,* edited by Ann Snitow, Christine Stansell, and Sharon Thompson, 100–113. New York: Monthly Review Press, 1983.

Diamond, Jared M. "Taiwan's Gift to the World." *Nature* 403, no. 6771 (February 2000): 709–10. https://doi.org/10.1038/35001685.

Díaz, Sandra, Josef Settele, Eduardo S. Brondízio, Hien T. Ngo, John Agard, Almut Arneth, Patricia Balvanera, et al. "Pervasive Human-Driven Decline of Life on Earth Points to the Need for Transformative Change." *Science* 366, no. 6471 (December 13, 2019): eaax3100. https://doi.org/10.1126/science.aax3100.

Dingo, Rebecca. "Networking the Macro and Micro: Toward Transnational Literacy Practices." *JAC* 33, no. 3/4 (2013): 529–52.

Dirlik, Arif. "Taiwan: The Land Colonialisms Made." *Boundary 2* 45, no. 3 (August 2018): 1–25. https://doi.org/10.1215/01903659-6915545.

Dolmage, Jay. *Disabled upon Arrival: Eugenics, Immigration, and the Construction of Race and Disability.* Columbus: The Ohio State University Press, 2018.

Driskill, Qwo-Li. "Doubleweaving Two-Spirit Critiques: Building Alliances between Native and Queer Studies." *GLQ: A Journal of Lesbian and Gay Studies* 16, no. 1–2 (January 1, 2010): 69–92. https://doi.org/10.1215/10642684-2009-013.

Driskill, Qwo-Li, Daniel Heath Justice, Deborah A. Miranda, and Lisa Tatonetti, eds. *Sovereign Erotics: A Collection of Two-Spirit Literature.* First Peoples: New Directions in Indigenous Studies. Tucson: University of Arizona Press, 2011.

Dubriwny, Tasha N. "Consciousness-Raising as Collective Rhetoric: The Articulation of Experience in the Redstockings' Abortion Speak-Out of 1969." *Quarterly Journal of Speech* 91, no. 4 (November 2005): 395–422. https://doi.org/10.1080/00335630500488275.

Ducharme, Jamie. "COVID-19 Is Making America's Loneliness Epidemic Even Worse." *Time,* May 8, 2020. https://time.com/5833681/loneliness-covid-19/.

Dun, Lia. "Kurama." In Chan, *Tender,* 19–21.

———. "Redrawing the Lines: How Anime Helped Shape My Nonbinary Identity." *Catapult,* July 25, 2019. https://catapult.co/stories/redrawing-the-lines-how-anime-helped-shape-my-nonbinary-identity.

———. "A Thousand Deaths, Not My Own." In Chan, *Flower of Ancestry,* 2:52–53.

Dunn, Thomas R. *Queerly Remembered: Rhetorics for Representing the GLBTQ Past.* Studies in Rhetoric/Communication. Columbia: University of South Carolina Press, 2016.

Edelman, Lee. *No Future: Queer Theory and the Death Drive.* Series Q. Durham: Duke University Press, 2004.

The Editors of Encyclopaedia Britannica. "Avalokiteshvara." In *Encyclopædia Britannica.* Encyclopædia Britannica, February 16, 2018. https://www.britannica.com/topic/Avalokiteshvara.

Emery, Neal. "Our Unsustainable Culture of Medical Specialization." *The Atlantic,* July 31, 2012. https://www.theatlantic.com/health/archive/2012/07/our-unsustainable-culture-of-medical-specialization/260504/.

Eng, David L. *The Feeling of Kinship: Queer Liberalism and the Racialization of Intimacy.* Durham: Duke University Press, 2010.

———. *Racial Castration: Managing Masculinity in Asian America.* Perverse Modernities. Durham: Duke University Press, 2001.

Eng, David L., and Shinhee Han. *Racial Melancholia, Racial Dissociation: On the Social and Psychic Lives of Asian Americans.* Durham: Duke University Press, 2019. Kindle.

Engebretsen, Elisabeth L., William F. Schroeder, and Hongwei Bao, eds. *Queer/Tongzhi China: New Perspectives on Research, Activism and Media Cultures.* Gendering Asia 11. Copenhagen: NIAS Press, 2015.

Farwell, Willard Bringham. *The Chinese at Home and Abroad.* San Francisco: A. L. Bancroft, 1885. https://archive.org/details/chinesehomeabroadoofarw/mode/2up.

Ferguson, Roderick A. *The Reorder of Things: The University and Its Pedagogies of Minority Difference.* Difference Incorporated. Minneapolis: University of Minnesota Press, 2012.

Fernandes, Sujatha. *Curated Stories: The Uses and Misuses of Storytelling.* Oxford Studies in Culture and Politics. New York: Oxford University Press, 2017.

Fleischman, Richard K., and Thomas N. Tyson. "The Interface of Race and Accounting: The Case of Hawaiian Sugar Plantations, 1835–1920." *Accounting History* 5, no. 1 (May 2000): 7–32. https://doi.org/10.1177/103237320000500102.

The Flight Deck: A Place for Artists with Purpose. "The Flight Deck." Accessed July 5, 2019. http://www.theflightdeck.org/.

Flynn, Elizabeth A., Patricia J. Sotirin, and Ann P. Brady, eds. "Introduction: Feminist Rhetorical Resilience-Possibilities and Impossibilities." In *Feminist Rhetorical Resilience,* 1–29. Logan: Utah State University Press, 2012.

Fortier, Anne-Marie. "'Coming Home': Queer Migrations and Multiple Evocations of Home." *European Journal of Cultural Studies* 4, no. 4 (November 2001): 405–24. https://doi.org/10.1177/136754940100400403.

France, David. *How to Survive a Plague: The Inside Story of How Activists and Scientists Tamed AIDS.* New York: Vintage, 2017.

Fujikane, Candace, and Jonathan Y. Okamura, eds. *Asian Settler Colonialism: From Local Governance to the Habits of Everyday Life in Hawai'i.* Honolulu: University of Hawai'i Press, 2008.

Garcia, J. Neil C. "Nativism or Universalism: Situating LGBT Discourse in the Philippines." *Kritika Kultura* 20 (2013): 48–68.

———. *Philippine Gay Culture: Binabae to Bakla, Silahis to MSM.* Queer Asia. Hong Kong: Hong Kong University Press, 2009.

García, Romeo. "Creating Presence from Absence and Sound from Silence." *Community Literacy Journal* 13, no. 1 (Fall 2018): 7–15.

Garland-Thomson, Rosemarie. "The Cultural Logic of Euthanasia: 'Sad Fancyings' in Herman Melville's 'Bartleby.'" *American Literature* 76, no. 4 (December 1, 2004): 777–806. https://doi.org/10.1215/00029831-76-4-777.

Gelinas, Karen. "Creating a Sustainable Buddhist Feminist *Thealogy*: Guanyin Devotion among American Women." PhD diss., University of the West, 2018. https://ir.uwest.edu/files/original/5eda6dd5825efd1b6fe2dcb247efeoeadb4c1a9d.pdf.

Gerdeman, Dina. "Distressed Employees? Try Resilience Training." HBS Working Knowledge, July 31, 2019. http://hbswk.hbs.edu/item/distressed-employees-try-resilience-training.

Gibson, Andrea. "A Letter to White Queers, A Letter to Myself." In *Pansy,* 35–37. Austin: Write Bloody Publishing, 2015.

Gila River Indian Community. "About: History." Accessed May 12, 2020. http://www.gilariver.org/index.php/about/history.

———. "Pima-Maricopa Irrigation Project." Accessed May 12, 2020. https://www.gilariver.com/.

Givens, Maria. "The Coronavirus Is Exacerbating Vulnerabilities Native Communities Already Face." *Vox,* March 25, 2020. https://www.vox.com/2020/3/25/21192669/coronavirus-native-americans-indians.

Goeller, Kimiko. "Reminders." In Chan, *Flower of Ancestry*, 2:50.

Goldstein, Dana. "Race, Sex, and the Virginia Tech Killer." *The American Prospect,* January 14, 2008. https://prospect.org/article/race-sex-and-virginia-tech-killer.

Gopinath, Gayatri. *Impossible Desires: Queer Diasporas and South Asian Public Cultures.* Perverse Modernities. Durham: Duke University Press, 2005.

———. *Unruly Visions: The Aesthetic Practices of Queer Diaspora.* Perverse Modernities. Durham: Duke University Press, 2018. Kindle.

Goss, Michael, Daniel L. Swain, John T. Abatzoglou, Ali Sarhadi, Crystal A. Kolden, A. Park Williams, and Noah S. Diffenbaugh. "Climate Change Is Increasing the Likelihood of Extreme Autumn Wildfire Conditions across California." *Environmental Research Letters* 15, no. 9 (August 20, 2020): 094016. https://doi.org/10.1088/1748-9326/ab83a7.

Gossett, Che, and Juliana Huxtable. "Existing in the World: Blackness at the Edge of Trans Visibility." In *Trap Door: Trans Cultural Production and the Politics of Visibility,* edited by Tourmaline, Eric A. Stanley, and Johanna Burton, 39–56. Cambridge, MA: MIT Press, 2017.

Gover, Angela R., Shannon B. Harper, and Lynn Langton. "Anti-Asian Hate Crime during the COVID-19 Pandemic: Exploring the Reproduction of Inequality." *American Journal of Criminal Justice* 45, no. 4 (August 2020): 647–67. https://doi.org/10.1007/s12103-020-09545-1.

Grant, Jaime M., Lisa Mottet, Justin Tanis, Jack Harrison, Jody L. Herman, and Mara Keisling. *Injustice at Every Turn: A Report of the National Transgender Discrimination Survey.* Washington, DC: National Center for Transgender Equality and National Gay and Lesbian Task Force, 2011.

Gumbs, Alexis Pauline. *Dub: Finding Ceremony.* Durham: Duke University Press, 2020. Kindle.

Gutiérrez y Muhs, Gabriella, Yolanda Flores Niemann, Carmen G. González, and Angela P. Harris, eds. *Presumed Incompetent: The Intersections of Race and Class for Women in Academia.* Boulder: University Press of Colorado, 2012.

Hahm, Katie. "Compton's Cafeteria." Resilience Archives: LGBTQ AAPI History Tour, May 28, 2017. https://www.historypin.org/en/person/89455/explore/pin/1074805.

———. "Trikone Marches in SF Pride for the First Time." Resilience Archives: LGBTQ AAPI History Tour, May 8, 2017. https://www.historypin.org/en/lgbtq-america/pacific-west/lgbtq-aapi-tour/geo/37.784642,-122.407327,19/bounds/37.783827,-122.408139,37.785457,-122.406515/paging/1/pin/1073219.

Halberstam, Jack. *Female Masculinity.* Durham: Duke University Press, 1998.

Hamraie, Aimi. *Building Access: Universal Design and the Politics of Disability.* Minneapolis: University of Minnesota Press, 2017.

Harper, Douglas. "Ecology (n.)." In *Online Etymology Dictionary.* Accessed September 21, 2020. https://www.etymonline.com/word/ecology.

———. "Morbid (adj.)." In *Online Etymology Dictionary.* Accessed September 6, 2020. https://www.etymonline.com/word/morbid.

Hauer, Mathew E. "Migration Induced by Sea-Level Rise Could Reshape the US Population Landscape." *Nature Climate Change* 7, no. 5 (May 2017): 321–25. https://doi.org/10.1038/nclimate3271.

Hill Collins, Patricia. *Black Feminist Thought: Knowledge, Consciousness, and the Politics of Empowerment.* 2nd ed. New York: Routledge, 2000.

Ho, Jennifer, and James Kyung-Jin Lee, eds. "The State of Illness and Disability in Asian America." Special issue, *Amerasia Journal* 39, no. 1 (2013).

Ho, Ming-sho. *Challenging Beijing's Mandate of Heaven: Taiwan's Sunflower Movement and Hong Kong's Umbrella Movement.* Philadelphia: Temple University Press, 2019.

Hom, Alice Y. [166]. Interview by Sine Hwang Jensen, January 31, 2016. Dragon Fruit Project. API Equality Northern California, San Francisco, California.

———. [169]. Interview by Sine Hwang Jensen, March 12, 2016. Dragon Fruit Project. API Equality Northern California, San Francisco, California.

Hong, Grace Kyungwon. "Existentially Surplus: Women of Color Feminism and the New Crises of Capitalism." *GLQ: A Journal of Lesbian and Gay Studies* 18, no. 1 (January 1, 2012): 87–106. https://doi.org/10.1215/10642684-1422152.

hooks, bell. *All about Love: New Visions*. New York: Harper Perennial, 2001.

———. *Feminism Is for Everybody: Passionate Politics*. 2nd ed. New York: Routledge, 2015.

Hsu, V. Jo. "Chinese Roots, Queer Kinships, and the Writing That Bends Toward Home." Color Bloq, December 2018. https://www.colorbloq.org/article/chinese-roots-queer-kinships-and-the-writing-that-bends-toward-home.

———. "Containment and Interdependence: Epidemic Logics in Asian American Racialization." *QED: A Journal in GLBTQ Worldmaking*, 7, no. 3 (Fall 2020): 125–34.

Huang, Shu-Min, and Shao-Hua Liu. "Discrimination and Incorporation of Taiwanese Indigenous Austronesian Peoples." *Asian Ethnicity* 17, no. 2 (April 2, 2016): 294–312. https://doi.org/10.1080/14631369.2015.1112726.

Hutcheon, Emily, and Bonnie Lashewicz. "Theorizing Resilience: Critiquing and Unbounding a Marginalizing Concept." *Disability & Society* 29, no. 9 (October 21, 2014): 1383–97. https://doi.org/10.1080/09687599.2014.934954.

Hutcheon, Emily, and Gregor Wolbring. "'Cripping' Resilience: Contributions from Disability Studies to Resilience Theory." *M/C Journal: A Journal of Media and Culture* 16, no. 5 (August 2013). https://doi.org/10.5204/mcj.697.

Indigenous Environmental Network. "Indigenous Principles of Just Transition." Accessed August 24, 2020. https://www.ienearth.org/justtransition/.

Jacobs, J. Bruce. "The History of Taiwan." *The China Journal*, no. 65 (2011): 195–203.

Johnson, Amber, and B. LeMaster, eds. *Gender Futurity, Intersectional Autoethnography: Embodied Theorizing from the Margins*. New York: Routledge, 2020.

Johnson, E. Patrick. "'Quare' Studies, or (Almost) Everything I Know about Queer Studies I Learned from My Grandmother." *Text and Performance Quarterly* 21, no. 1 (January 2001): 1–25. https://doi.org/10.1080/10462930128119.

Johnson, Martin. "FBI May Charge Man Who Attacked Asian Americans over Coronavirus with Hate Crime: Report." *The Hill*, April 1, 2020. https://thehill.com/homenews/state-watch/490692-fbi-may-charge-man-who-attacked-asian-americans-over-coronavirus-with.

Kafer, Alison. *Feminist, Queer, Crip*. Bloomington: Indiana University Press, 2013.

Karlis, Nicole. "Amid Growing Feelings of Isolation, Americans Flock to DNA Testing Services." *Salon*, June 23, 2018. https://www.salon.com/2018/06/23/americas-isolated-culture-may-explain-popularity-of-dna-testing/.

Karuka, Manu. *Empire's Tracks: Indigenous Nations, Chinese Workers, and the Transcontinental Railroad*. Oakland: University of California Press, 2019. Kindle.

Kawai, Yuko. "Stereotyping Asian Americans: The Dialectic of the Model Minority and the Yellow Peril." *Howard Journal of Communications* 16, no. 2 (April 2005): 109–30. https://doi.org/10.1080/10646170590948974.

Keira. "Return Address: The Space Between." In Chan, *Flower of Ancestry*, 2:24–25.

Kern, Leslie. *Feminist City: Claiming Space in a Man-Made World*. London; New York: Verso, 2020.

Khakpour, Porochista. *Sick: A Memoir.* New York: Harper Perennial, 2018.

Kim, Claire Jean. "The Racial Triangulation of Asian Americans." *Politics & Society* 27, no. 1 (March 1999): 105–38. https://doi.org/10.1177/0032329299027001005.

Kimmerer, R. W., and F. K. Lake. "The Role of Indigenous Burning in Land Management." *Journal of Forestry* 99, no. 11 (November 1, 2001): 36–41. https://doi.org/10.1093/jof/99.11.36.

King, Lisa, Rose Gubele, and Joyce Rain Anderson, eds. *Survivance, Sovereignty, and Story: Teaching American Indian Rhetorics.* Logan: Utah State University Press, 2015.

Klein, Ezra. "There Are No Good Choices." *Vox,* September 14, 2020. https://www.vox.com/21432760/coronavirus-2020-trump-government-response-covid-19-biden-america.

Kohll, Alan. "How You Can Build a More Resilient Workforce." *Forbes,* January 5, 2017. https://www.forbes.com/sites/alankohll/2017/01/05/how-you-can-build-a-more-resilient-workforce/.

Kondo, Dorinne K. *Worldmaking: Race, Performance, and the Work of Creativity.* Durham: Duke University Press, 2018. Kindle.

Kumārajīva. *The Lotus Sutra.* Translated by Tsugunari Kubo and Akira Yuyama. 3rd ed. BDK English Tripiṭaka Series. Maraga, CA: BDK America, 2007.

Lee, Erika. *America for Americans: A History of Xenophobia in the United States.* New York: Basic Books, 2019.

———. *The Making of Asian America: A History.* New York: Simon & Schuster, 2015.

Lee, Jamie A. *Producing the Archival Body.* New York: Routledge, 2021.

Lee, Wenshu. "Kuaering Queer Theory: My Autocritography and a Race-Conscious, Womanist, Transnational Turn." *Journal of Homosexuality* 45, no. 2–4 (September 23, 2003): 147–70. https://doi.org/10.1300/J082v45n02_07.

Leibowitz, Tovah. "Dapper Crip: Disability, Queer Masculinity, and Fashion." *DapperQ,* October 26, 2016. http://www.dapperq.com/2016/10/dapper-crip-disability-queer-masculinity-fashion/.

Lew, Steve. Interview by Dragon Fruit Project, May 2, 2014. Dragon Fruit Project. API Equality Northern California, San Francisco, California.

———. Interview by Yifan Mai, September 2015. Dragon Fruit Project. API Equality Northern California, San Francisco, California.

Lim, Song Hwee. "How to Be Queer in Taiwan: Translation, Appropriation, and the Construction of a Queer Identity in Taiwan." In *AsiaPacifiQueer: Rethinking Genders and Sexualities,* edited by Fran Martin, Peter A. Jackson, Mark McLelland, and Audrey Yue, 235–50. Champaign: University of Illinois Press, 2008. https://www.jstor.org/stable/10.5406/j.ctt1xch37.

Lin, Chao-Ching. "Political Indoctrination in the Curriculum during Four Periods of Elementary School Education in Taiwan." *The Social Studies* 94, no. 3 (2003). https://doi.org/10.1080/00377990309600196.

Lin, Fei-fan. "I Choose to Stand With Taiwan's Indigenous Peoples." Translated by V. Jo Hsu. *Facebook,* February 28, 2017. https://www.facebook.com/photo.php?fbid=10208891165985374&set=a.1160090091381&type=3&theater.

Lin, M. Personal interview with Jo Hsu, April 17, 2018.

Liu, Eric. *The Accidental Asian.* New York: Random House, 1998.

López, Gustavo, Neil G. Ruiz, and Eileen Patten. "Key Facts about Asian Americans, a Diverse and Growing Population." *Pew Research Center* (blog), September 8, 2017. https://www.pewresearch.org/fact-tank/2017/09/08/key-facts-about-asian-americans/.

Lorde, Audre. "A Litany for Survival." *Poetry Foundation,* 1978. https://www.poetryfoundation. org/poems/147275/a-litany-for-survival.

———. "The Master's Tools Will Never Dismantle the Master's House." In Moraga and Anzaldúa, *This Bridge Called My Back,* 94–97.

———. *Zami, a New Spelling of My Name.* Crossing Press Feminist Series. Trumansburg, NY: Crossing Press, 1982.

Lowe, Lisa. *The Intimacies of Four Continents.* Durham: Duke University Press, 2015. Kindle.

Lugones, María. *Pilgrimages/Peregrinajes: Theorizing Coalition against Multiple Oppressions.* Lanham, MD: Rowman & Littlefield, 2003.

Luhmann, Susanne. "Queering/Querying Pedagogy? Or, Pedagogy Is a Pretty Queer Thing." In *Queer Theory in Education,* edited by William F. Pinar, 141–55. Studies in Curriculum Theory. Mahwah, NJ: Lawrence Erlbaum, 1998.

Luibhéid, Eithne, and Lionel Cantú, eds. *Queer Migrations: Sexuality, U.S. Citizenship, and Border Crossings.* Minneapolis: University of Minnesota Press, 2005.

Lustgarten, Abrahm. "How Climate Migration Will Reshape America." *New York Times Magazine,* September 15, 2020. https://www.nytimes.com/interactive/2020/09/15/magazine/ climate-crisis-migration-america.html.

Manalansan, Martin F. *Global Divas: Filipino Gay Men in the Diaspora.* Perverse Modernities. Durham: Duke University Press, 2003.

Mao, LuMing. *Reading Chinese Fortune Cookie: The Making of Chinese American Rhetoric.* Logan: Utah State University Press, 2006.

Mao, LuMing, and Morris Young, eds. *Representations: Doing Asian American Rhetoric.* Logan: Utah State University Press, 2008.

Martin, Del, and Phyllis Lyon. *Lesbian/Woman.* 20th anniversary ed. Volcano, CA: Volcano Press, 1991.

Martinez, Aja Y. *Counterstory: The Rhetoric and Writing of Critical Race Theory.* CCC Studies in Writing & Rhetoric. Champaign: Conference on College Composition and Communication; National Council of Teachers of English, 2020.

Martinez, Diego A., Jeremiah S. Hinson, Eili Y. Klein, Nathan A. Irvin, Mustapha Saheed, Kathleen R. Page, and Scott R. Levin. "SARS-CoV-2 Positivity Rate for Latinos in the Baltimore–Washington, DC Region." *JAMA* 324, no. 4 (July 28, 2020): 392–95. https://doi.org/10.1001/ jama.2020.11374.

mata flores, jorge. "ancestral shifts." In Chan, *Tender,* 14–15.

McRuer, Robert. *Crip Theory: Cultural Signs of Queerness and Disability.* Cultural Front. New York: New York University Press, 2006.

Melamed, Jodi. *Represent and Destroy: Rationalizing Violence in the New Racial Capitalism.* Minneapolis: University of Minnesota Press, 2011.

Mingus, Mia. "Moving Toward the Ugly: A Politic Beyond Desirability." *Leaving Evidence* (blog), August 22, 2011. https://leavingevidence.wordpress.com/2011/08/22/moving-toward-the-ugly-a-politic-beyond-desirability/.

———. "Wherever You Are Is Where I Want to Be: Crip Solidarity." *Leaving Evidence* (blog), May 3, 2010. https://leavingevidence.wordpress.com/2010/05/03/where-ever-you-are-is-where-i-want-to-be-crip-solidarity/.

Mishra, Pankaj. "Land and Blood." *New Yorker,* November 18, 2013. https://www.newyorker.com/ magazine/2013/11/25/land-and-blood.

Mo, Cairo. "About the Artist." 2021. Accessed June 11, 2021. https://cairomo.net/about.html.

———. "The Queer Ancestors Project 2021 Exhibition." 2021. https://cairomo.net/qap.html#.

Mobile Homecoming. "About Mobile Homecoming Project." Accessed June 26, 2021. https://www.mobilehomecoming.org/aboutmhp.

Monberg, Terese Guinsatao. "Like the Molave: Listening for Constellations of Community through 'Growing Up Brown' Stories." *Enculturation*, no. 21 (April 20, 2016). http://enculturation.net/like-the-molave.

Monberg, Terese Guinsatao, and Morris Young. "Beyond Representation: Spatial, Temporal and Embodied Trans/Formations of Asian/Asian American Rhetoric." *Enculturation*, no. 27 (December 18, 2018). http://www.enculturation.net/beyond_representation.

Moraga, Cherríe. "La Güera." In Moraga and Anzaldúa, *This Bridge Called My Back*, 22–29.

———. *Loving in the War Years: Lo Que Nunca Pasó Por Sus Labios*. South End Press Classics Series. Cambridge, MA: South End Press, 2000.

Moraga, Cherríe, and Gloria Anzaldúa, eds. *This Bridge Called My Back: Writings by Radical Women of Color*. 4th ed. Albany: State University of New York Press, 2015.

Morrison, Toni. "Rootedness: The Ancestor as Foundation." In *Black Women Writers, 1950–1980: A Critical Evaluation*, edited by Mari Evans, 339–45. Garden City, NY: Anchor Press / Doubleday, 1984.

Muñoz, José Esteban. *Cruising Utopia: The Then and There of Queer Futurity*. Sexual Cultures. New York: New York University Press, 2009.

———. *Disidentifications: Queers of Color and the Performance of Politics*. Cultural Studies of the Americas. Minneapolis: University of Minnesota Press, 1999.

———. "Ephemera as Evidence: Introductory Notes to Queer Acts." *Women & Performance* 8, no. 2 (1996): 5–16.

Murthy, Vivek. "Work and the Loneliness Epidemic." *Harvard Business Review*, September 26, 2017, 3–7.

"MyHeritage DNA." Accessed December 29, 2019. https://www.myheritage.com/dna.

Nair, Yasmin. "The Politics of Storytelling." *Yasmin Nair* (blog), June 19, 2012. https://yasminnair.net/the-politics-of-storytelling/.

Nakano, Mia. Personal interview with Jo Hsu, May 15, 2018.

———. *Visible Resilience*. Visibility Project, 2017.

Nakano, Mia, and Visibility Project. *Visibility Project + Resilience Archives Work Sample*, 2019. https://vimeo.com/286240711.

Nakashima, Shō. "Kubi Dake Ni Natte Mo (Moro's Head)." In Chan, *Flower of Ancestry*, 2:3–4.

———. "Sacred Movements." In Chan, *Flower of Ancestry*, 2:42–43.

Ngai, Mae M. *Impossible Subjects: Illegal Aliens and the Making of Modern America*. Princeton, NJ: Princeton University Press, 2014.

Nguyen, Mimi Thi. *The Gift of Freedom: War, Debt, and Other Refugee Passages*. Next Wave: New Directions in Women's Studies. Durham: Duke University Press, 2012.

Nguyen, Viet Thanh. "Asian-Americans Need More Movies, Even Mediocre Ones." *New York Times*, August 21, 2018. https://www.nytimes.com/2018/08/21/opinion/crazy-rich-asians-movie.html.

Nicolazzo, Z. *Trans* in College: Transgender Students' Strategies for Navigating Campus Life and the Institutional Politics of Inclusion*. 1st ed. Sterling, VA: Stylus, 2017.

Nicolazzo, Z, Susan B. Marine, and Francisco J. Galarte. "Introduction." *TSQ: Transgender Studies Quarterly* 2, no. 3 (August 2015): 367–75. https://doi.org/10.1215/23289252-2926360.

Nishime, LeiLani. *Undercover Asian: Multiracial Asian Americans in Visual Culture.* The Asian American Experience. Urbana: University of Illinois Press, 2014.

Olson, Christa J. *Constitutive Visions: Indigeneity and Commonplaces of National Identity in Republican Ecuador.* University Park: Pennsylvania State University Press, 2014.

Omatsu, Glenn. "The 'Four Prisons' and the Movements of Liberation: Asian American Activism from the 1960s to the 1990s." In *Asian American Studies: A Reader,* edited by Min Zhou and Anthony Ocampo, 60–95. New York: New York University Press, 2016.

Ono, Kent A., and Vincent Pham. *Asian Americans and the Media.* Media and Minorities. Cambridge: Polity, 2009.

Oxford English Dictionary Online. "'comorbidity, n.'" Oxford: Oxford University Press, June 2020. https://www.oed.com/view/Entry/261449?redirectedFrom=comorbidity.

———. "'home, n.1 and adj.'" Oxford: Oxford University Press, June 2020. https://www.oed.com/view/Entry/87869?rskey=IUuO1y&result=1.

———. "'nonce, n.1.'" Oxford: Oxford University Press, March 2020. https://www.oed.com/view/Entry/127827?rskey=fiMobz&result=1&isAdvanced=false.

Panofsky, Aaron, and Joan Donovan. "Genetic Ancestry Testing among White Nationalists: From Identity Repair to Citizen Science." *Social Studies of Science* 49, no. 5 (October 2019): 653–81. https://doi.org/10.1177/0306312719861434.

Patsavas, Alyson. "Recovering a Cripistemology of Pain: Leaky Bodies, Connective Tissue, and Feeling Discourse." *Journal of Literary & Cultural Disability Studies* 8, no. 2 (2014): 203–218.

Peralta, Eyder. "Putting 'Deadliest Mass Shooting in U.S. History' into Some Historical Context." *NPR,* June 13, 2016. https://www.npr.org/sections/thetwo-way/2016/06/13/481884291/putting-deadliest-mass-shooting-in-u-s-history-into-some-historical-context.

Pérez, Kimberlee. "Staging the Family Unfamiliar: The Queer Intimacies in *Ramble-Ations: A One D'Lo Show.*" *Text and Performance Quarterly* 39, no. 4 (October 2, 2019): 371–87. https://doi.org/10.1080/10462937.2018.1457174.

Petersen, William. "Success Story, Japanese-American Style." *New York Times Magazine,* January 9, 1966, 20–43.

Pew Research Center. *The Rise of Asian Americans.* Pew Research Center's Social & Demographic Trends Project. June 19, 2012. http://www.pewsocialtrends.org/2012/06/19/the-rise-of-asian-americans/.

Piepzna-Samarasinha, Leah Lakshmi. *Care Work: Dreaming Disability Justice.* Vancouver: Arsenal Pulp Press, 2018.

Pinkney, London. "Fat Femmes Rise Up!: Interview with Sen M." *The Ana* 1, no. 1 (January 31, 2020): 48–51. https://wearetheana.com/issue-1.

Pohan, Gisele. Interview by Amy Sueyoshi, August 13, 2013. Dragon Fruit Project. API Equality Northern California, San Francisco, California.

Pough, Gwendolyn. "Do the Ladies Run This . . . ? Some Thoughts on Hip Hop Feminism." In *Catching a Wave: Reclaiming Feminism for the 21st Century,* edited by Rory Dicker and Alison Piepmeier, 232–43. Lebanon, NH: Northeastern University Press, 2003.

Povinelli, Elizabeth A. *Economies of Abandonment: Social Belonging and Endurance in Late Liberalism.* Durham: Duke University Press, 2011.

Powell, Malea. "Listening to Ghosts: An Alternative (Non)Argument." In *ALT DIS: Alternative Discourses and the Academy,* edited by Christopher Schroeder, Helen Fox, and Patricia Bizzell, 11–22. Portsmouth, NH: Boynton/Cook, 2002.

Powell, Malea, Daisy Levy, Andrea Riley-Mukavetz, Marilee Brooks-Gillies, Maria Novotny, Jennifer Fisch-Ferguson, and the Cultural Rhetorics Theory Lab. "Act I." *Enculturation,* no. 18 (October 25, 2014). http://enculturation.net/node/6097.

———. "Our Story Begins Here: Constellating Cultural Rhetorics." *Enculturation,* no. 18 (October 25, 2014). http://enculturation.net/our-story-begins-here.

Price, Margaret. "The Bodymind Problem and the Possibilities of Pain." *Hypatia* 30, no. 1 (February 2015): 268–84. https://doi.org/10.1111/hypa.12127.

Pritchard, Eric Darnell. *Fashioning Lives: Black Queers and the Politics of Literacy.* Carbondale: Southern Illinois University Press, 2017.

Purdy, James. "Three Gifts of Digital Archives." *Journal of Literacy and Technology* 12, no. 3 (November 2011): 24–49.

Pyle, Kai. "Naming and Claiming: Recovering Ojibwe and Plains Cree Two-Spirit Language." *TSQ: Transgender Studies Quarterly* 5, no. 4 (November 1, 2018): 574–88. https://doi.org/10. 1215/23289252-7090045.

Queen Sen Sen. "About." Art By Queen Sen Sen. Accessed May 1, 2020. https://www.facebook. com/pg/ArtbyQueenSenSen/about/?ref=page_internal.

———. "Sun—Protector of Queer & Trans Prisoners." In Chan, *Flower of Ancestry,* 2:30–31.

"Queer Ancestors Project." Accessed October 5, 2019. https://www.queerancestorsproject.org/.

Ragas, Brian. "Tita Aida Honored as Woman of the Year." *San Francisco Community Health Center* (blog), March 7, 2019. https://sfcommunityhealth.org/announcement/tita-aida-honored-as-woman-of-the-year/.

Randolph, Delia Grace, Johannes Refisch, Susan MacMillan, Caradee Yael Wright, Bernard Bett, Doreen Robinson, Bianca Wernecke, et al. *Preventing the Next Pandemic: Zoonotic Diseases and How to Break the Chain of Transmission.* Nairobi, Kenya: United Nations Environment Programme and International Livestock Research Institute, July 6, 2020. https://www.unep. org/resources/report/preventing-future-zoonotic-disease-outbreaks-protecting-environment-animals-and.

Rawson, KJ. "Archive This! Queering the Archive." In *Practicing Research in Writing Studies: Reflexive and Ethically Responsible Research,* edited by Katrina M. Powell and Pamela Takayoshi, 237–50. Research and Teaching in Rhetoric and Composition. New York: Hampton Press, 2012.

Reddy, Chandan. "Asian Diasporas, Neoliberalism, and Family: Reviewing the Case for Homosexual Asylum in the Context of Family Rights." *Social Text* 23, no. 3–4 (2005): 101–19. https://doi.org/10.1215/01642472-23-3-4_84-85-101.

———. *Freedom with Violence: Race, Sexuality, and the US State.* Perverse Modernities. Durham: Duke University Press, 2011.

Resilience Archives. "International Hotel." Resilience Archives: LGBTQ AAPI History Tour, May 22, 2016. https://www.historypin.org/en/lgbtq-america/pacific-west/lgbtq-aapi-tour/geo/37.784918,-122.409298,19/bounds/37.784103,-122.41011,37.785733,-122.408486/paging/1/pin/1025444.

———. "Mia Mingus in the Disability Visibility Project." Resilience Archives: LGBTQ AAPI History Tour, June 6, 2017. https://www.historypin.org/en/lgbtq-america/pacific-west/lgbtq-aapi-tour/geo/37.827178,-122.291308,8/bounds/36.140131,-123.954063,39.476522,-120.628553/search/tag:disabled/paging/1/pin/1075250.

———. "Performing Resilience Workshops Begin -2017." Resilience Archives: LGBTQ AAPI History Tour, March 9, 2017. https://www.historypin.org/en/lgbtq-america/pacific-west/lgbtq-aapi-tour/geo/37.783762,-122.408315,17/bounds/37.780502,-122.411562,37.787023,-122.405067/paging/1/pin/1074916.

———. "Valencia Lesbian Stroll." Resilience Archives: LGBTQ AAPI History Tour, June 6, 2017. https://www.historypin.org/en/lgbtq-america/pacific-west/lgbtq-aapi-tour/geo/37.827178,-122.291308,8/bounds/36.140131,-123.954063,39.476522,-120.628553/search/tag:2010s/paging/1/pin/1075251.

Revesz, Rachael. "Orlando Is Not the Deadliest Mass Shooting in US History." *The Independent,* June 16, 2016. http://www.independent.co.uk/news/world/americas/orlando-is-not-the-deadliest-mass-shooting-in-us-history-a7085571.html.

Riley-Mukavetz, Andrea. "Developing a Relational Scholarly Practice: Snakes, Dreams, and Grandmothers." *College Composition and Communication* 71, no. 4 (2020): 545–65.

———. "On Working From or With Anger: Or How I Learned to Listen to My Relatives and Practice All Our Relations." *Enculturation,* no. 21 (April 20, 2016). http://enculturation.net/on-working-from-or-with-anger.

Riley-Mukavetz, Andrea, and Malea Powell. "Making Native Space for Graduate Students: A Story of Indigenous Rhetorical Practice." In *Survivance, Sovereignty, and Story: Teaching American Indian Rhetorics,* edited by Lisa King, Rose Gubele, and Joyce Rain Anderson, 138–59. Logan: Utah State University Press, 2015.

Roberts, Dorothy E. *Killing the Black Body: Race, Reproduction, and the Meaning of Liberty.* 1st ed. New York: Vintage Books, 1997.

Roy, Arundhati. "The Pandemic Is a Portal." *Financial Times,* April 3, 2020. https://www.ft.com/content/10d8f5e8-74eb-11ea-95fe-fcd274e920ca.

Royster, Jacqueline Jones. *Traces of a Stream: Literacy and Social Change among African American Women.* Pittsburgh Series in Composition, Literacy, and Culture. Pittsburgh: University of Pittsburgh Press, 2000.

Rubin Museum of Art. "Fluid Depictions of Gender and Identity in Himalayan Art," June 13, 2016. https://rubinmuseum.org/blog/fluid-depictions-gender-identity-himalayan-art-lgbt.

Samuels, Ellen Jean. *Fantasies of Identification: Disability, Gender, Race.* Cultural Front. New York: New York University Press, 2014.

Sandahl, Carrie. "Queering the Crip or Cripping the Queer? Intersections of Queer and Crip Identities in Solo Autobiographical Performance." *GLQ: A Journal of Lesbian and Gay Studies* 9, no. 1–2 (2003): 25–56. https://doi.org/10.1215/10642684-9-1-2-25.

Sandoval, Chela. *Methodology of the Oppressed.* Minneapolis: University of Minnesota Press, 2000.

Saranillio, Dean Itsuji. "Why Asian Settler Colonialism Matters: A Thought Piece on Critiques, Debates, and Indigenous Difference." *Settler Colonial Studies* 3, no. 3–4 (November 2013): 280–94. https://doi.org/10.1080/2201473X.2013.810697.

Schalk, Sami. "Coming to Claim Crip: Disidentification with/in Disability Studies." *Disability Studies Quarterly* 33, no. 2 (March 27, 2013). https://doi.org/10.18061/dsq.v33i2.3705.

Schuessler, Jennifer. "Writing Dangerously." *New York Times* (blog), February 8, 2008. https://artsbeat.blogs.nytimes.com/2008/02/08/writing-dangerously/.

Sedgwick, Eve Kosofsky. *Epistemology of the Closet.* Berkeley: University of California Press, 2008.

Shah, Nayan. *Contagious Divides: Epidemics and Race in San Francisco's Chinatown.* American Crossroads 7. Berkeley: University of California Press, 2001.

Shange, Savannah. "Play Aunties and Dyke Bitches: Gender, Generation, and the Ethics of Black Queer Kinship." *The Black Scholar* 49, no. 1 (January 2, 2019): 40–54. https://doi.org/10.1080/00064246.2019.1548058.

Shilts, Randy. *And the Band Played On: Politics, People, and the AIDS Epidemic.* 20th anniv. ed. New York: St. Martin's Griffin, 2007.

Shuman, Amy. *Other People's Stories: Entitlement Claims and the Critique of Empathy.* Urbana: University of Illinois Press, 2010.

Simpson, Audra. "On Ethnographic Refusal: Indigeneity, 'Voice' and Colonial Citizenship." *Junctures,* no. 9 (December 2007): 67–80.

Simpson, Leanne. *As We Have Always Done: Indigenous Freedom through Radical Resistance.* Indigenous Americas. Minneapolis; London: University of Minnesota Press, 2017.

Singer, T. B. "The Profusion of Things: The 'Transgender Matrix' and Demographic Imaginaries in US Public Health." *TSQ: Transgender Studies Quarterly* 2, no. 1 (January 1, 2015): 58–76. https://doi.org/10.1215/23289252-2848886.

Solórzano, Daniel, and Tara J. Yosso. "Critical Race Methodology: Counter-Storytelling as an Analytical Framework for Education Research." *Qualitative Inquiry* 8, no. 1 (2002): 23–44.

Sontag, Susan. *Illness as Metaphor and AIDS and Its Metaphors.* New York: Picador USA, 2001.

Southwick, Steven M., and Dennis S. Charney. *Resilience: The Science of Mastering Life's Greatest Challenges.* 2nd ed. Cambridge; New York: Cambridge University Press, 2018.

Spade, Dean. *Normal Life: Administrative Violence, Critical Trans Politics, and the Limits of Law.* 2nd ed. Durham: Duke University Press, 2015.

———. "Toward a Critical Trans Politics: An Interview with Dean Spade." Interview by Rob Nichols, 2013. *Upping the Anti,* no. 14. http://uppingtheanti.org/journal/article/14-dean-spade/.

Stevenson, Angus, ed. "Resilience." In *Oxford Dictionary of English,* 1512. United Kingdom: Oxford University Press, 2010.

Storm, Carsten, ed. *Connecting Taiwan: Participation, Integration, Impacts.* Routledge Research on Taiwan. London; New York: Routledge Taylor & Francis Group, 2018.

"Success Story of One Minority in the U.S." *U.S. News and World Report,* December 26, 1966.

"Success Story: Outwhiting the Whites." *Newsweek,* June 21, 1971.

Sueyoshi, Amy. *Discriminating Sex: White Leisure and the Making of the American "Oriental."* The Asian American Experience. Urbana: University of Illinois Press, 2018. Kindle.

———. Personal interview with Jo Hsu, April 17, 2018.

Sullivan, Andrew. "Why Do Democrats Feel Sorry for Hillary Clinton?" *New York,* April 14, 2017. https://nymag.com/daily/intelligencer/2017/04/why-do-democrats-feel-sorry-for-hillary-clinton.html.

Suzuki, Shogo. "Japan's Socialization into Janus-Faced European International Society." *European Journal of International Relations* 11, no. 1 (March 2005): 137–64. https://doi.org/10.1177/1354066105050139.

Tallbear, Kimberly. "The Emergence, Politics, and Marketplace of Native American DNA." In *Routledge Handbook of Science, Technology, and Society,* edited by Daniel Lee Kleinman and Kelly Moore, 21–37. New York: Routledge, 2014.

Tam, Ruth. "Culture Clash: Asian Americans Balance Christianity and Culture in Rituals Honoring Their Ancestors." *Washington Post,* April 6, 2018. https://www.washingtonpost.com/news/post-nation/wp/2018/04/06/culture-clash-asian-americans-balance-christianity-and-culture-in-rituals-honoring-their-ancestors/.

"The Souls of Yellow Folk." Accessed August 6, 2019. https://wwnorton.com/books/9780393357554.

Thobani, Sitara. "Dorinne Kondo, 'Worldmaking: Race, Performance, and the Work of Creativity.'" New Books Network: Asian American Studies, June 24, 2019. https://newbooksnetwork.

com/dorinne-kondo-worldmaking-race-performance-and-the-work-of-creativity-duke-up-2018/.

Thom, Kai Cheng. *A Place Called No Homeland.* Vancouver: Arsenal Pulp Press, 2017.

———. "I Want to Find the Place Underneath Rage." Interview by Francesca Ekwuyasi. *Winter Tangerine,* December 8, 2017. http://www.wintertangerine.com/ucp-kaichengthom.

Ting, Jennifer P. "Bachelor Society: Deviant Heterosexuality and Asian American Historiography." In *Privileging Positions: The Sites of Asian American Studies,* edited by Gary Y. Okihiro et al., 271–79. Association for Asian American Studies. Pullman: Washington State University Press, 1995.

Toth, Robert C. "Peril to Identity: Japanese in U.S. Outdo Horatio Alger." *Los Angeles Times,* October 17, 1977.

Towle, Evan B., and Lynn Marie Morgan. "Romancing the Transgender Native: Rethinking the Use of the 'Third Gender' Concept." *GLQ: A Journal of Lesbian and Gay Studies* 8, no. 4 (2002): 469–97.

Trask, Haunani-Kay. "Settlers of Color and 'Immigrant' Hegemony: 'Locals' in Hawai'i." *Amerasia Journal* 26, no. 2 (January 2000): 1–26. https://doi.org/10.17953/amer.26.2.b31642r221215k7k.

Trauner, Joan B. "The Chinese as Medical Scapegoats in San Francisco, 1870–1905." *California History* 57, no. 1 (April 1, 1978): 70–87. https://doi.org/10.2307/25157817.

trivedi-pathak, madhvi. "Reminder for the Tenderhearted." In Chan, *Tender,* 1–3.

Tripp, Bill. "Our Land Was Taken. But We Still Hold the Knowledge of How to Stop Mega-Fires." *Guardian,* September 16, 2020, sec. Opinion. https://www.theguardian.com/commentisfree/2020/sep/16/california-wildfires-cultural-burns-indigenous-people.

Tuck, Eve. "Breaking Up With Deleuze: Desire and Valuing the Irreconcilable." *International Journal of Qualitative Studies in Education* 23, no. 5 (September 2010): 635–50. https://doi.org/10.1080/09518398.2010.500633.

Tuck, Eve, and K. Wayne Yang. "R-Words: Refusing Research." In *Humanizing Research: Decolonizing Qualitative Inquiry with Youth and Communities,* edited by Django Paris and Maisha T. Winn, 223–48. Thousand Oaks, CA: SAGE, 2014.

———. "Unbecoming Claims: Pedagogies of Refusal in Qualitative Research." *Qualitative Inquiry* 20, no. 6 (July 2014): 811–18. https://doi.org/10.1177/1077800414530265.

US Department of Health and Human Services. *National Diabetes Statistics Report, 2020: Estimates of Diabetes and Its Burden in the United States.* Centers for Disease Control and Prevention, 2020. https://www.cdc.gov/diabetes/pdfs/data/statistics/national-diabetes-statistics-report.pdf.

Velani, Nidhi Parixit. "Disha & Suchandra." In Chan, *Flower of Ancestry,* 2:18–19.

Visibility Project. "About." Accessed January 27, 2019. http://www.visibilityproject.org/about-2/.

Vivienne, Son. *Digital Identity and Everyday Activism: Sharing Private Stories with Networked Publics.* London: Palgrave Macmillan, 2016. https://doi.org/10.1057/9781137500748.

———. "'Little Islands of Empathy': Networked Stories of Gender Diversity and Multiple Selves." *Media International Australia* 168, no. 1 (August 2018): 19–30. https://doi.org/10.1177/1329878X18783019.

Vogel, Ezra F. *The Four Little Dragons: The Spread of Industrialization in East Asia.* The Edwin O. Reischauer Lectures 1990. Cambridge, MA: Harvard University Press, 1991.

Vuong, Ocean. *Night Sky with Exit Wounds.* Port Townsend, WA: Copper Canyon Press, 2016.

Wallis, Claudia. "Why Racism, Not Race, Is a Risk Factor for Dying of COVID-19." *Scientific American,* June 12, 2020. https://www.scientificamerican.com/article/why-racism-not-race-is-a-risk-factor-for-dying-of-covid-191/.

Walsh, Joe. "Trump Is Demanding China Pay 'Big Price' for Covid-19." *Forbes,* October 8, 2020. https://www.forbes.com/sites/joewalsh/2020/10/08/trump-is-demanding-china-pay-big-price-for-covid-19/.

Wan, William. "The Coronavirus Pandemic Is Pushing America into a Mental Health Crisis." *Washington Post,* May 4, 2020. Accessed August 7, 2020. https://www.washingtonpost.com/health/2020/05/04/mental-health-coronavirus/.

Wang, Chih-ming. "Affective Rearticulations: Cultural Studies in and from Taiwan." *Cultural Studies* 31, no. 6 (November 2, 2017): 740–63. https://doi.org/10.1080/09502386.2017.1375539.

Wang, Karin. "Parallel Journeys through Discrimination: Asian Americans and Modern Marriage Equality." In *Love Unites Us: Winning the Freedom to Marry in America,* edited by Kevin M. Cathcart and Leslie J. Gabel-Brett, 157–60. New York: New Press, 2016.

Weston, Kath. *Families We Choose: Lesbians, Gays, Kinship.* New York: Columbia University Press, 1997.

Wilkinson, Willy. Interview by Annie Kim Noguchi, 2012. Dragon Fruit Project. API Equality Northern California, San Francisco, California.

Williams, A. Park, John T. Abatzoglou, Alexander Gershunov, Janin Guzman-Morales, Daniel A. Bishop, Jennifer K. Balch, and Dennis P. Lettenmaier. "Observed Impacts of Anthropogenic Climate Change on Wildfire in California." *Earth's Future* 7, no. 8 (August 2019): 892–910. https://doi.org/10.1029/2019EF001210.

Wingard, Jennifer. *Branded Bodies, Rhetoric, and the Neoliberal Nation-State.* Lanham, MD: Lexington Books, 2015.

Wolfe, Patrick. *Traces of History: Elementary Structures of Race.* London; New York: Verso, 2016.

Wong, Alice. "Disability Visibility Project: Mia Mingus, Part 1." Disability Visibility Project, September 25, 2014. https://disabilityvisibilityproject.com/2014/09/25/disability-visibility-project-mia-mingus-alice-wong/.

———. "Disability Visibility Project: Mia Mingus, Part 3." Disability Visibility Project, September 27, 2014. https://disabilityvisibilityproject.com/2014/09/27/disability-visibility-project-mia-mingus-alice-wong-3/.

Wong, Anna May. "I Am Growing More Chinese—Each Passing Year! (1934)." In *Chinese American Voices: From the Gold Rush to the Present,* edited by Judy Yung, Gordon H. Chang, and Him Mark Lai, 1st ed., 177–82. Berkeley: University of California Press, 2006. https://www.jstor.org/stable/10.1525/j.ctt1pppwn.33.

Wong, Jade Snow. *Fifth Chinese Daughter.* Seattle: University of Washington Press, 1989.

Woodman, Abby Johnson. *Picturesque Alaska: A Journal of a Tour among the Mountains, Seas and Islands of the Northwest, from San Francisco to Sitka.* Boston: Houghton, Mifflin, 1890.

Wu, Ellen D. *The Color of Success: Asian Americans and the Origins of the Model Minority.* Princeton: Princeton University Press, 2015.

Yamada, Mitsuye. "Invisibility Is an Unnatural Disaster: Reflections of an Asian American Woman." In Moraga and Anzaldúa, *This Bridge Called My Back,* 30–35.

Yamashita, Karen Tei. *I Hotel.* 1st ed. Minneapolis: Coffee House Press, 2010.

Yancy, Clyde W. "COVID-19 and African Americans." *JAMA* 323, no. 19 (May 19, 2020): 1891–92. https://doi.org/10.1001/jama.2020.6548.

Yang, Andrew. "We Asian Americans Are Not the Virus, but We Can Be Part of the Cure." *Washington Post,* April 1, 2020. https://www.washingtonpost.com/opinions/2020/04/01/andrew-yang-coronavirus-discrimination/.

Yang, Wesley. *The Souls of Yellow Folk: Essays.* 1st ed. New York: Norton, 2018.

Yee, Jai Lei. "Ngin Ngin." In Chan, *Tender,* 30.

Yergeau, M. Remi. *Authoring Autism: On Rhetoric and Neurological Queerness.* Thought in the Act. Durham: Duke University Press, 2018. Kindle.

Yglesias, Matthew. "The Face of Seung-Hui Cho." *The Atlantic,* January 10, 2008. https://www.theatlantic.com/politics/archive/2008/01/-the-face-of-seung-hui-cho/47857/.

Yong, E. "America's Patchwork Pandemic Is Fraying Even Further." *The Atlantic,* May 20, 2020. https://www.theatlantic.com/health/archive/2020/05/patchwork-pandemic-states-reopening-inequalities/611866/.

Young, S. Hall. *The Mushing Parson.* Grand Rapids, MI: Felming H. Revell, 1927.

INDEX

442nd Infantry Combat Team, 19

跨 (crossing), 119, 123. *See also* kuaer pedagogies

家 (home), 9, 187. *See also* 作家 (writer); family/home

外省人 (outside province people), 161

誇 (proud), 119, 123. *See also* kuaer pedagogies

本省人 (this province people), 160

作家 (writer), 9

Abbey, Kristen, 136

ableism, 152, 171, 173, 175, 177; and racialization, 12–13, 15, 21, 29, 36, 45, 74–76, 95, 122, 140, 157, 189

abolition, 59–60, 65, 126

Aborigine, 160

academic careers, 3, 31, 64, 150

academic institutions, 2–4, 14, 29, 42, 155; aversion to embodiment, 166–67; Chinese schools, 155, 172; exclusivity of, 70–72, 142–43, 145, 156, 163–64; Native American boarding schools, 180

accessibility, 3, 40, 42; of archives, 84–85, 98–99, 102–3, 105–7; as practice of care, 62, 67–70, 175–76

accountability, 12, 14, 22, 72, 103, 111, 117, 140, 162

Act for the Government and Protection of Indians (1850), 192

activism, 43–44, 63, 72, 82, 89, 194; ancestral practice as, 117; and love, 39–40, 47–50, 52–53, 55, 58–59; organizers, 5, 72, 84, 96, 190; and police violence, 186, 188; and scholarly lineage, 4, 7, 164, 166, 171; storytelling as, 13, 22–25, 27, 29, 67n102, 108, 138; in Taiwan, 162; visibility as, 95, 101–2, 118, 138

adolescence, 3, 61, 152, 168

affective grammars, 41, 60, 62–63, 124

affective ties, 26, 35, 39, 60, 128, 161

affirmative action, 26, 195

African Americans, 15–17, 21, 191. *See also* Blackness

Ahmed, Sara, 8, 35, 166

Ahsan, Bahaar, 124–26, 140

Ahuja, Bex, 93, 108

Aida, Tita, 49–52, 54, 57, 59, 71, 195

Akimel O'odham, 144–45

Alaska Natives, 114. *See also* Indigenous peoples

Alexander, M. Jacqui, 11

217

INTERSECTIONAL RHETORICS

KARMA R. CHÁVEZ, SERIES EDITOR

This new series takes as its starting point the position that intersectionality offers important insights to the field of rhetoric—including that to enhance what we understand as rhetorical practice, we must diversify the types of rhetors, arguments, frameworks, and forms under analysis. Intersection works on two levels for the series: (1) reflecting the series' privileging of intersectional perspectives and analytical frames while also (2) emphasizing rhetoric's intersection with related fields, disciplines, and research areas.

www.ingramcontent.com/pod-product-compliance
Lightning Source LLC
Chambersburg PA
CBHW020702270326
41928CB00005B/219